D1128812

ELECTRONIC AMERICA

ISSN 1554-4397

ELECTRONIC AMERICA

John W. Weier

INFORMATION PLUS® REFERENCE SERIES
Formerly published by Information Plus, Wylie, Texas

6/05

Detroit • New York • San Francisco • San Diego • New Haven, Conn. • Waterville, Maine • London • Munich

THOMSON
GALE

Electronic America
John W. Weier
Paula Kepos, Series Editor

Project Editor
John McCoy

Permissions
Margaret Abendroth, Edna Hedblad, Emma Hull

Composition and Electronic Prepress
Evi Seoud

Manufacturing
Drew Kalasky

LIBRARY OF CONGRESS CATALOGING-IN-PUBLICATION DATA

ISBN 0-7876-5103-6 (set)
ISBN 0-7876-9092-9
ISSN 1554-4397

Printed in the United States of America
10 9 8 7 6 5 4 3 2 1

TABLE OF CONTENTS

PREFACE

Electronic America is part of the *Information Plus Reference Series*. The purpose of each volume of the series is to present the latest facts on a topic of pressing concern in modern American life. These topics include today's most controversial and most studied social issues: abortion, capital punishment, care for the elderly, crime, the environment, health care, immigration, minorities, national security, social welfare, women, youth, and many more. Although written especially for the high school and undergraduate student, this series is an excellent resource for anyone in need of factual information on current affairs.

By presenting the facts, it is Thomson Gale's intention to provide its readers with everything they need to reach an informed opinion on current issues. To that end, there is a particular emphasis in this series on the presentation of scientific studies, surveys, and statistics. These data are generally presented in the form of tables, charts, and other graphics placed within the text of each book. Every graphic is directly referred to and carefully explained in the text. The source of each graphic is presented within the graphic itself. The data used in these graphics are drawn from the most reputable and reliable sources, in particular from the various branches of the U.S. government and from major independent polling organizations. Every effort has been made to secure the most recent information available. The reader should bear in mind that many major studies take years to conduct, and that additional years often pass before the data from these studies are made available to the public. Therefore, in many cases the most recent information available in 2005 dated from 2002 or 2003. Older statistics are sometimes presented as well, if they are of particular interest and no more-recent information exists.

Although statistics are a major focus of the *Information Plus Reference Series* they are by no means its only content. Each book also presents the widely held positions and important ideas that shape how the book's subject is discussed in the United States. These positions are explained in detail and, where possible, in the words of their proponents. Some of the other material to be found in these books includes: historical background; descriptions of major events related to the subject; relevant laws and court cases; and examples of how these issues play out in American life. Some books also feature primary documents, or have pro and con debate sections giving the words and opinions of prominent Americans on both sides of a controversial topic. All material is presented in an even-handed and unbiased manner; the reader will never be encouraged to accept one view of an issue over another.

HOW TO USE THIS BOOK

During the late twentieth century and early twenty-first century the United States was transformed by the rapid development and adoption of new electronic devices, programs, and other technologies. Computers, cell phones, CD-ROMs, cable television, e-mail, MP3s, DVDs, viruses, robots, spam, peer-to-peer networks, and massive multiplayer online role-playing games were in limited use in 1980, if they existed at all. By 2004 they had all become more common, and many were ubiquitous. Their effect on America, and the world, has been profound. New types of industries developed to produce and make use of these technologies. Existing businesses used them to become more efficient. New technologies also opened the door to new kinds of crime and criminals, and with them a need for changes in U.S. government and law enforcement. Last but not least, the average American found that the new technology made it increasingly easy for them to communicate and find information, as well as to enjoy themselves, to be frustrated, or even to be victimized, in new and different ways.

Electronic America consists of ten chapters and three appendices. Each of the chapters is devoted to a particular aspect of the changes in the United States brought about by high technology and its applications. For a summary of the information covered in each chapter, please see the synopses provided in the Table of Contents at the front of the book. Chapters generally begin with an overview of the basic facts and background information on the chapter's topic, then proceed to examine sub-topics of particular interest. For example, Chapter 2: America Discovers New Ways to Communicate begins by contrasting the options most Americans had for communicating with each other in 1985 with those available twenty years later. It then moves on to examine the history of e-mail, followed by a detailed examination of who uses e-mail and how in the twenty-first century. This includes substantial coverage of spam and the efforts to control it. Next in the chapter are sections on Instant Messaging and Voice over Internet Protocol (VoIP). Mobile phones are the subject of the next section, with extensive detail on the nature of mobile phones, their development over time, and their usage in twenty-first century America and attendant concerns. The chapter concludes with a discussion of changes in communications that were taking place in 2004, such as the development of third generation wireless technology. Readers can find their way through a chapter by looking for the section and sub-section headings, which are clearly set off from the text. Or, they can refer to the book's extensive index, if they already know what they are looking for.

Statistical Information

The tables and figures featured throughout *Electronic America* will be of particular use to the reader in learning about this topic. These tables and figures represent an extensive collection of the most recent and valuable statistics on new technology and its impact on the United States—for example, graphics in the book cover how many Americans use the Internet and how usage differs depending on demographic characteristics; enrollment in distance learning programs by type of institution; and the results of a survey on the frequency and types of electronic crimes perpetrated against American businesses. Thomson Gale believes that making this information available to the reader is the most important way in which we fulfill the goal of this book: to help readers understand the issues and controversies surrounding new technology in America and reach their own conclusions.

Each table or figure has a unique identifier appearing above it, for ease of identification and reference. Titles for the tables and figures explain their purpose. At the end of each table or figure, the original source of the data is provided.

In order to help readers understand these often complicated statistics, all tables and figures are explained in the text. References in the text direct the reader to the relevant statistics. Furthermore, the contents of all tables and figures are fully indexed. Please see the opening section of the index at the back of this volume for a description of how to find tables and figures within it.

Appendices

In addition to the main body text and images, *Electronic America* has three appendices. The first appendix is the Important Names and Addresses directory. Here the reader will find contact information for a number of government and private organizations that can provide further information on aspects of recreation. The second appendix is the Resources section, which can also assist the reader in conducting his or her own research. In this section, the author and editors of *Electronic America* describe some of the sources that were most useful during the compilation of this book. The final appendix is the index.

ADVISORY BOARD CONTRIBUTIONS

The staff of Information Plus would like to extend their heartfelt appreciation to the Information Plus Advisory Board. This dedicated group of media professionals provides feedback on the series on an ongoing basis. Their comments allow the editorial staff who work on the project to continually make the series better and more user-friendly. Our top priorities are to produce the highest-quality and most useful books possible, and the Advisory Board's contributions to this process are invaluable.

The members of the Information Plus Advisory Board are:

- Kathleen R. Bonn, Librarian, Newbury Park High School, Newbury Park, California

- Madelyn Garner, Librarian, San Jacinto College— North Campus, Houston, Texas

- Anne Oxenrider, Media Specialist, Dundee High School, Dundee, Michigan

- Charles R. Rodgers, Director of Libraries, Pasco-Hernando Community College, Dade City, Florida

- James N. Zitzelsberger, Library Media Department Chairman, Oshkosh West High School, Oshkosh, Wisconsin

COMMENTS AND SUGGESTIONS

The editors of the *Information Plus Reference Series* welcome your feedback on *Electronic America*. Please direct all correspondence to:

Editors
Information Plus Reference Series
27500 Drake Rd.
Farmington Hills, MI 48331-3535

CHAPTER 1

THE INTERNET AND THE ELECTRONIC AGE

The Internet was a Cold War military project. It was designed for the purposes of military communication in a United States devastated by a Soviet nuclear strike. . . . When I look at the Internet—that paragon of cyberspace today—I see something astounding and delightful. It's as if some grim fallout shelter had burst open and a full-scale Mardi Gras parade had come out.

—Bruce Sterling, in "Literary Freeware—Not for Commercial Use" (with William Gibson), *Speeches to the National Academy of Sciences Convocation on Technology and Education,* Washington, D.C., May 10, 1993)

Since the 1980s, innovations in electronics and communications technologies have utterly transformed the way in which Americans lead their lives. Computers and the Internet have dramatically reduced the time needed to complete dozens of mundane tasks, such as finding directions, searching library catalogs, or researching products. Cell phones, e-mail, and instant messaging now enable people to communicate with each other at any time or place. Affordable microprocessors have improved the efficiency and features on everything from coffee makers to stereos to dishwashers to automobiles.

The speed with which these new technologies have proliferated through American homes and offices is nothing short of astounding. Cell phones, which were once novelties occupying the middle front seat of a car, can now be found in the pockets of many fifteen-year-olds. Computers and the Internet, once only accessible to those who worked in government installations, large corporations, and academic institutions, are present in most American homes. According to the U.S. Census Bureau, only 8.2% of American households had computers in 1984. As can be seen in Figure 1.1, this number increased to 51% by the year 2000. The Internet, which was not available to homes in 1984, had forty-four million U.S. customers by the turn of the twenty-first century, according to Eric C. Newburger in *Home Computers and Internet Use in the United States: August 2000* (Washington,

DC: U.S. Census Bureau, September 2001). More recent estimates, derived by the Pew Internet & American Life Project (Pew/Internet; www.pewinternet.org) in 2004, revealed that 73% of American adults (148 million people) had computers and 63% of adults (128 million people) used the Internet.

The Internet and Daily Life, an August 2004 Pew/Internet study, found that 88% of online adult Americans believed that the Internet played a crucial role in their lives, and 64% said their daily routines and activities would be affected if they could not use the Internet. Table 1.1, taken from *America's Online Pursuits* (Washington, DC: Pew/Internet, December 2003), reveals that the Internet has become more and more integrated into people's lives. The activities that most people engaged in on the Internet were such typical uses as sending or reading e-mail, searching for an answer to a question, or researching a product or service. The use of the Internet to engage in activities other than these standard operations, however, rose the fastest. The number of wired adult Americans who used the Internet to bank online grew 127% between 2000 and 2002. The number of users who looked for religious or spiritual information increased 94%; the number who bought or made a travel reservation jumped 87%, and the number who participated in an auction went up 85%. Perhaps the most interesting of these statistics was the rise in the number of adult Americans who purchased a product on the Internet. Despite a recession during this period, the number of people who bought products online rose 63%.

While the spread of technology has affected most people in a positive way, significant pitfalls have developed as well. As these technologies have been thoroughly embraced by the well educated and wealthy, typically disadvantaged groups have been left at a bigger disadvantage. The Internet and computer databases have also made fraud much easier. The number of cases of identity theft in the United States has exploded in recent years. Each day thieves steal hundreds of social security and credit card

TABLE 1.1

Growth of online pursuits, 2000–02

Estimated growth in users who have ever done these activities (2000–2002)

Activity	First time we asked this Have done this (millions)	Most recent time Have done this (millions)	Growth %
Bank online	15 (March 2000)	34 (October 2002)	127%
Look for religious or spiritual info	18 (March 2000)	35 (November 2002)	94%
Buy or make a reservation for travel	31 (March 2000)	58 (December 2002)	87%
Participate in an online auction	13 (March 2000)	24 (December 2002)	85%
Check sports scores or info	30 (March 2000)	52 (September 2002)	73%
Download music files to your computer	21 (June–July 2000)	36 (October 2002)	71%
Buy a product	41 (March 2000)	67 (December 2002)	63%
Look for health or medical info	46 (March 2000)	73 (December 2002)	59%
Look for political news or info	30 (March 2000)	47 (November 2002)	57%
Look for info from a government site	40 (March 2000)	66 (November 2002)	56%
Research a product or service	64 (March 2000)	97 (December 2002)	52%
Get news	52 (March 2000)	78 (December 2002)	50%
Research for your job	42 (March 2000)	61 (November 2002)	45%
Play a game	29 (March 2000)	42 (June–July 2002)	45%
Surf the web for fun	54 (March 2000)	78 (January 2002)	44%
Look for info on a hobby or interest	65 (March 2000)	91 (January 2002)	40%
Buy or sell stocks	10 (March 2000)	14 (September 2002)	40%
Research for school or training	47 (March 2000)	63 (September 2002)	34%
Send an instant message	39 (March 2000)	52 (June–July 2002)	33%
Get financial info	38 (March 2000)	50 (September 2002)	32%
Send or read email	78 (March 2000)	102 (December 2002)	31%
Search to answer a question	79 (Sept–Dec 2000)	98 (September 2002)	24%
Participate in a chat room or discussion	24 (March 2000)	29 (June–July 2002)	21%

Note: Listening to music online is not included in this chart because the most recent data we have is from 2001. Creating content online has also been excluded due to the relatively short period of time in which we have asked about it.

SOURCE: Mary Madden and Lee Rainie, "Overall Growth of Online Pursuits," in *America's Online Pursuits,* Pew Internet and American Life Project, December 22, 2003, http://www.pewinternet.org/pdfs/PIP_Online_Pursuits_Final.pdf (accessed October 25, 2004). Used by permission of the Pew Internet and American Life Project, which bears no responsibility for the interpretations presented or conclusions reached based on analysis of the data.

FIGURE 1.1

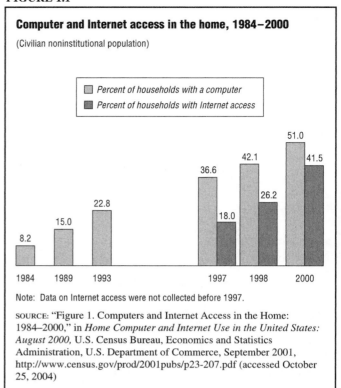

Computer and Internet access in the home, 1984–2000

(Civilian noninstitutional population)

Note: Data on Internet access were not collected before 1997.

SOURCE: "Figure 1. Computers and Internet Access in the Home: 1984–2000," in *Home Computer and Internet Use in the United States: August 2000,* U.S. Census Bureau, Economics and Statistics Administration, U.S. Department of Commerce, September 2001, http://www.census.gov/prod/2001pubs/p23-207.pdf (accessed October 25, 2004)

numbers by simply surfing the Internet or by sending out fraudulent e-mails. According to a report entitled *Consumer Fraud in the United States: An FTC Survey*, released by the U.S. Federal Trade Commission (FTC) in August 2004, identity theft accounted for 43% of the cases of fraud in the United States. In the year prior to the release of the report, nearly ten million Americans were victims of identity theft. According to the study, the cost to Americans of these fraudulent activities came to $48 billion.

Another problem that appears to be growing worse is the number of viruses and worms making their way around the Internet. The CERT Coordination Center at Carnegie Mellon University in Pittsburgh, Pennsylvania, reported that malicious computer incidents (hacking attempts, viruses, and worms directed at specific organizations) increased from 21,756 in 2000 to 137,529 in 2003. (See Table 1.2.) Not only do viruses, worms, and hackers cost time and energy, but they also put valuable information at risk. To make matters worse, in October 2004, the first mobile phone virus was detected in Southeast Asia. The virus, known as Cabir, infects mobile phone software and could be used to steal information from mobile phone address books.

Despite such difficulties, technological innovation is showing no sign of slowing down. It is likely that within the next decade, Americans will be carrying powerful portable computers that are nearly as small as present-day organizers. Price tags at the grocery store will give off radio signals that will automatically register the merchandise on a credit card when the buyer leaves the market. Robotic appliances, such as lawnmowers and vacuum cleaners, will automate some of the more tedious domestic chores.

THE HISTORY OF THE INTERNET

At the center of the information technology and electronics revolution lies the Internet. Many believe the

TABLE 1.2

Number of Internet worms, viruses, and hacking attempts reported, 1988–2003

1988–1989

Year	1988	1989
Incidents	6	132

1990–1999

Year	1990	1991	1992	1993	1994	1995	1996	1997	1998	1999
Incidents	252	406	773	1,334	2,340	2,412	2,573	2,134	3,734	9,859

2000–2003

Year	2000	2001	2002	2003
Incidents	21,756	52,658	82,094	137,529

Total incidents reported (1988–2003): 319,992

An incident may involve one site or hundreds (or even thousands) of sites. Also, some incidents may involve ongoing activity for long periods of time.

SOURCE: "Incidents Reported," in *Cert/CC Statistics 1988–2004,* CERT Coordination Center, Carnegie Mellon Software Engineering Institute, February 13, 2004, http://www.cert.org/stats/cert_stats.html#incidents (accessed October 25, 2004). Reproduced by special permission of the Carnegie Mellon Software Engineering Institute.

Internet had its origins on October 4, 1957, when the Russians launched the Sputnik satellite into orbit with four military rockets. The news of Sputnik, a beeping steel sphere the size of an ottoman, sent the United States into a frenzy. At the time, the United States and the Union of Soviet Socialist Republics (USSR) were engaged in what has become known as the cold war, a period of sustained military buildup and ideological conflict, and Americans were fearful that Soviet satellite technology could be used to spy on the United States or to launch missile attacks on American targets. The one advantage the United States thought it had, technological superiority, now seemed tenuous.

In response, the U.S. government formed the Advanced Research Projects Agency (ARPA) within the Department of Defense a year after the Sputnik launch. The central mission of this new agency was to develop state-of-the-art technology to stay well ahead of the Soviet Union. One of the first things on ARPA's agenda was to create a system by which the ARPA operational bases could communicate with one another and their contractors via computer. They wanted the system to be resilient enough to survive a nuclear attack

John Licklider, a scientist at the Massachusetts Institute of Technology (MIT), was appointed to oversee the computer research program at ARPA in 1962. He conferred with some of the leading minds in networking technology at the time, including the MIT graduate student Leonard Kleinrock and Paul Baran of RAND. Their solution, first published in 1967, was a nationwide network of ARPA computers known as ARPANET. In this network, a user on any computer terminal in the network would be able to send a message to multiple users at other computer terminals. If any one computer was knocked out in a nuclear

attack, the remaining stations could still communicate with one another.

For this network to function properly, the researchers established that the computers would have to transmit information by first breaking the information down into discrete packets. These packets were then to be sent along high-speed phone lines and reassembled upon reaching their destination at another computer. At the time, telephone conversations traveled across dedicated telephone wires in one long stream of data from one user to another like a single train traveling along a track. While this was adequate for chatting with distant relatives, it did not work well when one computer attempted to send data to multiple other computers on the network. By packetizing information, the information became much more flexible. Much like cars on a highway, the packets could be routed easily to multiple computers. If one packet of information went bad in transmission, it did not disrupt the stream of data transmitting from one computer to another and could easily be resent. Packets could also carry information about themselves and where they were going; they could be compressed for speed; and they could be encrypted for security purposes.

After two years of engineering the parts needed for ARPANET, the researchers at ARPA set up the first four computer centers in the network. They were located at the University of California, Los Angeles (UCLA), Stanford Research Institute, the University of California, Santa Barbara (UCSB), and at the University of Utah. Between these nodes, AT&T had laid down telephone lines capable of transmitting data at 50 kilobytes per second. The first test of the system commenced on October 29, 1969, when Charley Kline at UCLA tried logging into the Stanford system. Upon encountering the letter "G" in the word "LOGIN," the system crashed.

A Loose Affiliation of Networks

Needless to say, the researchers at UCLA worked out the problems, and a little over two years later, the ARPANET was fully functional and had forty nodes linked to it. Figure 1.2 shows the ARPANET in September 1971. Throughout the early and mid-1970s, the development of networking technologies progressed slowly. Ray Tomlinson invented the first e-mail program in order to send typed messages across the network in 1971, and a year later, the first computer-to-computer chat took place at UCLA. Bob Metcalfe at Xerox in 1973 developed the first Ethernet to connect computers and printers in a large organization together. Mike Lesk at AT&T Bell Labs in 1976 put together a program entitled Unix-to-Unix-copy protocol (UUCP) that allowed Unix computers, typically used by academics, to communicate with one another over the phone lines.

Such technological developments as these allowed people and organizations that were not connected through ARPANET to set up networks of their own by the late 1980s

FIGURE 1.2

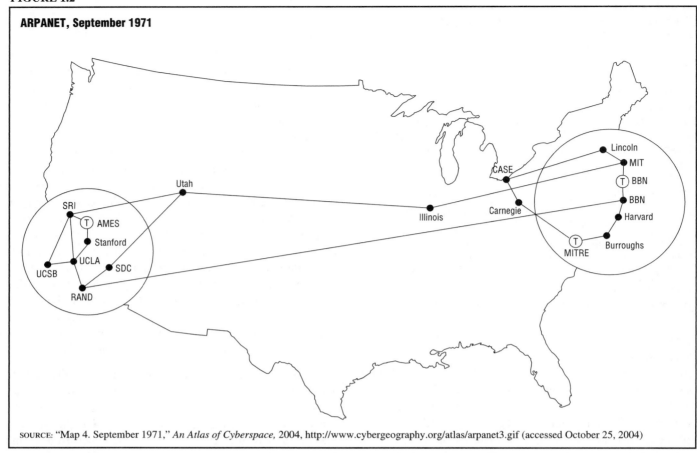

ARPANET, September 1971

SOURCE: "Map 4. September 1971," *An Atlas of Cyberspace,* 2004, http://www.cybergeography.org/atlas/arpanet3.gif (accessed October 25, 2004)

and the early 1990s. One of the largest of these was the Computer Science and Research Network (CSNET), established by a number of universities with help from the National Science Foundation (NSF). These universities, which included the University of Wisconsin and Purdue, recognized the advantages in resource sharing and communication the ARPANET provided the Ivy League and West Coast schools and wanted to develop similar capabilities. Usenet was established initially to connect researchers at Duke and the University of North Carolina and eventually spread all over the country. BITNET was formed to connect computers in the City University of New York system. Most of these smaller networks used standard telephone lines to operate. They were primarily set up to transfer scientific data, share computing resources, post items on bulletin boards, and provide e-mail.

One big problem was that these different networks could not readily communicate with one another. Each network used different methods to identify the computers within the network. A computer in one network could not even recognize the computers in different networks, and information packets sent out from one network could not navigate the other networks. The situation would be analogous to a state in the United States having its own postal services and unique postal address system indecipherable to people living outside of that state. A letter sent to a relative in that state would never reach its destination.

During the 1970s, two clever engineers, Vint Cerf and Bob Kahn, devised the Transmission Control Program and the Internet Protocol (TCP/IP). This suite of programs created a universal address system that could be installed on any existing network. Once installed, the machines on the network could recognize and send information to a machine on any other network, provided they also had TCP/IP. In 1983 ARPANET started using TCP/IP, which was already being used by CSNET. The merger created the first collection of interconnected computer networks, and the "Internet" was born. To this day, each machine on the Internet has a unique IP address that identifies that machine on a network. Servers typically have permanent IP numbers assigned to them, while most personal computers are given a different number by an Internet service provider (ISP) each time the user begins a new session.

In the year the Internet was born, home computing was still in its infancy. Commodore 64 had just made its debut, sporting a one megahertz microprocessor and 64 kilobytes of random access memory (RAM). Relatively few people owned home computers. Most of them used their machines for basic business applications, such as word processors and spread sheets, and for playing games. Home users did not have direct access to the Internet. Relatively low speed modems were widely available in the mid- to late 1980s, and people could dial directly into servers owned by CompuServe, Quantum Computer Services (later to be renamed America Online [AOL]), and Prodigy. These services allowed people to post messages, go into chat rooms, play games, or send and receive e-mail. None of these services connected to the Internet, and e-mails could only be sent among people on the same service.

The only people who could surf the Internet freely were those who had access to powerful mainframe computers through a university, the government, or a large corporation. The Internet, however, was a very uninviting place in the 1980s. Users connecting to the Internet had to know exactly what they were looking for to get it. To reach another computer or server on the Internet, users had to key in the IP address for that computer, which consisted of a string of up to twelve numbers, such as 216.183.103.150. To maneuver around on a server, commands had to be typed in computer code on a prompt line, and cryptic directories had to be sifted through. There were no Web browsers, colorful Internet pages, or search engines.

By 1984 the dedicated name server (DNS), developed by the University of Wisconsin, was introduced, making the Internet somewhat more user friendly. A DNS is a computer server on the Internet with a database that pairs domain names with IP addresses, giving people the ability to type in a name instead of a twelve digit number to reach a destination on the Internet. An Internet browser in 2004 contacts one of many DNSs each time an address, such as www.yahoo.com, is entered into the address bar. Most Internet service providers have a name server filled with the names and IP address numbers of widely used sites. Once the browser makes the request of the name server, the name server sends back the IP address number, which for Yahoo is 216.109.118.70. The Internet browser then uses this IP address to access the site the user wants to visit (Yahoo in this case).

Along with these name servers, a dedicated name system was also put into place so that no two names would be the same. Domain names with a minimum of two levels were decided on. The top-level designated the country or economic sector a computer is in (.com or .gov), and a unique second-level domain name designated the organization itself (NASA or Google). Host names, such as "www," specified the actual machine in the domain. Information Sciences Institute was put in charge of managing the root dedicated name server in 1985 for all domains to make sure that no two were alike and to track who was registered for what name. Some of the first domain names to be registered were symboics.com, mit.edu, think.com, and berkeley.edu.

A Major Expansion in the Mid-1980s

In 1986 Internet use expanded exponentially when the NSF installed new super computers and a new backbone for the U.S. Internet service, giving rise to NSFNet. Today,

FIGURE 1.3

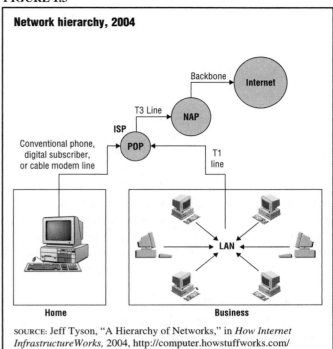

SOURCE: Jeff Tyson, "A Hierarchy of Networks," in *How Internet InfrastructureWorks,* 2004, http://computer.howstuffworks.com/internet-infrastructure1.htm (accessed October 25, 2004)

Internet service providers (ISPs) and cable companies have their own backbones, which are all tied into one another. When a home user connects to the Internet via phone, digital subscriber line (DSL), or cable, they connect to a bank of modems called a point of presence (POP) that is owned by the service provider (See Figure 1.3.) Each POP from each service provider, be it AOL or Comcast, feeds into a citywide network access point (NAP). These NAPs are connected to one another via backbones that consist of bundles, or trunks, of fiber optic cables that carry cross-country transmissions. The first NSF-funded backbone consisted of 56 kilobytes per second wire to connect the access points. The wire was laid down by AT&T. The NSF also provided five supercomputers to route traffic between the NAPs and bundles. In 1988 the NSF upgraded NSFNet when they installed supercomputers that could handle 1.544 gigabytes of traffic per second and fiber-optic line that could transfer information at 1.5 megabytes per second. Computers are only able to recognize and deal with information in digital binary form, wherein all data is made up entirely of ones and zeros. Computers process the long lines of complex, binary computer code in bite-sized quantities known as bytes. Each byte consists of a string of eight ones and zeros that can be used to represent binary numbers from zero to 255. In binary, one is 00000001, two is 00000010, nineteen is 00010011, and 255 is 11111111. A thousand bytes equals a kilobyte, a million bytes equals a megabyte, and a billion bytes equals a gigabyte.

The creation of the NSFNet ended the transmission bottlenecks that existed in the early Internet. The network also provided access for most major research institutions and universities. Academic departments and government agencies across the country jumped at the chance to set up servers and share information with their colleagues. From 1986 to 1987 the number of hosts (machines with a distinct IP address) on the Internet jumped from 5,000 to nearly 28,000.

The NSF strictly prohibited the use of its site for commercial purposes. Though such a rule may seem harsh, it had the intended consequence of fostering the development of private Internet providers. In 1987 UUNET became the first commercial Internet provider, offering service to Unix computers. Nineteen eighty-nine saw the introduction of The World, which was the first commercial provider of dial-up access, and computer scientists at McGill University in Montreal invented Archie, the first Internet search engine for finding computer files.

An Internet for Everyone

In 1991 Tim Berners-Lee at CERN, the European Organization for Nuclear Research, located in Switzerland, introduced the three technologies that would give rise to the World Wide Web. The first of Berners-Lee's technologies was the Web browser, a program that allowed a user to jump from one server computer on the Internet to another. The second was the hypertext markup language (HTML), which was a programming language for creating Web pages with graphics and links to other Web pages. The third was the hypertext transfer protocol (HTTP), a command used by the browser to retrieve the HTML information contained on the server's Web site. In concert, these three innovations led to the Web as it became known in the early twenty-first century. On his server, Berners-Lee created the first Web site at CERN. As the technology spread, many more Web servers and sites quickly came into being.

With these technologies, people were no longer required to use complex computer codes and sift through cryptic directories to retrieve information from other computers on the Internet. A user with the browser on his or her computer was able to simply type in the name of a server on the Internet along with the HTTP command (i.e., http://www.yahoo.com), and the browser began the process of gathering information automatically. The browser first contacted a DNS server to get the IP address of the server. Once the browser connected with the Web server, the browser sent out the HTTP command. The HTTP told the server to send the browser the HTML code for the specified Web site. Upon receiving the HTML code, the browser read the code and simply formed the page the owners of the server wanted the computer user to see (Yahoo's home page, for instance).

At the same time that these great strides were being made in establishing the Internet, the U.S. government began to take a more active role in its development. In 1991 Senator Al Gore (D-Tennessee) introduced the U.S. High Performance Computing Act into Congress. The act set aside over $2 billion for further research into computing and to improve the infrastructure of the Internet. Though most of it was earmarked for such large agencies as the NSF and NASA, some of the funds were placed into the hands of independent software developers.

Marc Andreesen used a federal grant received through this act to develop the Mosaic X Web browser, which was released in 1993. The browser was one of the first commercial browsers to employ the HTML program language and the HTTP, and it became the first browser to be embraced by the general public. It was easy to set up, easy to use, and backed by a full customer support staff. It displayed images in an attractive way and contained many of the standard features used on Microsoft's Internet Explorer today, such as the address prompt and "back" and "forward" buttons. Tens of thousands of copies of Mosaic X were sold.

Once Mosaic X became popular, more and more Web sites employing HTML and HTTP were posted. According to Internet historian Robert H. Zakon (http://www.zakon.org/robert/internet/timeline/), in June 1994 there were approximately 2,700 Web sites; by June 1995 there were an estimated 23,500. Growth in hosts during the same period reflected an increase from 3.2 million in July 1994 to 6.6 million in July 1995. The Web was growing at such a rapid rate that the NSF created the Internet Network Information Center (InterNIC) as an agency to handle domain names. The InterNIC contracted with Network Solutions to handle domain registration. By 1995 the companies that ran the older dial-up services for home users, such as CompuServe, American Online, and Prodigy, brought their clients to the Internet and offered Internet service for all. Internet network providers, such as MCI and Qwest, began laying fiber optic cables and communications networks at a breakneck pace. Advertising appeared on the Web for the first time (the first banner being for ZIMA), e-shopping appeared on the Internet, and many companies such as Netscape went public.

In the following years the Internet has gained a firm foothold in American life. As of July 2004, Zakon estimated the number of Web servers at more than 52 million, and the number of hosts, computers with a registered IP address, at more than 285 million.

THE DIGITAL DIVIDE

Although the Internet has swept into American households at a faster rate than almost any other technology, many people are still not wired. According a memo by director Lee Rainie of the Pew Internet & American Life Project (April 13, 2004), 27% of American adults did not use a computer, and 37% still did not go online. As can be

TABLE 1.3

Adult computer users, by selected characteristics, 2004

% of U.S. adults in each group who use computers

Men	73%
Women	72%
Generation	
Gen Y (ages 18–27)	85%
Gen X (ages 28–39)	87%
Trailing boomers (ages 40–49)	84%
Leading boomers (ages 50–58)	76%
Matures (ages 59–68)	57%
After work (ages 69+)	24%
Race and ethnicity	
Whites	73%
Blacks	62%
Hispanics (English speaking)	75%
Household income	
<$30,000	55%
$30,000–$49,999	82%
$50,000–$74,999	92%
$75,000+	93%
Community type	
Urban	75%
Suburban	76%
Rural	61%
Educational attainment	
Less than high school	39%
High school graduate	67%
Some college courses	84%
College graduate/graduate degree	91%

N=2,204.

SOURCE: Lee Rainie, "Computer Penetration Demographics," in *Pew Internet Project Data Memo,* Pew Internet and American Life Project, April 13, 2004, http://www.pewinternet.org/pdfs/PIP_April2004_Data_Memo.pdf (accessed October 25, 2004). Used by permission of the Pew Internet and American Life Project, which bears no responsibility for the interpretations presented or conclusions reached based on analysis of the data.

TABLE 1.4

Adult Internet users, by selected characteristics, 2004

% of U.S. adults in each group who use the Internet

Men	65%
Women	61%
Generation	
Gen Y (ages 18–27)	78%
Gen X (ages 28–39)	78%
Trailing boomers (ages 40–49)	71%
Leading boomers (ages 50–58)	62%
Matures (ages 59–68)	47%
After work (ages 69+)	17%
Race and ethnicity	
Whites	64%
Blacks	46%
Hispanics (English speaking)	63%
Household income	
<$30,000	41%
$30,000–$49,999	69%
$50,000–$74,999	86%
$75,000+	89%
Community type	
Urban	65%
Suburban	67%
Rural	48%
Educational attainment	
Less than high school	24%
High school graduate	54%
Some college courses	78%
College graduate/graduate degree	85%

N=2,204.

SOURCE: Lee Rainie, "Internet Penetration Demographics," in *Pew Internet Project Data Memo,* Pew Internet and American Life Project, April 13, 2004, http://www.pewinternet.org/pdfs/PIP_April2004_Data_Memo.pdf (accessed October 25, 2004). Used by permission of the Pew Internet and American Life Project, which bears no responsibility for the interpretations presented or conclusions reached based on analysis of the data.

seen in Table 1.3 and Table 1.4, demographic differences existed between computer users who were connected to the Internet and those who were not. The biggest discrepancies were in age, income, and educational attainment. Race, gender, and community type factored in to a lesser extent. The 2000 U.S. Census uncovered similar results, which can be viewed in Table 1.5. Both surveys reveal that those in typically disadvantaged demographics have the least exposure to the Internet. This leads to a concern that, without the Internet at their disposal, people in these demographic segments will become even more disadvantaged. Not only are they disconnected from e-mail, which has become a common form of communication, but they also do not benefit from such online services as employment Web sites and research resources that many users take for granted.

Wealth and Education

Wealth lies at the very heart of this digital divide. According to the data memo issued by Rainie of Pew/Internet in April 2004, nearly 89% of the people in households that made over $75,000 reported they used the Internet, compared with 41% of people who lived in households earning less than $30,000 a year. (See Table 1.4.) This gap in Internet use has shown only marginal improvement over the past four years. A tracking survey completed by Pew/Internet in spring 2000 revealed that 31% in the lowest income bracket used the Internet, while 78% of those in the highest bracket were online. Of those who did not go online, 30% said the reason was that ISPs charge too much. Major differences also existed in how varying income groups online used the Internet. The Pew/Internet study *America's Online Pursuits* revealed that 75% of those in the $30,000 and under category reported they went online just for fun, while only 58% in the $75,000 and over category agreed they used the Internet for fun. Perhaps not surprisingly, wealthier households used the Internet more to seek financial information or to purchase reservations. Only half (49%) of online Americans with household incomes in the lowest bracket tried to buy something online, as opposed to three quarters (74%) in the highest bracket. Those with the highest income in the survey were five times more likely to purchase stocks online than those with the smallest salaries.

TABLE 1.5

Households with computers and Internet access, by selected characteristic, 2001

[In percent. Based on the Current Population Survey and subject to sampling error.]

Characteristic	Households with computers				Households with Internet access			
	Total	Rural	Urban	Central city	Total	Rural	Urban	Central city
All households	56.5	55.6	56.7	51.5	50.5	48.7	51.1	45.7
Age of householder:								
Under 25 years old	51.1	41.3	53.0	50.9	44.7	33.5	46.7	45.3
25 to 34 years old	62.5	61.5	62.8	57.5	57.3	55.4	58.8	53.9
35 to 44 years old	69.9	71.2	69.4	62.1	62.6	62.3	63.4	54.3
45 to 54 years old	66.9	68.0	66.4	59.9	60.9	61.1	61.3	53.4
55 years old or over	39.1	38.0	39.5	35.5	33.9	32.1	35.0	29.9
Householder race/ethnicity:								
White[1]	61.1	58.0	62.4	60.0	55.4	51.0	56.8	54.8
Black[1]	37.1	31.5	37.7	33.9	30.8	24.4	30.9	27.4
American, Indian, Eskimo, Aleut[1]	44.7	37.6	49.5[2]	49.5	38.7	31.4	41.5	44.1
Asian or Pacific Islander[1]	72.7[2]	69.4	72.8	67.4	68.1	68.2	64.1[2]	63.1
Hispanic	40.0	36.6	40.3	38.1	32.0	29.9	32.6	29.8
Household type:								
Married couple with children under 18	78.9	78.6	79.0	72.4	71.6	69.7	73.6	64.6
Male householder with children under 18	55.1	53.6	55.6	51.8	44.9	39.9	47.2	44.3
Female householder with children under 18	49.2	51.0	48.9	41.6	40.0	40.9	42.3	33.5
Family households without children	58.8	55.0	60.4	55.2	53.2	48.9	55.3	49.7
Nonfamily households	39.2	31.6	40.9	41.4	35.0	26.9	36.2	37.0
Education of householder:								
Elementary	16.0	13.4	17.1	16.9	11.2	10.4	11.6	11.5
Some high school	28.2	27.6	28.4	25.5	22.7	22.4	22.6	19.8
High school graduate or GED	46.5	50.0	45.0	39.0	39.8	42.1	39.3	32.5
Some college	64.5	68.5	63.2	58.4	57.7	60.2	57.3	52.0
Bachelor's degree or more	79.8	81.1	79.5	76.7	75.2	75.1	75.0	72.0
Household income:								
Under $5,000	25.9	17.9	28.2	24.5	20.5	12.5	23.0	20.2
$5,000 to $9,999	19.2	16.4	20.1	20.6	14.4	11.0	15.5	14.5
$10,000 to $14,999	25.7	24.3	26.3	24.3	19.4	18.1	20.7	19.3
$15,000 to $19,999	31.8	29.4	32.6	33.9	23.6	21.0	25.3	24.6
$20,000 to $24,999	40.1	40.0	40.1	36.4	31.8	31.7	32.4	28.7
$25,000 to $34,999	49.7	49.4	49.9	49.9	42.2	40.5	43.7	41.3
$35,000 to $49,999	64.3	64.7	64.2	64.4	56.4	55.0	57.5	56.2
$50,000 to $74,999	77.7	78.1	77.6	75.8	71.4	70.6	71.7	70.5
$75,000 and over	89.0	89.0	88.9	86.4	85.4	84.8	85.5	83.8

[1]Non-Hispanic.
[2]Figure does not meet standards of reliability or precision.

SOURCE: "No. 1158. Households with Computers and Internet Access by Selected Characteristic: 2001," in *Statistical Abstract of the United States: 2003*, U.S. Census Bureau, Economics and Statistics Administration, U.S. Department of Commerce, Spring 2003, http://www.census.gov/prod/2004pubs/03statab/inforcomm.pdf (accessed October 25, 2004)

With most consumer-buying trends in the United States, wealth and education typically go hand in hand. Internet use is no exception. Looking at Table 1.4, only 24% of people with less than a high school education used the Internet, while 85% of college graduates went online. According to a Pew/Internet survey conducted in spring 2000 and published as *Who's Not Online*, very few (17%) adults with less than a high school degree used the Internet, versus a large majority (75%) of those with college degrees. Americans with a good deal of education utilized the Internet in much same way as those with high incomes. The December 2003 Pew/Internet study *America's Online Pursuits* revealed that college graduates preferred to go online more to bank, trade stocks, and make reservations than did those with less education. Using the Internet for job research or to answer a question tended to increase incrementally with education level as well. Only 80% of wired high school graduates utilized the Internet to answer a question they had by going online, whereas 87% of those with a college education reported using the Internet to investigate a query.

Age

Age was the third major factor that played a role in who used the Internet. As can be seen in Table 1.4, Internet usage was lower for older Americans. The transition, however, was not gradual. Seventy-one percent of those aged forty to forty-nine used the Internet in 2004, which was nearly as much as Gen-Xers (ages twenty-eight to thirty-nine). People aged fifty to fifty-eight were not that far behind at 62%. However, Internet usage suddenly fell off by 15% for those aged fifty-nine to sixty-eight. Only 17% of the people over age sixty-nine used the Internet. The reason for this low Internet usage in this highest age bracket was fairly obvious. The Internet was neither available at home nor common in the workplace until the late 1990s, when many of those over seventy had already left the workforce. They had long ago adopted other ways to do their work, get directions, and look up information.

Once seniors decide to take the plunge, however, they generally spend as much time online as younger users. Most seniors who did use the Internet were white, highly educated, and lived in households with higher incomes. The spring 2000 Pew/Internet tracking survey revealed that 22% of white seniors over age sixty-five were online and only 11% of African-Americans over sixty-five were online. These numbers are expected to change significantly over time, as new generations become retirees. Young and middle-aged Internet users are expected to continue using the Internet at the volume they do today and may even use their increasing spare time to take further advantage of the Internet.

Race and Ethnicity

Differences in Internet usage between different races and ethnicities—while not as dramatic as differences between different age and income groups—are significant and persistent. Table 1.4 shows that in 2004 white people and English-speaking Hispanics were roughly on par with one another in terms of Internet usage at 64% and 63% respectively. This was a dramatic change from 2000, when only 43% of Hispanics were online compared to 50% of whites. African-Americans trailed behind in both years. Their usage rate climbed from 34% in 2000 to 46% in 2004, a smaller increase than that shown by whites or Hispanics. Generally, Internet usage between races and ethnicities varies greatly with income, education, age, and even community type. Figure 1.4, released by the U.S. Commerce Department, shows that the difference in Internet usage in 2001 among different racial and ethnic groups was fairly small at the higher income brackets. For Americans making over $75,000, 89.8% of Asian-Americans, 86.2% of whites, 77% of African-Americans, and 75.6% of Hispanics were wired. At lower incomes, however, the discrepancies became enormous. A full 45% of Asians with an income of $15,000 or below still utilized the Internet. Only 20.8% of whites in this income group were online, and the percentage of African-Americans in this income group using the Internet was just 9.2%. A March 2004 Pew/Internet report entitled *Older Americans and the Internet* revealed that fewer African-Americans and Hispanics over age sixty-five were using the Internet than their white peers, and a February 2004 Pew/Internet report entitled *Rural Areas and the Internet* concluded that African-Americans living in rural areas did not use the Internet as much as those in the cities and suburbs.

America's Online Pursuits indicated that people of different races and ethnicities used the Internet in different

FIGURE 1.4

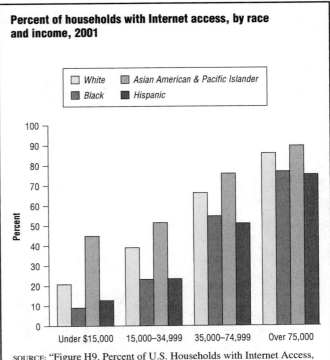

Percent of households with Internet access, by race and income, 2001

SOURCE: "Figure H9. Percent of U.S. Households with Internet Access, by Income, by Race/Hispanic Origin, 2001," in *A Nation Online: How Americans Are Expanding Their Use of the Internet,* Economics and Statistics Administration, U.S. Department of Commerce, 2001, http://www.ntia.doc.gov/ntiahome/dn/hhs/ChartH9.htm (accessed October 25, 2004)

ways. Whites tended to use the Internet to make online purchases, bank online, or buy stocks more than African-Americans and English-speaking Hispanics. In making online reservations, however, Hispanics came out on top. Some 59% of online Hispanics said they used the Internet at some point to make a travel purchase online, compared with 48% of wired African-Americans and 52% of wired whites. Both African-Americans and Hispanics used the Internet more than whites for entertainment purposes, such as downloading music or looking for sports information. In the gaming arena, 34% of online whites had played online games, versus 54% of Hispanics and 48% of blacks.

Gender

Differences in gender were not so apparent when looking at the number of overall users. As Table 1.4 reveals, 65% of the adult male population of this country was online in 2004 as opposed to 61% of women. The real differences came in how the two genders used the Internet. According *America's Online Pursuits* men were much more likely to seek financial information online, while women were more likely to look for religious information. When it came to seeking health information online, wired women beat out wired men 74% to 58%. On the other hand, 81% of wired men pursued information on hobbies online compared with 73% of women.

FIGURE 1.5

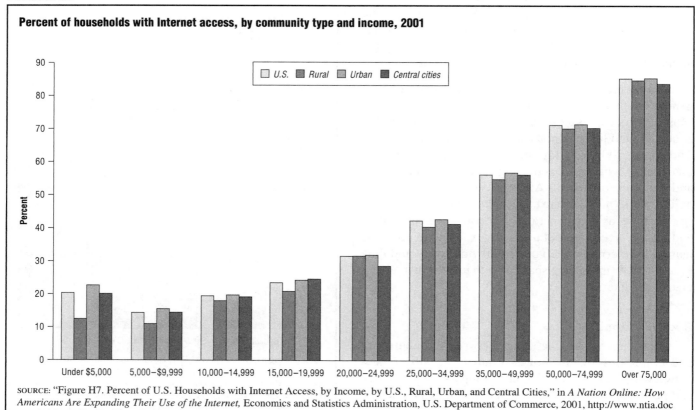

Percent of households with Internet access, by community type and income, 2001

SOURCE: "Figure H7. Percent of U.S. Households with Internet Access, by Income, by U.S., Rural, Urban, and Central Cities," in *A Nation Online: How Americans Are Expanding Their Use of the Internet,* Economics and Statistics Administration, U.S. Department of Commerce, 2001, http://www.ntia.doc .gov/ntiahome/dn/hhs/ChartH7.htm (accessed October 25, 2004)

Community Type

Internet usage also diverged according to the type of community people lived in. While urban and suburban Internet usage was relatively on par at 65% and 67%, rural Internet usage came in only at 48% in 2004. (See Table 1.4.) The February 2004 Pew/Internet report *Rural Areas and the Internet* revealed that, as a whole, wired rural adults were more likely to look for spiritual information and less likely to conduct financial transactions online. The report also suggested that the low number of rural Internet users was not due to a lack of Internet service in remote regions. The discrepancy had more to do with the fact that rural Americans were, in general, older and less wealthy than urbanites or suburbanites. Seniors accounted for 22% of people living in rural areas, as opposed to 16% in suburban populations. Forty-seven percent of rural residents had household incomes of $30,000 or less, compared with 29% of suburbanites and 39% of urbanites. Figure 1.5, released by the U.S. Commerce Department, supports these findings. The level of Internet usage for those with incomes greater than $75,000 was nearly the same regardless of community type in 2001. In this income bracket, 85.5% of urbanites and 84.8% of rural Americas went online. Just as with race, the discrepancies between the groups grew as yearly income waned. Only 12.5% of people making under $5,000 in rural areas used the Internet, whereas 22.7% of low-income urbanites were wired.

These trends occurred on a regional scale as well. According to *Internet Use by Region in the United States* (Washington, DC: Pew/Internet, August 2003), the regions with the lowest Internet usage were the South (48%) and the Lower Midwest (55%). (See Table 1.6.) The regions with the highest Internet usage were the Pacific Northwest (68%), New England (66%), and California (65%). For the most part, these regional trends could be ascribed to wealth and education. California and New England had large populations of wealthy and educated people, and the South had some of the lowest incomes and education levels. The exception to this rule was the Pacific Northwest where the number of Internet users tended to be disproportionately high in relation to income and education. Table 1.7 shows Internet use by state, and the results reflect the regional findings. Mississippi and Arkansas had the lowest percentage of Internet users in 2001 at 36.1% and 36.9% respectively. The states with the highest percentage of Internet users were Alaska and New Mexico with 64.1% and 61.6% Internet users.

THE FUTURE OF COMPUTING AND THE INTERNET

In the immediate future, the typical Internet connection is likely to become much faster. An April 2004 Pew/Internet data memo by senior research specialist

TABLE 1.6

Adults with Internet access, by region, 2002

Some 59% of American adults had Internet access at the end of 2002, up from about 50% in 2000. The use of the Internet by Americans over age 18 varies by region, however, as shown below.

Region	Adults with Internet access in December 2002 (%)
New England (Connecticut, Maine, Massachusetts, New Hampshire, Vermont, Rhode Island)	66%
Mid-Atlantic (Delaware, New Jersey, New York, Pennsylvania)	58
National Capital (Maryland, Virginia, Washington, DC)	64
Southeast (Florida, Georgia, North Carolina, South Carolina)	57
South (Alabama, Arkansas, Kentucky, Louisiana, Mississippi, Tennessee, West Virginia)	48
Industrial Midwest (Illinois, Indiana, Michigan, Ohio)	56
Upper Midwest (Minnesota, North Dakota, South Dakota, Wisconsin)	59
Lower Midwest (Iowa, Kansas, Missouri, Nebraska, Oklahoma)	55
Border states (Arizona, New Mexico, Texas)	60
Mountain states (Colorado, Idaho, Montana, Nevada, Utah, Wyoming)	64
Pacific Northwest (Oregon, Washington)	68
California	65

SOURCE: Tom Spooner, Peter Meredith, and Lee Rainie, "Internet Penetration by U.S. Region," in *Internet Use by Region in the United States,* Pew Internet and American Life Project, August 27, 2003, http://www .pewinternet.org/pdfs/PIP_Regional_Report_Aug_2003.pdf (accessed October 25, 2004). Used by permission of the Pew Internet and American Life Project, which bears no responsibility for the interpretations presented or conclusions reached based on analysis of the data.

TABLE 1.7

Households with computers and Internet access, 1998 and 2001

[In percent. Based on survey and subject to sampling error.]

State	1998		2001	
	Computers	Internet access	Computers	Internet access
U.S.	42.1	26.2	56.5	50.5
AL	34.3	21.6	43.7	37.6
AK	62.4	44.1	68.7	64.1
AZ	44.3	29.3	59.4	51.9
AR	29.8	14.7	46.8	36.9
CA	47.5	30.7	61.5	55.3
CO	55.3	34.5	64.7	58.5
CT	43.8	31.8	58.7	55.0
DE	40.5	25.1	58.4	52.5
DC	41.4	24.2	49.3	41.4
FL	39.5	27.8	55.9	52.8
GA	35.8	23.9	52.4	46.7
HI	42.3	27.9	63.1	55.2
ID	50.0	27.4	62.8	52.7
IL	42.7	26.5	53.0	46.9
IN	43.5	26.1	53.2	47.3
IA	41.4	21.8	59.4	51.0
KS	43.7	25.7	57.5	50.9
KY	35.9	21.1	49.8	44.2
LA	31.1	17.8	45.7	40.2
ME	43.4	26.0	62.8	53.3
MD	46.3	31.0	64.1	57.8
MA	43.4	28.1	59.1	54.7
MI	44.0	25.4	58.3	51.2
MN	47.6	29.0	64.6	55.6
MS	25.7	13.6	41.9	36.1
MO	41.8	24.3	55.3	49.9
MT	40.9	21.5	56.0	47.5
NE	42.9	22.9	55.6	45.5
NV	41.6	26.5	58.2	52.5
NH	54.2	37.1	55.0	50.2
NJ	48.1	31.3	61.2	57.2
NM	42.2	25.8	67.7	61.6
NY	37.3	23.7	50.6	43.1
NC	35.0	19.9	50.1	44.5
ND	40.2	20.6	53.0	46.5
OH	40.7	24.6	57.6	50.9
OK	37.8	20.4	49.9	43.8
OR	51.3	32.7	65.8	58.2
PA	39.3	24.9	53.5	48.7
RI	41.0	27.1	58.6	53.1
SC	35.7	21.4	52.2	45.0
SD	41.6	23.9	55.3	47.6
TN	37.5	21.3	51.3	44.8
TX	40.9	24.5	53.7	47.7
UT	60.1	35.8	67.7	54.1
VT	48.7	31.8	60.4	53.4
VA	46.4	27.9	58.8	54.9
WA	56.3	36.6	66.5	60.4
WV	28.3	17.6	48.0	40.7
WI	43.0	25.1	56.4	50.2
WY	46.1	22.7	58.1	51.0

SOURCE: "No. 1159. Households with Computers and Internet Access: 1998 and 2001," in *Statistical Abstract of the United States: 2003,* U.S. Census Bureau, Economics and Statistics Administration, U.S. Department of Commerce, Spring 2003, http://www.census.gov/prod/2004pubs/03statab/inforcomm.pdf (accessed October 25, 2004)

John Horrigan reported that forty-eight million people had high-speed broadband connections at home and sixty-eight million had access at home or on the job. The number of people with broadband Internet connections represented 55% of all Internet users and 34% of the American population. Figure 1.6 shows that in June 2000 only a little more than five million people had broadband; by March 2004 forty-eight million adults had broadband connections at home.

When broadband first became available, its early users tended to be those who had been online for more than three years, and those whom the Pew Internet & American Life Project dubbed as the "Young Tech Elite." These were people thirty-five and under with good incomes, college degrees, and the latest gadgets and information services. By 2004, however, people were adopting broadband faster, and they were not all necessarily part of the "Young Tech Elite." Relatively inexpensive DSL services that hook up right into the phone lines are making high-speed Internet more affordable for all. At the rate with which broadband subscriptions are rising, dial-up lines may soon be a thing of the past.

Another Internet trend that is picking up momentum in the first decade of the twenty-first century is the use of wireless connections. For many, the Internet has become an essential part of everyday life, and people increasingly want to be able to log on to the Internet from any location, in private or public spaces. It is therefore not surprising that more Americans are turning to wireless technologies. According to a May 2004 Pew/Internet memo by Horrigan, at that time nearly 28% of American adults were using either laptop computers with wireless modems or cell phones that enabled them to surf the Web or check e-mail.

FIGURE 1.6

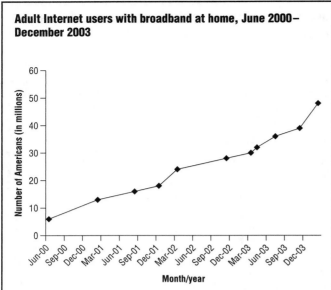

Adult Internet users with broadband at home, June 2000– December 2003

SOURCE: John Horrigan, "American Adults with Broadband at Home," in *Pew Internet Project Data Memo,* Pew Internet and American Life Project, April 2004, http://www.pewinternet.org/pdfs/PIP_Broadband04 .DataMemo.pdf (accessed October 25, 2004). Used by permission of the Pew Internet and American Life Project, which bears no responsibility for the interpretations presented or conclusions reached based on analysis of the data.

Nearly 18% of Internet users in the United States said they have used a wireless laptop to access the Internet, and 10% said they go online from a location other than home. The number of wireless hotspots has been on the rise as well. Statistics published by Gartner Inc. on the Web (www.dataquest.com) revealed that the number of wireless local area networks grew from 1,200 globally to more than 151,000 between 2001 and 2005.

Despite these numbers, however, wireless access to the Internet outside of the house is typically slow or spotty due to the limited 150 to 300 foot range of wireless fidelity (Wi-Fi) hotspots and the slow speed of dial-up modems. Several emerging technologies may allow people to access high-speed Internet on their laptops wherever they go. According to Anil Ananthaswamy in "Broadband Web Link Goes Wireless" (*New Scientist*, April 17, 2004), several large companies, including Intel and AT&T, are promoting a new technology that will enable a laptop to connect wirelessly to a base station over twenty miles away. The technology, called Wi-MAX (Worldwide Interoperability for Microwave Access), uses base station transmitters much like those in a mobile phone network. Any laptop computer equipped with a Wi-MAX receiver should be able to instantly log on to one of these stations and receive high-speed Internet access from miles away. With enough transmitters in place, logging on anywhere in a city with high-speed access may soon be as easy as it is at home. Another technology closer to market is the third generation (3G) cell phone service. This service will allow cell phones to receive and send signals that contain as much information as a broadband Internet connection. With a 3G modem equipped to a computer, people may soon be able to get high-speed access for the Internet through the cellular network.

In the long term, however, the future of the Internet will likely be the Internet2. Internet2 is not a new Internet, but a collaboration of dozens of academic institutions and corporations working together to develop technologies that will be integrated into the Internet and allow it to move forward. One project the consortium is working on is version six of the Internet Protocol (IPv6). The number of computers, cell phones, and other devices using the Internet has grown exponentially in recent years. Each time one of these devices logs onto the Internet, it requires its own address. Right now the current Internet protocol only allows for a little over four billion addresses, which will soon be insufficient to accommodate all users. Ipv6 introduces a new Internet address system that will allow for trillions upon trillions of new addresses. The Internet2 has also had a hand in setting up and creating technologies to be used on Abilene. Abilene is a new high-performance backbone network laid down by Qwest Communications, which connects a number of universities and government installations. The fiber optic cables in this backbone can carry information at a rate of 10 gigabytes per second. Internet2 is designing networks, software, and hardware that can utilize Abeline with the idea that one day this will be the standard. With such a network, the Internet will likely have no speed limits. Americans should be able to watch high definition television via the Internet, teleconference with friends and family at any time, and easily access entire libraries of music and books online.

CHAPTER 2
AMERICA DISCOVERS NEW WAYS TO COMMUNICATE

In 1985 American adults typically had one phone number for the house and one for work. By 2004, many tech-savvy Americans had added such alternate communications as a cell phone, a fax line, an instant messaging account, an e-mail address for business, another for home, and still another to ward off spam. Communication has undeniably been one of the central motivations behind the technical strides that have taken place since the beginning of the cold war. The Internet was first conceived as a way of connecting computers for the purpose of communication, and e-mail was the first application to gain acceptance and widespread use on the Internet. In *Spam: How It Is Hurting Email and Degrading Life on the Internet* (Washington, DC: Pew Internet & American Life Project, October 2003), researcher Deborah Fallows reported that nearly thirty billion e-mails were flying across the Internet on a given day. When looking at what activities online Americans participate in the most on a daily basis, e-mail generally beats out every other activity two to one. That does not even take into account the nearly fifty-four million Americans who reported using instant messaging in 2003.

The Internet is not the only communications system to flourish. Since the early 1980s an entirely new phone system has sprung up across America as well. Table 2.1 reveals that the number of cellular sites in the United States grew from 5,616 sites to 139,338 sites between 1990 and 2002, and the amount of revenue brought in by the cellular phone system rose from $4.5 billion to $76.5 billion. The number of cell phone subscribers jumped from 5.3 million subscriptions in 1990 to 33 million in 1998 to approximately 140 million subscribers in 2002. In terms of percentage, the rise in cell phone customers outstripped the increase in Internet customers and was roughly equivalent to the rise in home computers since the early 1980s.

In some ways these new forms of communication have made life easier. Most Americans no longer have to hunt down a phone booth and dig for change when searching for that elusive restaurant. Nor do most travelers have to worry about being stranded on a deserted roadway miles from a phone. Using e-mail, online Americans can now easily stay in touch with anyone in any country around the world. At the same time, however, Americans now have to comb through offensive spam on a daily basis, concern themselves with unleashing viruses on the computer, and endure annoying cell phone chimes everywhere they go.

E-MAIL

E-mail was the first of these new communications technologies to emerge. Not more than two years after the initial ARPANET test in 1969, Ray Tomlinson of ARPANET created the first e-mail program. Tomlinson got the idea from a program that had been floating around on time-share computers. These computers, prevalent in the early sixties, consisted of a number of remote terminals all connected to a central host computer where all the office files and programs were stored. The remote terminals, which were typically spread throughout the office building, consisted of little more than a screen and a keyboard, and the office workers shared the resources of the central computer. Programs were written for these systems wherein people could leave messages for one another within the core computer. Tomlinson simply adapted one of these static internal mail programs into a program that could send messages to other computers on the ARPANET. The first mass e-mail Tomlinson sent out with his program was a message to all ARPANET terminals informing them of the availability of "electronic mail." He told them to address one another using the following convention: "user's log-in name@host computer name." This same convention is still used today.

The first e-mail program was not very user-friendly. The e-mails did not have subject lines or date lines, they had to be opened in the order that they were received and

TABLE 2.1

Cellular telecommunications industry, 1990–2002

[Calendar year data, except as noted (5,283 represents 5,283,000). Based on a survey mailed to all cellular, personal communications services, and enhanced special mobile radio (ESMR) systems. For 2002 data, the universe was 2,481 systems and the response rate was 87 percent. The number of operational systems beginning 2000 differs from that reported for previous periods as a result of the consolidated operation of ESMR systems in a broader service area instead of by a city-to-city basis.]

Item	Unit	1990	1995	1997	1998	1999	2000	2001	2002
Systems	Number	751	1,627	2,228	3,073	3,518	2,440	2,587	2,481
Subscribers	1,000	5,283	33,786	55,312	69,209	86,047	109,478	128,375	140,766
Cell sites[1]	Number	5,616	22,663	51,600	65,887	81,698	104,288	127,540	139,338
Employees	Number	21,382	68,165	109,387	134,754	155,817	184,449	203,580	192,410
Service revenue	Mil. dol.	4,548	19,081	27,486	33,133	40,018	52,466	65,016	76,508
Roamer revenue[2]	Mil. dol.	456	2,542	2,974	3,501	4,085	3,883	3,936	3,896
Capital investment	Mil. dol.	6,282	24,080	46,058	60,543	71,265	89,624	105,030	126,922
Average monthly bill[3]	Dollars	80.90	51.00	42.78	39.43	41.24	45.27	47.37	48.40
Average length of call[3]	Minutes	2.20	2.15	2.31	2.39	2.38	2.56	2.74	2.73

[1]The basic geographic unit of a wireless PCS or cellular system. A city or county is divided into smaller "cells," each of which is equipped with a low-powered radio transmitter/receiver. The cells can vary in size depending upon terrain, capacity demands, etc. By controlling the transmission power, the radio frequencies assigned to one cell can be limited to the boundaries of that cell. When a wireless PCS or cellular phone moves from one cell toward another, a computer at the switching office monitors the movement and at the proper time, transfers or hands off the phone call to the new cell and another radio frequency.
[2]Service revenue generated by subscribers' calls outside of their system areas.
[3]As of December 31.

SOURCE: "No. 1150. Cellular Telecommunications Industry: 1990 to 2002," in *Statistical Abstract of the United States: 2003,* U.S. Census Bureau, Economics and Statistics Administration, U.S. Department of Commerce, Spring 2003, http://www.census.gov/prod/2004pubs/03statab/inforcomm.pdf (accessed October 25, 2004)

they read as strings of continuous text. Despite these flaws, the e-mail application caught on in the ARPANET community quickly, and the talented computer scientists in the organization worked out most of the kinks. Within a couple of years, users could list messages by subject and date, delete selected messages, and forward messages to other users. E-mail soon became the most popular application for the busy researchers working at ARPANET. When communicating by e-mail, they did not have to worry about the formalities or the long delays inherent in letter writing. Unlike a phone conversation, no time was wasted on small talk, and a copy of the communication could be retained. Finally, people could send e-mails to one another at any time of day or night. By the late 1970s, e-mail discussion groups had formed within the ARPANET community. Two of the more popular were the science fiction group and a group that discussed the potential future social ramifications of e-mail.

In the late 1970s and early 1980s, other networks began to develop, such as Usenet and BITNET, which consisted of mainframe computers that connected to one another over telephone lines. The central purpose of these networks was to connect universities and government agencies that were not on ARPANET. Some of these networks, such as Usenet, were set up for the express purpose of sending e-mail and posting messages on newsgroups. Usenet consisted of computers of various sizes all over the country. A relatively small number of large, powerful computers formed the backbone of the network, and a large number of smaller computers logged on to the network through the larger ones. To send an e-mail from Indiana to South Carolina, for instance, a person on a small computer in Indiana would first dial into

and post an e-mail onto the nearest large computer. The person operating the large computer in Indiana would then pass the e-mail via modem along with other messages from the region to all the other large computers in the network, including those in or near South Carolina. When the recipient of the e-mail logged into the network through the nearest large computer, the e-mail would then automatically be downloaded.

By the late 1980s, e-mail was available commercially for home users to a limited extent. Such companies as Quantum Computer Services (now known as America Online, or AOL) and Prodigy set up chat room and e-mail services that could be enjoyed by people with home computers. Quantum Link, for instance, was a service compatible with the Commodore 64 computer. Home users dialed into local Quantum Link mainframes, which were located in most major cities around the country. The mainframes were interconnected via open phone lines, so that anyone using the service could e-mail or chat with anyone else logged onto the service across country. A member, however, could not contact someone on another commercial service or on the much larger Internet.

E-mail Becomes Widespread

The development of NSFInternet and the standardization of Internet protocols (TCP/IP) in the mid-1980s brought most of the smaller academic networks such as BITNET together, allowing people throughout academia and government agencies to communicate with one another via e-mail. The invention of the World Wide Web, Mosaic, and the widespread use of more powerful personal computers allowed home users access to Internet e-mail by the early 1990s. In 1994 AOL began offering people a limited service on the Web with the ability to send and receive e-mail. Within a year, all the established dial-up services such as CompuServe and Prodigy moved their e-mail subscribers onto the larger Internet.

Since the mid-1990s e-mail has become the most used application on the Internet. According to a poll conducted by the Pew Research Center in 1996, fifty million adult Americans had used e-mail. A Pew/Internet survey in spring 2000 revealed that the number of Internet users who took advantage of e-mail leapt to seventy-eight million people. Still another Pew/Internet survey, conducted in June 2003, showed e-mail use among Americans was at 117 million people. Most people said that e-mail helped them to maintain social ties with friends, communicate better on their jobs, and interact more effectively with local governments.

Who Uses E-mail?

A December 2003 Pew/Internet study entitled *America's Online Pursuits* reported that different demographic groups incorporate e-mail into their lives to varying degrees. In 2002 95% of online women sent and received e-mail, while only 90% of men did so. Women also saw e-mail in a more positive light then men and were more likely to say they looked forward to checking their mail. Along racial lines, however, the differences were greater. Only 87% of online African-Americans used e-mail, compared with 93% of whites on the Internet. A higher percentage of English-speaking Hispanics in general sent and received e-mail than whites. However, 54% of whites used e-mail on a daily basis, compared with 39% of online Hispanics.

Trends for e-mail use by age do not reflect trends for general Internet use. Figure 2.1 shows that of all age groups online in December 2002, those over sixty-five years of age had embraced e-mail the most. A March 2004 Pew/Internet survey report entitled *Older Americans and the Internet* revealed that 94% of online seniors sent or received e-mail, compared with 91% of all Internet users. E-mail is by far the Internet activity that seniors engage in more than any other. E-mail use, just like Internet use, varies with wealth and education. Thirty-nine percent of high school graduates sent e-mail on a typical day according to the December 2003 Pew/Internet report of American's online activities. The same study revealed that some 61% of college graduates were e-mailing daily. Furthermore, only 37% of adult Americans making less than $30,000 per year used e-mail. In households with incomes of more than $75,000 per year, 58% of people sent and received e-mail.

Spam

By far the biggest problem facing e-mail today is spam, which is generally defined as unsolicited e-mail

FIGURE 2.1

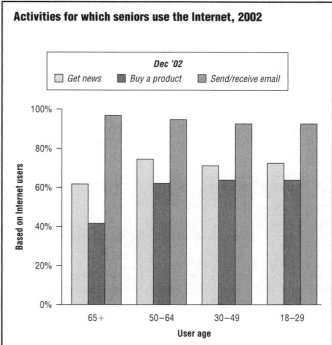

SOURCE: "More Seniors Use E-mail Than Do Other Activities Online," in *America's Online Pursuits,* Pew Internet and American Life Project, December 22, 2003, http://www.pewinternet.org/pdfs/PIP_Online _Pursuits_Final.pdf (accessed October 25, 2004). Used by permission of the Pew Internet and American Life Project, which bears no responsibility for the interpretations presented or conclusions reached based on analysis of the data.

sent in bulk. Many people, including Orson Swindle of the Federal Trade Commission (FTC), believe that spam may be on the verge of making e-mail an impractical means of communication. In 2003 Fallows had reported in *Spam: How It Is Hurting Email and Degrading Life on the Internet* that spam had reached epidemic proportions. As noted in *Spam*, the research marketing firm Radicati Group found that nearly half of the thirty billion e-mails passing back and forth on the Internet each day consisted of spam. The spam most Internet users saw in their e-mail boxes was only a fraction of the total spam sent to them. MSN and AOL both reported that each day they trashed 2.4 billion spam messages that would have otherwise reached their customers' electronic mailboxes. For AOL customers, this amounted to about sixty-seven spam e-mails per inbox or 80% of e-mail traffic. As stated in the Pew/Internet report, the price to American businesses to deal with all this spam totaled between $10 billion and $87 billion annually as of 2003.

Spam means many things to many people. According to Fallows in *Spam*, most people (92%) in 2003 agreed to the statement that spam is "unsolicited commercial e-mail from a sender they do not know or cannot identify." Beyond this basic definition, however, opinions varied widely. As Table 2.2 shows, some 78% of adults believed that unsolicited mail containing health, beauty, or medical offers was not

TABLE 2.2

E-mail recipients' definition of spam, 2003

Sender or subject matter	% who consider it spam
Unsolicited commercial email (UCE) from a sender you don't know	92%
UCE from a political or advocacy group	74
UCE from a non-profit or charity	65
UCE from a sender with whom you've done business	32
UCE from a sender you have given permission to contact you	11
UCE containing adult content	92
UCE with investment deals, financial offers, moneymaking proposals	89
UCE with product or service offers	81
UCE with software offers	78
UCE with health, beauty, or medical offers	78
Unsolicited email with political messages	76
Unsolicited email with religious information	76
A personal or professional message from one you don't know	74

Notes: For items 1–5, N=624. For items 6–13, N=648. UCE is unsolicited commercial email. E-mailers' definition of spam depends on the sender and the subject matter of the message.

SOURCE: "What E-mailers Consider Spam," in *Spam: How It Is Hurting E-mail and Degrading Life on the Internet,* Pew Internet and American Life Project, October 22, 2003, http://www.pewinternet.org/pdfs/PIP_Spam_Report.pdf (accessed October 25, 2004). Used by permission of the Pew Internet and American Life Project, which bears no responsibility for the interpretations presented or conclusions reached based on analysis of the data.

FIGURE 2.2

Percentage of e-mail received on a typical day that is spam, 2003

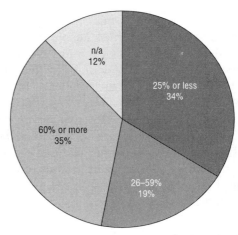

SOURCE: "Percentage of E-mail That Is Spam Received on a Typical Day," in *Spam: How It Is Hurting E-mail and Degrading Life on the Internet,* Pew Internet and American Life Project, October 22, 2003, http://www.pewinternet.org/pdfs/PIP_Spam_Report.pdf (accessed October 25, 2004). Used by permission of the Pew Internet and American Life Project, which bears no responsibility for the interpretations presented or conclusions reached based on analysis of the data.

spam. If the sender of the spam was promoting a nonprofit organization or charity, then only 65% of the recipients considered the e-mail spam. People were even less judgmental toward organizations with which they conducted business. Only 32% of e-mailers agreed that unsolicited e-mails sent from someone they did business with is spam. On the other hand, there were those (11%) who believed that an unsolicited e-mail from someone who was given permission to contact them was still spam.

Figure 2.2 shows a breakdown of the percentage of people's daily e-mail that was made of spam in 2003. Roughly a third (34%) of the e-mailing population said their e-mail consisted of 25% spam or less, and another third (35%) replied that their e-mail was made of 60% spam or more. As to the amount of time people spent on spam, Figure 2.3 reveals that 35% of e-mailers took less than five minutes a day clearing out the spam in 2003. Some 13% said they spent between fifteen minutes and thirty minutes on spam, and 15% said they spent over a half-hour or more. Overall, spam affected people's private accounts more than their work accounts. A third of people said their personal e-mails received more than 80% spam on a typical day, compared with 5% of people who responded that their work e-mail received this much spam. Only 7% of people said they received no spam in their personal e-mail inboxes, and nearly 40% said they received no spam in their work e-mail inboxes.

The vast majority of adults who received spam did not like it. Twenty-seven percent of people surveyed in the 2003 Pew/Internet study agreed spam is a "big problem." Most people (59%) said spam was "annoying, but not a

big problem," and only a small number of people (14%) responded that it was not a problem at all. Table 2.3 shows the single biggest objection people had to spam was that it was unsolicited. They were also upset at the volume of spam, its offensive and oftentimes obscene nature, and the fact that spam took time to deal with. Nearly one-third of all adult e-mailers expressed concern that in an attempt to cope with spam, either they or their service provider's e-mail filters were accidentally deleting legitimate e-mails. Still other people claimed that they miss out on e-mail because spam clogs their e-mail accounts to the point where they cannot receive any more mail. All of this amounts to a continued erosion of trust in e-mail. If spam volume continues to grow, it could eventually become heavy enough to jeopardize the system itself.

The problem is that sending out spam costs next to nothing per message sent. Even if 1% of people respond to a spam attack, be it for a legitimate digital cable filter or a fraudulent credit card scam, the spammer stands to make a lot of money or bring in a lot of credit card numbers. The October 2003 Pew/Internet report on spam revealed that 7% of people said they occasionally responded to spam ads. Bringing this number down to zero would likely be impossible. Until an effective law is put into place, the lucrative spam industry will probably continue to thrive. People will still get paid to build and sell huge lists of e-mail addresses. Software makers will continue to make money putting together programs that generate random lists of e-mail addresses and programs

FIGURE 2.3

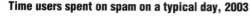

Time users spent on spam on a typical day, 2003

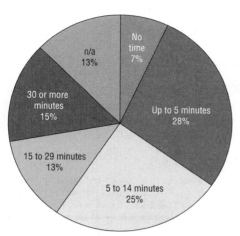

SOURCE: "Time Users Spend on Spam in a Typical Day," in *Spam: How It Is Hurting E-mail and Degrading Life on the Internet,* Pew Internet and American Life Project, October 22, 2003, http://www.pewinternet.org/pdfs/PIP_Spam_Report.pdf (accessed October 25, 2004). Used by permission of the Pew Internet and American Life Project, which bears no responsibility for the interpretations presented or conclusions reached based on analysis of the data.

TABLE 2.3

Aspects of spam that bother e-mail recipients, 2003

Bothersome aspects of spam	% e-mailers bothered
Unsolicited nature of spam	84%
Deceptive or dishonest content	80
Potential damage to computer	79
Volume of spam	77
Offensive or obscene content	76
Compromise to privacy	76
Can't stop it	75
Time it takes to deal with it	69

N=1,272.

SOURCE: "Aspects of Spam That Bother E-mailers," in *Spam: How It Is Hurting E-mail and Degrading Life on the Internet,* Pew Internet and American Life Project, October 22, 2003, http://www.pewinternet.org/pdfs/PIP_Spam_Report.pdf (accessed October 25, 2004). Used by permission of the Pew Internet and American Life Project, which bears no responsibility for the interpretations presented or conclusions reached based on analysis of the data.

that help spammers find easily exploitable e-mail servers with lists of e-mail accounts.

A group of some of computer scientists and engineers met at the Massachusetts Institute of Technology in the spring of 2003 to begin researching technologies that can stop spam. In addition, representatives from AOL, Yahoo, and Microsoft met to share intelligence on blocking spam in 2003.

ANTI-SPAM LEGISLATION. The federal government has also become involved in limiting spam. On January 1, 2004, the "Controlling the Assault of Non-Solicited Pornography and Marketing Act of 2003" (CAN-SPAM Act) went into effect. This Congressional act, enforced by the FTC and the states' attorneys general, lays out a number of provisions that commercial e-mail senders (spammers) must follow. One provision states that commercial e-mail senders must clearly identify unsolicited e-mail as solicitations or advertisements for products and services. Commercial e-mail senders must also provide a way for the recipient of the mail to opt out of receiving any more e-mails from them, and all e-mails must contain a legitimate address and use honest subject lines. While these provisions address the issue of spam, enforcement has been very difficult. Creating a false identity on the Internet is easy, and once spammers know someone is tracking them down, they can easily relocate their operations to a different state or country. As of October 13, 2004, emarketer.com, one of the premier Web sites devoted to Internet marketing, reported that the level of compliance of CAN-SPAM has only managed to reach the 4% mark.

INSTANT MESSAGING

Instant messaging (IM) is a tool that allows people to communicate via text messages in near real time over the Internet, and it is typically available on personal computers and on selected cell phones. *How Americans Use Instant Messaging* (Washington, DC: Pew Internet & American Life Project, September 2004) revealed that roughly fifty-four million people (42% of online, adult Americans) used instant messaging. In 2000 IM only had forty-one million users. Some 36% of these IM users reported that they use IM every day, and 63% used it several times a week. Twenty-four percent of those who used IM spent more time on IM than on e-mail. Table 2.4 shows the IM services people used the most in July 2004 and where they liked to use it. AOL was the most popular service, followed by Yahoo and Microsoft.

Generally, most instant messaging programs allow a user to block instant messages from anyone but the people the user wishes to converse with on a regular basis. Those who used instant messaging typically only used it to stay in touch with people they knew well. The September 2004 Pew/Internet report stated that two-thirds of IM users (66%) regularly used the service to communicate with between one and five people, and only roughly one-tenth (9%) contacted more than ten people regularly with IM. In addition, most people preferred to do their instant messaging at home for quick, one-on-one conversations. Seventy-seven percent of the IM community used IM at home, as opposed to 21% at work. Only 22% of IM enthusiasts in 2004 typically sent and received instant messages for more than an hour a day, and 47% percent said their typical IM sessions lasted for less than fifteen minutes.

IM provided people some unique advantages that other communication devices did not. Because of its compact size on the computer screen and its instant nature,

TABLE 2.4

Instant messaging (IM) users and the most popular applications, July 2004

	All locations		Home		Work		University	
	Unique visitors (000)	% reach among Internet users	Unique visitors (000)	% reach	Unique visitors (000)	% reach	Unique visitors (000)	% reach
Unduplicated total	67,921	43.3	53,360	38.8	14,391	28.9	5,754	49.2
AOL Instant Message (proprietary service)	25,090	16.0	21,236	15.5	3,171	6.4	1,888	16.1
Yahoo! Messenger	22,135	14.1	17,564	12.8	4,582	9.2	1,338	11.4
AOL Instant Messenger (AiM service)	21,363	13.6	16,600	12.1	4,234	8.5	2,491	21.3
MSN Messenger applications	17,167	10.9	13,307	9.7	4,132	8.3	1,361	11.6
ICQ	3,956	2.5	2,311	1.7	1,449	2.9	658	5.6
PalTalk	624	0.4	490	0.4	142	0.3	21	0.2
Trillian	404	0.3	239	0.2	133	0.3	52	0.4

SOURCE: "July Data on IM Users and the Most Popular Applications," in *How Americans Use Instant Messaging*, Pew Internet and American Life Project, September 1, 2004, http://www.pewinternet.org/pdfs/PIP_Instantmessage_Report.pdf (accessed October 25, 2004). Used by permission of the Pew Internet and American Life Project, which bears no responsibility for the interpretations presented or conclusions reached based on analysis of the data.

people reported that IM was easy to use while multitasking. Thirty percent of adult Americans said that they multitask while using IM. Instant messaging also has a clandestine aspect to it. A person can type a message without anyone knowing what he or she is doing. Nearly a quarter of all IM users said they use IM to converse with someone they were in close proximity to—typically because a class or meeting was in progress.

Table 2.5 shows that IM users in 2004 did not fall along the same demographic lines as Internet users. A higher percentage of African-Americans than whites used instant messaging, and English-speaking Hispanics used IM at the highest rate. Over half of online adult Americans with incomes less than $30,000 reported using IM. Forty-nine percent of those online adults with less than a high school degree took part in instant messaging, which was more than any other educational group. Unlike almost all Internet activities, years of experience on the Internet did not seem to matter when it came to IM. Of course, some of these trends, such as income and Internet experience, were likely due to the age of people who preferred IM. Instant messaging appealed to 62% of Internet users aged eighteen to twenty-seven. In fact, 57% of that age group actually used instant messaging more than e-mail. IM use then dropped off sharply with those aged twenty-eight to thirty-nine and stayed low through retirees.

VOICE OVER INTERNET PROTOCOL (VOIP)

Another type of Internet communications technology emerging in the early years of the twenty-first century is voice over Internet protocol (VoIP). VoIP is an application that allows the user to make phone calls over the Internet. The user attaches the phone to an adapter that sits between the phone and the computer. When a call is in progress, the adapter breaks down the voice stream into data packets that can then be routed over the Internet just like e-mail to their destination. (Regular phone conversations typically travel as streams of continuous data over a dedicated phone line that connects two people directly.) If the person on the other end of the call is also equipped with VoIP, then the entire conversation is treated by the Internet as nothing more than an instant message or an e-mail. If the person using VoIP, however, dials to a traditional phone, then the call must be converted into a continuous voice stream by a telecom company before the call reaches its destination.

VoIP is likely to become a technology that gains wide acceptance with little fanfare. In "Talk Becomes Cheap" (*Popular Science*, August 2004), Nicole Davis stated that four million people worldwide are already making calls on VoIP. According to a June 2004 Pew/Internet and New Millennium Research Council data memo, technology research firm Gartner Inc. reported that 150,000 Americans subscribed to VoIP in 2003. This number would grow to one million by the end of 2004 and reach six million by 2005. The same Pew/Internet memo revealed that approximately thirty-four million people (17% of all Americans) had heard of VoIP, and nearly fourteen million Americans had used VoIP at some point in their lives.

According to Davis in *Popular Science*, VoIP will have to overcome a few obstacles in order to become mainstream. Most important, the user of the service is required to have broadband, which as of late 2004 was installed in roughly only 30% of American homes. Second, not all telecommunications companies have installed gateways to convert VoIP to voice stream and back again on all their phone systems, so some normal phones with local area codes cannot take VoIP calls. Not all providers accept 911 calls over VoIP either. Finally, VoIP shuts down when the power dies, which could prove disastrous in a hurricane, earthquake, or other massive power outage.

TABLE 2.5

Instant messaging (IM) users by selected characteristics, May–June 2004

	The percent of internet users in each group who are IM users (e.g. 42% of online men are IM users)	The proportion of the IM population each group makes up (e.g. 50% of all IM-ers are men)
Men	42%	50%
Women	42%	50
Race/ethnicity		
Whites	41%	73%
Blacks	44	8
Hispanics	52	9
Other	40	10
Age		
Gen Y (ages 18–27)	62%	31%
Gen X (ages 28–39)	37	28
Trailing boomers (ages 40–49)	33	20
Leading boomers (ages 50–58)	29	12
Matures (ages 59–68)	25	7
After work (age 69+)	29	3
Household income		
Less than $30,000	53%	31%
$30,000–$50,000	42	24
$50,000–$75,000	36	19
$75,000+	39	27
Educational attainment		
Did not graduate from HS	49%	8%
High school grad	44	31
Some college	48	32
College degree+	34	29
Community type		
Urban	45%	30%
Suburban	42	49
Rural	40	21
Type of internet connection at home		
Broadband	46%	41%
Dialup	39	59

N=1,399. The percentages in the right column do not at times add up to 100 because of rounding.

SOURCE: "Who Uses Instant Messaging," in *How Americans Use Instant Messaging,* Pew Internet and American Life Project, September 1, 2004, http://www.pewinternet.org/pdfs/PIP_Instantmessage_Report.pdf (accessed October 25, 2004). Used by permission of the Pew Internet and American Life Project, which bears no responsibility for the interpretations presented or conclusions reached based on analysis of the data.

MOBILE PHONES

The cell phone is the only information technology present since the mid-1980s that has outpaced the Internet in terms of use. The development of the modern cell phone began in the mid-1940s, nearly twenty years before scientists even conceived of an Internet. In 1946 the Bell System introduced the first commercial radio-telephone service in St. Louis, Missouri. The radio-telephone, typically mounted under the front dashboard of a car or truck, received incoming telephone calls via radio waves transmitted from a large tower planted on a downtown building. A bell rang and a light went off on the radio-telephone to signify an incoming call. When the person using the radio-telephone answered, his or her side of the conversation was transmitted to one of several receiving stations around the city that were all open to the same frequencies. Both the incoming and outgoing signals were relayed through a switchboard and routed into the national phone system. From the start, this system had a number of limitations. Calls had to be routed through a live switchboard operator, both parties involved in a conversation could not talk at once, and only three conversations could take place citywide at any given time with the bandwidth restrictions.

History and Development

The idea for the modern mobile cellular phone network was first posited in 1947 by D. H. Ring at Bell Laboratories in an internal memorandum. The memo proposed a system that would overcome many of the flaws inherent in the radio-telephone. The plan called for a network of low-powered cellular towers that could receive and transmit telephone calls via radio waves to and from mobile phones. Each tower would have a three-mile broadcast radius. As the user of the mobile phone traveled across these cells, the call was to be automatically routed from one tower to the next and the phone would switch frequencies. To accommodate more customers using a limited number of frequencies, towers that were out of range of one another were to send and receive radio signals of the same frequency. That way two people three miles apart or more could carry on separate conversations using the same frequency without interfering with one another's reception.

In order to implement this vision on a large scale and make a profit, AT&T would require more frequencies on the radio spectrum than the Federal Communications Commission (FCC) then allowed for two-way radio communications. The radio spectrum is essentially a long ribbon of frequencies that stretch from 3 kilohertz to 300 gigahertz. Only one device in an area, be it a radio station or a television station, can use a particular part of this ribbon to broadcast or else interference will arise. The FCC regulates what type of devices can operate over various sections of the radio spectrum. Cell phones generally eat up a big part of each spectrum because each cell phone requires two signals at two different frequencies—one signal for the incoming signal and one for the outgoing signal. With the limits the FCC imposed in 1947, only twenty-seven cellular phone conversations could take place in a metropolitan area equipped with Bell Lab's proposed cellular system. When AT&T approached the FCC and asked them for additional room on the radio spectrum, the FCC held fast and did not grant them additional frequencies.

Over the next twenty years, mobile phone technology did not show rapid advances. The Richmond Radiotelephone Company in 1948 implemented the first automated radio-telephone service that did not require a live switchboard operator. In 1964 the Bell System rolled out the Improved Mobile Telephone Service to replace their aging radio-telephone network. This system allowed for both people to talk at once during a call. The bandwidth each phone occupied on the radio spectrum was narrowed, so more than a few people in a city could use it.

Technological Developments after 1960

AT&T once again approached the FCC in 1958, this time asking for 75 megahertz of spectrum located in the 800 megahertz range of the radio spectrum. At the time, hardly anyone in the United States used this part of the spectrum for broadcasting. The FCC did not review the proposal until 1968. They then considered it for two years and made a tentative decision to let AT&T use that part of spectrum for two-way radio in 1970. Meanwhile, the Bell System, Motorola, and several other companies began engineering the technologies necessary for the cell phone network. In 1969 the Bell System installed the first cell phone system aboard a train. The system consisted of a set of payphones placed on the Metroliner trains that ran between New York City and Washington, D.C. Cell phone towers were set up along the track. As the train sped along, telephone conversations were routed from tower to tower just as described in the 1947 memo. Four years after this first cellular phone went into use, Martin Cooper at Motorola developed the first personal, handheld cellular phone. Motorola erected a single prototype cellular tower in New York to test the phone. Cooper made his first call to his rival at Bell Labs, who was attempting to create a similar device.

In 1978 the FCC allowed AT&T to test an analog cellular telephone service. AT&T chose Chicago, Illinois, for their trial run, and set up ten cellular towers, which covered 21,000 square miles of the Chicagoland area. Customers who wanted to use the service leased large, car-mounted telephones. The trial run was a success, and Ameritech, the regional Bell in metropolitan Chicago, launched the first commercial cellular service in 1983. Two months after Ameritech began service, Motorola offered service as well in the Washington-Baltimore area. Most people had car-mounted phones. The alternatives were large portable phones that were so big they had to be carried around in a suitcase. At first, none of the cellular systems being put in place were compatible with one another and roaming outside of the calling area was not a possibility.

In the late 1980s the Telecommunications Industry Association established some basic standards for cell-phone companies. The standards paved the way for a continuous, cross-country network that everyone could use regardless of which company was providing the service (often times with extra roaming charges). The first standard was for analog phones. Analog phones process signals in much the same way as car radios or traditional phones do. When a person speaks into the cell phone, the microphone turns the signal into a continuous stream of electrical impulses, which travels out from the phone's

antennae and to the cellular tower. Both these outgoing signals and the incoming signals on modern analog phones take up 30 kilohertz of space on the radio wave spectrum.

Modern Cell-Phone Networks

By 1990 the number of people using cell phones increased dramatically to over five million subscribers, according to the U.S. Census. (See Table 2.1.) With the analog standard and the frequency limitations imposed by the FCC, less than one hundred people in each network were able to use one cellular tower at once. If the number of cell phones maintained the same rate of growth, then cell-phone companies would soon require new technologies that allowed more cell-phone conversations to take place in a given area. The cell-phone companies' solution was to adopt digital technology.

A digital signal is a signal that is broken down into impulses representing ones and zeros. When a digital cell phone receives a digital signal, a chip inside the phone known as a digital signal processor (DSP) reads these ones and zeros and then constructs an analog signal that travels to the phone's speaker. Conversely, the DSP also processes analog signals coming from the phone's microphone, converting them into ones and zeros, before sending the signal to a cell tower. By breaking down the signal into ones and zeros, more telephone calls can be handled by one frequency. The process is analogous to breaking down and cutting up boxes to allow more to fit inside a trash can. The first digital system widely used by the cell phone companies was the time division multiple access (TDMA) method. Figure 2.4 and Figure 2.5 show the difference between the older, frequency division multiple access (FDMA) and TDMA. FDMA requires each phone to use a different frequency. TDMA allows three cell-phone conversations to be contained in the same thirty-kilohertz-wide band that held only one analog conversation. By the early 1990s cellular companies were erecting digital cellular towers enabled with TDMA across the country.

By 1995 the number of cell-phone users had grown to nearly thirty-four million people by U.S. Census estimates, and the TDMA systems were looking as if they might hit capacity as well. In response, the FCC auctioned off more frequency bands in the radio wave spectrum in the 1850 megahertz to the 1900 megahertz range. Services set up on these bands were known as personal communications services (PCS). PCS networks were designed for handheld mobile phones instead of car phones and had smaller cells than the original cellular network. The PCS networks also employed an updated version of TDMA and a newer technology known as code division multiple access (CDMA). Both could pack up to eight calls into one frequency band. With so many bands available, cell-phone companies introduced a multitude of features standard into their phones, such as the ability to send instant messages, surf the Web, play games, send e-mail, and check the identity of callers.

FIGURE 2.4

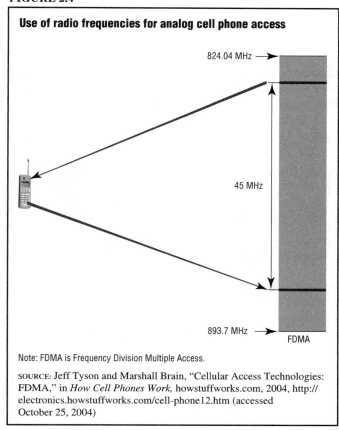

Use of radio frequencies for analog cell phone access

824.04 MHz →

45 MHz

893.7 MHz →

FDMA

Note: FDMA is Frequency Division Multiple Access.

SOURCE: Jeff Tyson and Marshall Brain, "Cellular Access Technologies: FDMA," in *How Cell Phones Work,* howstuffworks.com, 2004, http://electronics.howstuffworks.com/cell-phone12.htm (accessed October 25, 2004)

FIGURE 2.5

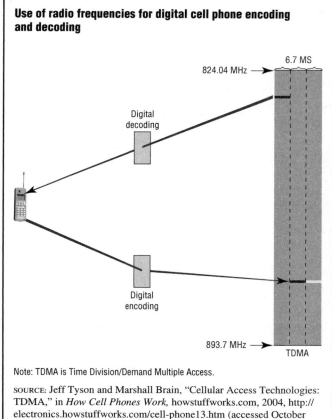

Use of radio frequencies for digital cell phone encoding and decoding

6.7 MS

824.04 MHz →

Digital decoding

Digital encoding

893.7 MHz →

TDMA

Note: TDMA is Time Division/Demand Multiple Access.

SOURCE: Jeff Tyson and Marshall Brain, "Cellular Access Technologies: TDMA," in *How Cell Phones Work,* howstuffworks.com, 2004, http://electronics.howstuffworks.com/cell-phone13.htm (accessed October 25, 2004)

Issues and Concerns

Though cell phones have brought a great deal of convenience to modern life, they have become a source of trouble as well. Many believe that cell phones contribute to automobile accidents because drivers cannot concentrate on the road appropriately while speaking on a cell phone. While Congress continued to debate whether or not to institute a nationwide ban of handheld cell-phone use in automobiles, many states already had laws in place by late 2004. Figure 2.6 displays the states that had instituted cell phone driving laws as of July 2004. As can be seen, Washington, D.C., New Jersey, and New York all had full bans on the use of handheld cell phones while driving. Maine banned teen drivers from talking on cell phones while driving. Seven states banned cell phones just for drivers of school buses. In addition, cell-phone restrictions for drivers were being considered by the legislatures of Iowa, Hawaii, Louisiana, and North Carolina in 2004.

As cell-phone makers add such features as Internet access and video games, many believe cell phones are also becoming a bigger distraction and a source of potential trouble for children. In "Cell Phones and Kids: Do They Mix?," an MSNBC article published August 20, 2004, Bob Sullivan outlined some of the concerns parents face with regards to kids and cell phones. While parents have a fairly easy time monitoring what children do on the computer, cell phones are a different story. Given the portable nature of cell phones, children can easily play games or surf the Internet from any location, without their parents' knowledge. In addition, cell-phone Internet browsers have no parental controls, and cell-phone games do not have content ratings. The best way to monitor children's cell-phone use, Sullivan concluded, is to check the activity reported on monthly bills.

Finally, some health concerns associated with cell-phone use emerged at the beginning of the twenty-first century. In "Nerve Cell Damage in Mammalian Brain after Exposure to Microwaves from GSM Mobile Phones" (*Environmental Health Perspectives,* June 2003), Lief Salford and his colleagues at Lund University in Sweden demonstrated that cell-phone radiation caused brain damage in rats. The scientists mounted a European cell phone to the side of the rats' cage for two hours a day for fifty days to emulate the amount of exposure a habitual cell-phone user would receive. The rats' brains showed significant blood vessel leakage as well as areas of damaged neurons.

THE FUTURE OF COMMUNICATIONS

Integration is likely to be the future of communications technology. As of 2004 many people were using BlackBerry devices that combine Internet and cellular

FIGURE 2.6

State distracted driving laws, July 2004

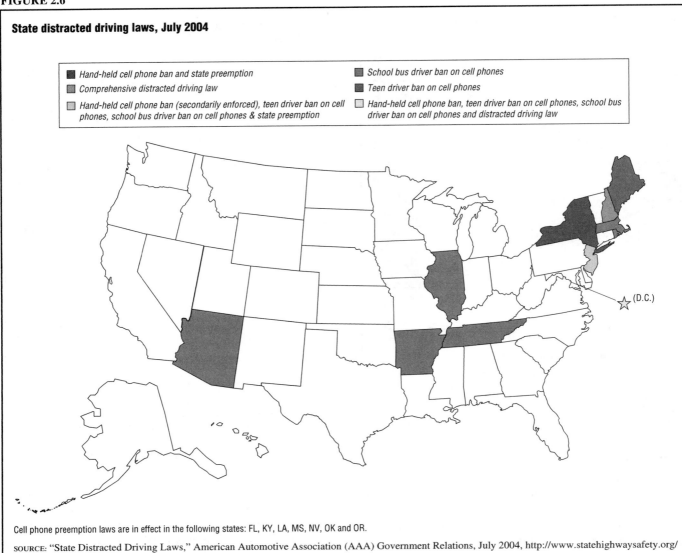

■ *Hand-held cell phone ban and state preemption*
■ *Comprehensive distracted driving law*
▨ *Hand-held cell phone ban (secondarily enforced), teen driver ban on cell phones, school bus driver ban on cell phones & state preemption*
■ *School bus driver ban on cell phones*
■ *Teen driver ban on cell phones*
□ *Hand-held cell phone ban, teen driver ban on cell phones, school bus driver ban on cell phones and distracted driving law*

Cell phone preemption laws are in effect in the following states: FL, KY, LA, MS, NV, OK and OR.

SOURCE: "State Distracted Driving Laws," American Automotive Association (AAA) Government Relations, July 2004, http://www.statehighwaysafety.org/html/media/maps.ppt#1 (accessed October 25, 2004).

technology. A BlackBerry is a wireless, handheld device that downloads e-mail on the Web by dialing into a cell-phone network and then connecting to the Internet. Black-Berry devices also have personal organizer capabilities, including an address book and planner. As of late 2004, many companies offered BlackBerry–cell phone hybrids with a cell phone built into the BlackBerry device, so that both e-mail and cell-phone calls could be received on the same device.

The third generation of wireless technology, commonly referred to as 3G, should allow for even more integration of Internet technologies into cell phones. As of 2004, 3G was being set up for commercial use in the United States. An advanced form of CDMA, 3G will allow more people to share a broader bandwidth of frequencies on the current cell-phone networks. The FCC is working to free up more of the radio frequency spectrum for this new network. The additional bandwidth

should dramatically increase the amount of information that can flow between the phone and the cellular tower, making broadband Internet access and streaming video possible on cell phones. With the new system in place, Americans will likely be using their cell phones to download and play music and movie files, watch newscasts, and shop online. Continued development of smaller electronics and display screens should bring even higher quality cameras, video games systems, and Web cameras to cell phones.

The biggest technological issue facing cell-phone makers in the first decade of the twenty-first century is limited battery life. The more features phones have, the more energy they need to run. According to Steve Morgenstern in "Got Juice?" (*Popular Science*, October 2004), battery energy density since 1990 has tripled, whereas processor speeds, display screens, and memory have increased in complexity hundreds of times. The more complex an electronics device becomes, the more power it needs to run. Unless battery technology increases dramatically, batteries may soon set the limit for how many features can be packed into a cell phone.

CHAPTER 3

INFORMATION TECHNOLOGY AND AMERICAN BUSINESS

The explosive growth of electronic and communications technologies since the 1980s was fueled in no small part by corporate America's desire to make money. Throughout the 1980s and 1990s, such high-tech companies as Microsoft and Intel strove to create affordable computers, Internet technologies, cell phones, and a variety of electronics-based products for use in the office and at home. A huge market segment, commonly referred to as the information technology (IT) industry, grew up around the production of these new technologies. From 1996 to 2001 alone the IT-producing industries' real domestic output increased 41% from $589 billion to $829 billion. (See Table 3.1.) The U.S. Department of Commerce reported in *Digital Economy 2003* that the IT industries, which made up approximately 8% of the American economy in the late nineties, were responsible for about 30% of domestic growth over those years.

As information technologies spread through American offices and corporations, they transformed other industries outside of the IT sector as well. In the financial industries, such innovations as scanners and interconnected bank networks greatly reduced the number of paper checks in circulation daily. The retail industry discovered a new way to sell merchandise. Some $44 billion in retail sales took place over the Internet in 2002, as stated in *E-Stats*, a U.S. Census report on electronic commerce. The same report revealed that in 2002, $752 billion in business-to-business manufacturing shipments were ordered online.

The Internet did not affect all businesses positively. Travel agencies, for instance, saw an enormous drop in revenue due to online reservations sites. According to *Travelers' Use of the Internet* (Washington, DC: Travel Industry Association of America, September 2004), 44.6 million Americans had booked at least one travel service or product online during the previous year, and 40% of those travelers made all their travel reservations online. The growth in online bookings led to an 18.6% drop in the number of travel agency jobs in the United States between 1998 and 2003. According to figures published by the Bureau of Labor Statistics in *Occupational Employment and Wage Estimates*, 120,850 travel agents were employed in 1998 compared with 98,410 in 2003.

Information technologies, however, had their biggest impact on the productivity of American business as a whole. Every industry from trucking to real estate to health care to manufacturing incorporated new technologies that helped make doing business more efficient and affordable. Entire medical and law libraries were replaced by online databases that could be searched in minutes. Retail inventories, which used to be counted by hand, were linked directly to cash registers, ultimately cutting down on inventories and expensive storage costs. Bookkeeping and accounting, which was once an arduous task completed in thick, paper ledgers, was done in a fraction of the time and at a fraction of the cost on computer accounting programs.

INFORMATION TECHNOLOGY INDUSTRY

While IT has been around since International Business Machines (IBM) began mass-producing computers in the early 1950s, it did not become a large part of the U.S. economy until the 1990s. A number of high-tech companies, such as Microsoft and Dell, had positioned themselves as the commercial leaders in Internet, personal computer, and cell phone technologies during the 1980s. When use of the World Wide Web became common in 1994 and the price of electronics began to drop, Americans flocked to these technologies. Revenues in the high-tech industries increased at a rate not seen in any industry since the postwar boom of the 1950s. Microsoft had sales of $140 million in 1985. Ten years later its revenue had increased to $6 billion; by 2004, when Microsoft produced the operating systems for over 90% of computers, its revenue topped $32 billion. Cisco Systems, the leading

TABLE 3.1

Gross domestic product of information technology producing industries, by industry, 1996–2001 and estimated 2002 and 2003

	1996	1997	1998	1999	2000	2001	2002 est.	2003 est.
				($millions)				
Total Gross Domestic Product*	7,780,300.0	8,288,600.0	8,812,500.0	9,313,100.0	9,953,100.0	10,199,400.0	10,555,100.0	11,040,634.6
Year-to-year GDI change (%)		6.5%	6.3%	5.7%	6.9%	2.5%	3.5%	4.6%
Industry								
Hardware								
Computers and equipment, calc. machines	51,151.5	56,140.3	66,727.0	62,262.7	54,966.8	46,390.4	43,699.8	46,234.3
Computers and equipment wholesale sales	59,767.0	68,224.1	72,395.8	77,211.5	72,212.3	58,795.6	55,400.9	58,614.2
Computer and equipment retail sales	4,794.1	5,465.7	6,110.2	6,431.1	6,410.0	5,581.3	5,785.2	6,120.7
Electron tubes	1,564.9	1,568.4	1,619.4	1,758.0	1,362.1	1,180.6	1,324.2	1,561.7
Printed circuit boards	5,048.3	5,062.3	5,047.7	5,557.1	6,626.8	4,731.7	5,307.3	6,259.2
Semiconductors	51,601.8	64,135.3	59,977.2	68,021.7	67,896.6	44,118.2	49,485.0	58,360.3
Passive electronic components	15,332.2	12,996.1	12,351.3	12,657.7	14,778.6	11,037.2	12,379.8	14,600.2
Industrial instruments for measurement	3,146.2	4,914.9	4,761.8	4,581.3	4,801.6	4,567.2	4,137.9	4,241.8
Instruments for measuring electricity	5,684.8	8,991.8	8,755.0	9,010.4	10,346.8	8,236.5	7,462.3	7,649.6
Laboratory analytical instruments	3,040.5	4,111.2	4,480.6	4,715.0	4,730.3	4,723.1	4,279.1	4,386.5
Total hardware	201,131.5	231,610.1	242,226.0	252,206.5	244,131.9	189,361.8	189,261.4	208,028.6
Software and computer services								
Computer programming services	29,412.5	34,967.9	47,654.0	56,405.1	63,261.8	61,145.4	61,818.0	62,693.1
Prepackaged software	47,683.4	52,261.5	61,408.5	69,063.2	75,961.1	77,709.1	78,563.9	80,200.9
Prepackaged software wholesale sales	3,483.8	3,818.2	4,051.7	4,321.2	4,041.5	3,290.6	3,100.6	3,174.6
Prepackaged software retail sales	647.7	710.2	794.0	835.7	832.9	725.3	751.7	769.6
Computer integrated system design	34,039.8	43,940.7	58,225.6	66,114.9	75,136.8	73,733.1	74,544.2	75,600.4
Computer processing, data preparation	23,106.2	24,391.8	26,299.2	30,028.7	33,602.5	37,850.1	38,266.5	38,808.7
Information retrieval services	5,252.9	6,892.9	9,729.7	16,354.3	25,312.6	26,155.7	26,443.4	26,818.1
Computer services management	10,150.4	11,789.0	9,278.9	11,882.5	12,779.5	14,891.0	15,054.8	15,268.1
Office machinery rental and leasing	4,160.1	4,820.9	6,495.8	7,292.2	7,846.8	6,635.5	6,708.5	6,803.6
Computer maintenance and repair	5,941.1	6,631.8	7,961.3	8,480.2	8,494.3	8,652.2	8,747.4	8,871.3
Computer related services, nec	2,460.0	3,385.2	6,060.6	7,496.6	9,330.4	9,548.0	9,653.0	9,789.7
Total software and computer services	166,338.0	193,610.1	237,959.3	278,274.6	316,600.2	320,336.0	323,651.9	328,798.2
Communications equipment								
Household audio and video equipment	1,731.2	2,372.8	2,663.0	2,855.0	3,221.2	3,143.0	2,668.4	2,601.4
Telephone equipment, exc. ext. modems	16,958.9	23,766.1	25,415.7	32,744.8	35,843.0	28,005.2	23,776.4	22,087.2
Radio & TV communications equipment	18,016.1	24,273.9	22,839.9	23,122.9	26,756.9	22,751.6	19,316.1	17,943.8
Magnetic and optical and recording media	2,302.1	2,300.2	2,242.3	1,902.5	1,440.6	989.9	840.4	819.3
Total communications equipment	39,008.3	52,713.0	53,160.9	60,625.2	67,261.7	54,889.7	46,601.4	43,451.7
Communications services								
Telephone and telegraph communications	163,900.0	166,700.0	173,900.0	193,700.0	208,000.0	218,500.0	224,846.0	240,980.0
Cable and other pay TV services	18,665.4	21,490.0	32,216.0	36,876.2	41,819.5	45,823.4	47,211.9	50,616.8
Total communications services	182,565.4	188,190.0	206,116.0	230,576.2	249,819.5	264,323.4	272,057.9	291,596.8
Total IT-producing industries	589,043.2	666,123.2	739,462.2	821,682.5	877,813.3	828,910.9	831,572.6	871,875.2
Share of the economy	7.6%	8.0%	8.4%	8.8%	8.8%	8.1%	7.9%	7.9%

*Gross Domestic Product here is Gross Domestic Income.

SOURCE: "Appendix Table 1.2. Information Technology Producing Industries Gross Domestic Product By Industry," in *Digital Economy 2003,* Economics and Statistics Administration, U.S. Department of Commerce, https://www.esa.doc.gov/reports/AppendixTable1.2.xls (accessed November 11, 2004)

commercial maker of Internet routers and switches, grew at an even faster rate. Between 1990 and 2001, the company's revenue grew a whopping 31,784% from sales of $69 million to sales of $22 billion. Dell Inc., the 2003 top seller of home computers, saw sales increase from $300 million in 1989 to $41 billion in fiscal year 2004.

The growth of these companies along with the rest of the IT-producing industries had a tremendous impact on the economy. Table 3.2 shows a list of the types of businesses that make up the IT-producing industries. According to *Digital Economy 2003* (Washington, DC: U.S. Department of Commerce, 2003), the IT industries as a whole made up roughly 8% to 9% of the United States domestic economy between 1996 and 2000. These industries, however, were responsible for 1.4% of the nation's

4.6% annual average real gross domestic product (GDP) growth over these years. GDP is one of the basic yardsticks used to measure the U.S. economy and is defined as the value, or sale price, of all goods produced in a country less the cost of the materials that went into making those goods. In other words, the IT sector, which made up a little under a one-tenth of the economy, accounted for over one-third of the economic growth. Between 1993 and 2000, employment in the IT industries expanded rapidly as well. IT companies hired people at twice the rate of all private industries and added more than 1.8 million jobs to the workforce. Table 3.3 lists employment of IT industries from 1993 to 2002. Most jobs were added in the software and computer services sectors, followed by computer hardware and communication services.

TABLE 3.2

Information technology producing industries, 2003

Hardware industries	Software/services industries
Computers and equipment	Computer programming
Wholesale trade of computers and equipment*	Prepackaged software
Retail trade of computers and equipment*	Wholesale trade of software*
Calculating and office machines	Retail trade of software*
Magnetic and optical recording media	Computer-integrated system design
Electron tubes	Computer processing, data preparation
Printed circuit boards	Information retrieval services
Semiconductors	Computer services management
Passive electronic components	Computer rental and leasing
Industrial instruments for measurement	Computer maintenance and repair
Instruments for measuring electricity	Computer related services, nec
Laboratory analytical instruments	
	Communications services industries
Communications equipment industries	Telephone and telegraph
Household audio and video equipment	communications
Telephone and telegraph equipment	Cable and other TV services
Radio and TV communications equipment	

*Wholesale and retail from computer manufacturer sales from branch offices.

SOURCE: "Box 1.1. Information Technology Producing Industries," in *Digital Economy 2003*, Economics and Statistics Administration, U.S. Department of Commerce, April 2004, http://www.esa.doc.gov/reports/DEChap1.pdf (accessed November 11, 2004)

The End of the IT Boom

Toward the turn of the century many Americans thought that the IT boom could continue indefinitely. They invested enormous sums of money in IT and IT-related stocks. From late 1998 to early 2000 Microsoft and Dell's stock doubled in value, and Cisco Systems's stock quadrupled. The NASDAQ, a stock index that tracks the value of numerous IT stocks, rose from 2,490 on August 10, 1999, to a peak value of 5,048 on Friday, March 10, 2000—one of largest increases of a major stock index in history. Many Americans invested not only in large, well-established corporations, but also in small e-commerce companies such as Pets.com and eToys. Many of these "dot-coms" were brand new businesses that had yet to produce any profits. People invested in them in the hope that these "dot-coms" would enjoy the sort of huge rise in value that made early investors into Dell or Microsoft millionaires.

On Monday, March 13, 2000, the NASDAQ dropped nearly 150 points to 4,907. The index dropped for several more days, rebounded to a point close to its former high, and then proceeded to fall intermittently for the next two-and-a-half years, finally hitting bottom on October 9, 2002, at 1,114. Other stock indexes, such as the Dow Jones Industrial Average and Standard and Poor's 500, followed this downward trend, ultimately returning to 1998 levels. The entire country slipped into recession. The stock bubble burst because investors began to fear that a large number of IT and IT-related companies were not living up to expectations and pulled their money out of the market.

By 2001 many of the "dot-coms" were out of business, and many established IT companies began posting losses. From 2001 to 2002 Cisco Systems lost more than $3.4 bil-

lion, and Dell's annual earnings dipped by roughly $700 million. According to the Commerce Department in *Digital Economy 2003*, the main reason for the slowdown in the IT industries was that the private business sector stopped buying equipment. Throughout the 1990s just about every type of business—from law firms to paper producers to grocery stores to auto shops—was either buying or updating their computers, printers, and networks. Businesses that did not make such investments quickly became outdated and inefficient and did not survive. By the turn of the twenty-first century, many companies outside of the IT industries were done buying IT equipment. In addition, the components that make up the infrastructure for the Internet—fiber optic cables, routers, and switches—had largely been laid down by the late 1990s, so the need for these components greatly diminished as well.

The numbers in Table 3.1 support the Commerce Department's assessment. This table shows the GDP by sector for all IT-producing industries. As can be seen, those industries that produced hardware components and communications equipment were the hardest hit. The GDP for these industries dropped 22% and 18% respectively from 2000 to 2001. The industries that did reasonably well through this recessionary period were the software and services sector and the communications services sector. Although American businesses as a whole had bought much of their hardware, many still had the need for new software, Internet service, and computer maintenance.

Lost Jobs

In order to cut their losses in this down market, IT companies began laying off many of the workers they had hired during the 1990s. *Digital Economy 2003* stated that nearly 600,000 jobs were shed in the IT industries between 2000 and 2002. This job loss accounted for nearly one-quarter of all the jobs lost during this recession. The rate of job loss in the IT industries was six times that of all private industry. Not surprisingly, Table 3.3 shows that the industry that lost the most jobs was computer hardware, which shed nearly 320,000 jobs.

While many of the jobs that were lost simply ceased to exist, two additional trends combined to decrease the number of traditional employment positions. "Outsourcing" indicates work contracted to nonemployees such as temporary workers; "offshoring" refers to situations in which the positions are assumed by workers located in another country where wages are cheaper. With the advent of e-mail, the Internet, and low-cost international phone calls, offices separated by continents could easily be linked through cyberspace. Geography was no longer such a big concern for a company. In India, for instance, there were large numbers of highly educated people who were well versed in English and computer science and were more than happy to work for a fraction of the typical

TABLE 3.3

Employment in the information technology producing industries, 1993–2002

	2002 NAICS code	Employment (000s)										Average annual rate of growth (%)		
		1993	1994	1995	1996	1997	1998	1999	2000	2001	2002	93–00	00–01	01–02
Computer hardware														
Electronic computers	334111	189.0	175.9	166.2	165.7	172.6	178.3	171.3	168.6	159.3	138.4	-1.6	-5.5	-13.1
Computer storage devices	334112	34.6	35.5	37.7	38.5	39.6	39.0	40.5	38.0	37.0	32.8	1.3	-2.6	-11.4
Computer terminals	334113	24.2	24.7	25.8	26.1	26.8	26.6	25.5	25.2	23.8	21.3	0.6	-5.6	-10.5
Other computer peripheral equipment	334119	57.9	61.6	65.8	74.3	77.8	78.4	72.8	70.1	66.1	57.2	2.8	-5.7	-13.5
Computer and software wholesalers	423430	211.0	211.2	221.1	236.0	258.9	287.0	302.0	298.4	280.0	251.4	5.1	-6.2	-10.2
Computer and software retailers	443120	120.4	127.3	137.7	148.1	164.8	175.3	187.8	191.4	178.9	162.0	6.8	-6.5	-9.5
Electron tubes	334411	24.8	24.5	24.0	22.9	21.9	20.7	20.6	20.4	19.1	16.2	-2.8	-6.4	-15.2
Bare printed circuit boards	334412	96.7	102.0	115.3	123.8	132.1	134.0	126.5	139.5	120.2	83.9	5.4	-13.8	-30.2
Semiconductors and related devices	334413	210.5	217.0	231.5	255.5	272.9	279.9	268.0	289.2	292.1	254.8	4.6	1.0	-12.8
Electronic capacitors	334414	16.4	16.7	18.2	17.4	17.0	15.9	15.2	16.9	14.4	11.0	0.4	-14.8	-23.6
Electronic connectors	334417	15.3	15.9	17.3	18.5	20.3	20.4	21.9	24.2	23.7	18.1	6.8	-2.1	-23.6
Printed circuit assemblies	334418	52.7	53.8	55.2	56.9	60.0	62.0	61.8	64.4	60.8	51.2	2.9	-5.6	-15.8
Miscellaneous electronic components	334415,6,9	103.0	105.5	109.5	111.6	115.6	116.9	116.5	121.7	115.1	96.2	2.4	-5.4	-16.4
Industrial process variable instruments	334513	59.6	61.1	63.3	65.2	65.6	67.2	68.9	70.1	67.4	61.2	2.3	-3.9	-9.2
Electricity and signal testing instruments	334515	69.6	68.0	68.0	71.0	72.0	72.5	65.2	65.8	65.1	54.8	-0.8	-1.1	-15.8
Analytical laboratory instruments	334516	38.6	36.8	36.0	36.5	36.9	37.3	36.5	35.7	35.4	33.6	-1.1	-0.7	-5.2
Semiconductor machinery	333295	18.1	19.3	22.4	24.3	24.9	25.2	23.1	24.7	23.2	19.6	4.5	-6.1	-15.5
Office machinery	333313	14.7	14.9	15.6	15.8	16.2	16.1	15.4	15.3	14.7	12.7	0.6	-3.9	-13.6
Total computer hardware		**1,357.2**	**1,371.7**	**1,430.6**	**1,508.2**	**1,595.9**	**1,652.8**	**1,639.5**	**1,679.6**	**1,596.4**	**1,376.4**	**3.1**	**-5.0**	**-13.8**
Software and computer services														
Software publishers	511210	125.9	136.8	157.2	174.8	195.2	214.9	235	260.6	268.9	256	11.0	3.2	-4.8
ISPs and web search portals	518111,2	39.7	41.2	48.6	59.6	70.4	86.4	132.2	194.3	176.8	142.1	25.5	-9.0	-19.6
Data processing and related services	518210	223.4	226.9	242.6	252	268.4	282.8	307.1	315.7	316.8	305.3	5.1	0.3	-3.6
Computer and software wholesalers	423430	11.9	11.9	12.5	13.3	14.6	16.2	17.0	16.8	15.8	14.2	5.1	-6.2	-10.2
Computer and software retailers	443120	15.7	16.6	18.0	19.4	21.5	22.9	24.5	25.0	23.4	21.2	6.8	-6.5	-9.5
Custom computer programming services	541511	199.4	220.6	255.7	286.4	331.8	388.6	464.2	540.0	562.9	511.8	15.3	4.2	-9.1
Computer systems design services	541512	190.1	209.4	242.6	285.2	343.2	408.1	468.7	502.9	520.3	462.4	14.9	3.5	-11.1
Computer facilities management services	541513	51.8	51.4	52.8	54.5	55.4	58.6	63.9	64.9	64.6	58.4	3.3	-0.5	-9.6
Other computer-related services	541519	43.6	49.9	60.2	75.3	96.3	119.6	136.1	146.5	150.1	130.1	18.9	2.5	-13.3
Office machine rentals and leasing	532420	10.5	10.6	11.0	11.5	12.0	12.8	12.9	13.1	12.9	13.0	3.3	-1.5	0.6
Computer and office machine repair	811212	39.9	41.4	44.6	48.2	51.2	51.4	51.0	47.7	48.3	46.6	2.6	1.3	-3.5
Total software and computer services		**951.9**	**1,016.7**	**1,145.7**	**1,280.2**	**1,460.0**	**1,662.2**	**1,912.6**	**2,127.5**	**2,160.8**	**1,961.0**	**12.2**	**1.6**	**-9.2**
Communications equipment														
Telephone apparatus	334210	92.4	92.0	93.8	96.2	100.8	105.6	101.6	106.5	97.2	70.6	2.0	-8.7	-27.4
Broadcast and wireless communications equipment	334220	93.3	100.2	110.6	112.4	113.8	110.8	104.4	107.3	102.5	89.1	2.0	-4.5	-13.1
Audio and video equipment	334310	57.2	57.6	53.8	52.9	52	53.2	52.4	52.1	47.4	41.6	-1.3	-9.0	-12.2
Fiber optic cable manufacturing	335921	14.7	15.4	15.8	15.9	16.4	16.9	17.9	20.4	20.2	15.1	4.8	-1.2	-25.1
Software reproducing	334611	20.3	21.8	23.7	24.8	25.4	26.3	26.9	28.2	27.1	25.3	4.8	-4.1	-6.4
Magnetic and optical recording media	334613	5.4	5.7	6.2	6.5	6.7	6.9	7.1	7.4	7.1	6.7	4.8	-4.1	-6.4
Total communications equipment		**283.3**	**292.8**	**304.0**	**308.8**	**315.1**	**319.7**	**310.3**	**322.0**	**301.5**	**248.4**	**1.8**	**-6.4**	**-17.6**

TABLE 3.3

Employment in the information technology producing industries, 1993–2002 [CONTINUED]

	2002 NAICS code	1993	1994	1995	1996	1997	1998	1999	2000	2001	2002	Average annual rate of growth (%)		
												93–00	00–01	01–02
Employment (000s)														
Communications services														
Wired telecommunications carriers	517110	624.5	621.9	611.1	603.2	629.9	652.1	688.1	719.2	732.2	662.4	2.0	1.8	−9.5
Cellular and other wireless carriers	517212	47.4	60.3	75.9	92.5	111.0	121.1	134.3	155.7	171.0	168.7	18.5	9.8	−1.3
Telecommunications resellers	517310	170.5	171.8	171.2	171.6	181.3	188.7	200.2	213.6	214.1	185.7	3.3	0.2	−13.3
Cable and other program distribution	517510	75.8	80.4	86.6	94.6	96.9	102.4	110.9	123	129.2	128	7.2	5.0	−0.9
Satellite and other telecommunications services	517410.910	15.1	15.3	16.5	17.5	19.3	20.4	20.5	21.2	25.2	28.9	5.0	18.9	14.7
Communications equipment repair and leasing	811213	18.1	18.2	19.2	20.3	20.9	20.8	20.6	19.8	20.1	19.4	1.3	1.5	−3.1
Total communications services		**951.4**	**967.9**	**980.5**	**999.7**	**1,059.3**	**1,105.5**	**1,174.6**	**1,252.5**	**1,291.8**	**1,193.1**	**4.0**	**3.1**	**−7.6**
All IT-producing industries (Year to year rate of change)		3,543.8	3,649.0 3.0%	3,860.8 5.8%	4,096.9 6.1%	4,430.4 8.1%	4,740.3 7.0%	5,037.0 6.3%	5,381.6 6.8%	5,350.4 −0.6%	4,779.0 −10.7%	6.2	−0.6	−10.7
All private industries		91,855	95,016	97,866	100,169	103,113	106,021	108,686	110,996	110,707	108,886	2.7	−0.3	−1.6
IT share of all private industries		3.9%	3.8%	3.9%	4.1%	4.3%	4.5%	4.6%	4.8%	4.8%	4.4%			

Note: NAICS is North American Industry Classification System.

SOURCE: "Appendix Table 2.2. IT-Producing Industry Employment, 1993–2002," in *Digital Economy 2003*, Economics and Statistics Administration, U.S. Department of Commerce, April 2004, http://www.esa.doc.gov/reports/appendixtable2.2.xls (accessed November 11, 2004)

American hourly wage. Companies such as Dell moved high-paying technical assistance jobs, low- to mid-level computer programming jobs, and even technical documentation jobs to other countries.

According to Mark Gongloff in "U.S. Jobs Jumping Ship" (*CNN/Money*, July 2003), nearly 40% of U.S. companies have either contracted IT services or have run a pilot offshore outsourcing program. Deducing the number of jobs that have moved overseas since 2000, however, was all but impossible. The Bureau of Labor Statistics (BLS), the government agency in charge of recording who loses their jobs and why, only began counting the number of jobs moved overseas in 2004. In "Mass Layoff Statistics in the United States and Domestic and Oversees Relocation" (Washington, DC: Bureau of Labor Statistics, December 2004), Sharon P. Brown reported that 10,722 U.S. positions in private, nonfarm industry had been eliminated between January and September 2004 because the work had been moved to another country.

IT Becomes a Mature Industry

By 2003 the IT industries showed signs of recovery. As can be seen in Table 3.1, the GDP in the IT-producing industries grew by 4.6% to $871.9 billion in 2003 as business spending on IT equipment began to accelerate. In the first nine months of 2003, IT spending by the private sector rose 2.3% on average. Consumer/household spending on IT equipment, which did not abate as sharply during the recession, grew faster through 2002 and into 2003. In addition, the IT industries did not cut back on research and development during the recession. Consequently, many new products were in their pipelines by the end of recession. Nevertheless, employment numbers in the IT industries had not recovered significantly by 2003. In *Digital Economy 2003*, the Commerce Department reported that these developments taken together point to the fact that the IT industry had settled into maturity. Future growth, the report predicted, would likely be more modest and less volatile than it was in the 1980s and 1990s.

THE IMPACT OF INFORMATION TECHNOLOGY ON AMERICAN BUSINESSES

The rise of the IT industries, though dramatic, did not impact the American economy nearly as much as the products that these industries produced. Nearly every task in a modern office, regardless of the business, employs some piece of technology that either was not present before the proliferation of information technologies or was only present in a very limited way. These technologies have had a profound effect on the productivity of businesses as well as individual employees.

In *Digital Economy 2003* the Commerce Department reported that the annual growth of productivity per employee in the private sector increased sharply during the 1990s. Fig-

FIGURE 3.1

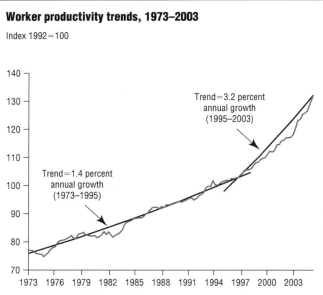

Worker productivity trends, 1973–2003

Index 1992 = 100

Trend = 3.2 percent annual growth (1995–2003)

Trend = 1.4 percent annual growth (1973–1995)

SOURCE: "Figure 4.1. Average Annual Productivity Growth Accelerated in Non-farm Business Sector after 1995," in *Digital Economy 2003*, Economics and Statistics Administration, U.S. Department of Commerce, April 2004, https://www.esa.doc.gov/reports/DE-Chap4.pdf (accessed November 11, 2004)

ure 3.1 is a chart of productivity growth of the private, nonfarm business sector from 1973 to 2003. Between 1973 and 1995 the productivity of workers in America increased at a rate of roughly 1.4% each year. Then in 1995, which was just about the time the Internet became widespread, this entire curve shifted and the productivity of workers began to grow at 3.2% per year. The growth in value of what the average worker in the United States produced each year increased by 1.8%.

To determine if this sudden acceleration in worker productivity was indeed due to the introduction of IT technologies into the workforce, the Commerce Department separated all private industry into those that were IT-intensive, such finance and retail, and those that were less IT-intensive, such as construction. The authors of the study found that IT-intensive industries, which already had a relatively high worker productivity growth per year, increased in productivity much faster than less IT-intensive industries in 1995. During the recessionary period in 2000 and 2001, the IT-intensive industries' worker productivity did not wane. On the other hand, yearly growth in worker productivity in non-IT intensive industries had not occurred prior to 1995; it then rose 1% per year until 2000 before turning negative. Such results suggest that the introduction of IT technology into the workplace has not only improved worker productivity for the long term, but has also increased the rate at which it improves.

How IT Has Increased Productivity

The ways in which Information Technoloy increased productivity and made businesses more profitable are

TABLE 3.4

Shipments, sales, and revenues, by total and e-commerce, 2002–01

[Shipments, sales and revenues are in billions of dollars.]

Description	Value of shipments, sales, or revenue				Year to year percent change		% Distribution of e-commerce	
	2002		2001					
	Total	E-commerce	Total	E-commerce	Total	E-commerce	2002	2001
Total*	**14,675**	**1,157**	**14,585**	**1,080**	**0.6**	**7.1**	**100.0**	**100.0**
B-to-B*	6,582	1,072	6,672	1,010	−1.3	6.1	92.7	93.5
Manufacturing	3,840	752	3,971	724	−3.3	3.8	65.0	67.0
Merchant wholesale	2,742	320	2,701	286	1.5	11.7	27.7	26.5
B-to-C*	8,093	85	7,913	70	2.3	21.4	7.3	6.5
Retail	3,230	44	3,157	34	2.3	29.3	3.8	3.2
Selected services	4,863	41	4,756	36	2.2	15.0	3.5	3.3

*We estimate B-to-B and B-to-C e-commerce by making several simplifying assumptions: manufacturing and wholesale e-commerce is entirely B-to-B, and retail and service e-commerce is entirely B-to-C. We also ignore definitional differences among shipments, sales, and revenues. The resulting B-to-B and B-to-C estimates, while not directly measured, show that almost all the dollar volume of e-commerce activity involves transactions between businesses.

SOURCE: "U.S. Shipments, Sales, Revenues and E-Commerce: 2002 and 2001," in *United States Department of Commerce E-Stats,* U.S. Census Bureau, Economics and Statistics Administration, U.S. Department of Commerce, April 2004, http://www.census.gov/eos/www/papers/2002/2002finaltext.pdf (accessed November 11, 2004)

nearly endless. The reduction of paper in the workplace saved many large corporations millions of dollars. Word processors and desktop publishing software dramatically reduced the time necessary to complete many mundane office tasks, particularly in the communications industry. Computer systems in factories allowed manufacturers precise control over production lines, increasing efficiency and thus saving millions of dollars. Interoffice and Internet networks gave corporations weekly and sometimes even daily access to sales numbers and profit margins, enabling them to make faster decisions to increase profitability. If a line of clothing was not selling, for instance, the company would see the figures immediately and pull the line from the stores, rather than allow it to take up valuable retail space.

The improvements in efficiency created by information technologies even hit the open road. *Digital Economy 2003* included a study that employed data from the U.S. Census's Vehicle Inventory and Use Surveys. The study examined the use of onboard computers on trucks. Standard onboard computers recorded how truck drivers operate the trucks they drive. Owners of trucking fleets used these standard computers to keep tabs on their drivers to make sure they were not mistreating the trucks. Advanced onboard computers, which debuted around the turn of the twenty-first century, added several new features, including GPS locators that allowed the dispatcher to determine where the truck was in real time and communicate schedule changes to the driver. Armed with advanced onboard computers, the dispatcher could see where the entire fleet was and make scheduling decisions to fully utilize the trucks and avoid situations where the trucks were idle and waiting for cargo. The Commerce Department report analyzed the impact these various onboard computers had on the companies that used them. The study found that when advanced onboard computers were used instead of the

standard onboard computers, truck utilization increased by 13%. Industry wide, the use of advanced computers added up to a 3% increase in the amount of truck utilization, which translated to $16 billion in extra revenue per year.

E-COMMERCE

Electronic-commerce (E-Commerce), which is simply the sale of goods and services over the Internet, has grown steadily every year since the debut of the World Wide Web in 1991. Though most attention has been given to online retail, most electronic commerce actually occurs in business-to-business transactions as can be seen in Table 3.4. Figure 3.2 is a breakdown of e-commerce as a percentage of the value of sales in each industry that did business online in 2002. By far, most e-commerce occurred in manufacturing, where shipments ordered online accounted for 19.6% ($752 billion) of the total value of all manufacturing shipments. Merchant wholesalers came in second, with electronic commerce representing 11.7% ($320 billion) of business, and retail trade finished third with 1.4% ($44 billion) of all sales originating from e-commerce. Selected service revenue were sales made by a number of sectors in the service industry and included such businesses as travel brokers and online publications.

Manufacturers are companies that take raw materials and manufacture products used by other businesses. For instance, a soft-drink company typically buys its cans from a manufacturer that manufactures the cans from raw aluminum. Dell buys computer components from dozens of manufacturers around the world in order to put together its computers. The reason so many manufacturers use the Internet to conduct business transactions is that the Internet cuts costs and streamlines the processes involved in buying and selling manufactured goods. E-commerce allows the buyer to easily compare competitors' prices,

FIGURE 3.2

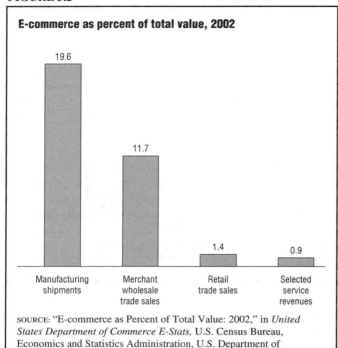

E-commerce as percent of total value, 2002

SOURCE: "E-commerce as Percent of Total Value: 2002," in *United States Department of Commerce E-Stats,* U.S. Census Bureau, Economics and Statistics Administration, U.S. Department of Commerce, April 2004, http://www.census.gov/eos/www/papers/2002/2002finaltext.pdf (accessed November 11, 2004)

reduces the costs of writing up and sending paper purchase orders and invoices, maintains an electronic copy of each sale, and cuts down the time it takes for the goods to reach the buyer. As can be seen in Table 3.5, goods shipped through e-commerce rose from 2001 to 2002, whereas the total value of manufacturing shipments declined. By far, transportation equipment topped the list with over $297 billion being shipped as a result of electronic transactions. This was followed by computer and electronic products, chemicals, food, and tobacco and beverages.

Merchant wholesale trade sales made up the second largest block of e-commerce transactions in 2002. Wholesalers act as a mediator between manufacturers and retailers. Wholesalers typically buy large quantities of goods from a number of manufacturers and then resell these goods to retail outlets. Table 3.6 is a historical chart of U.S. merchant wholesale trades from 1998 to 2002 broken down into total sales and e-commerce sales. In just five years, the number of sales conducted by e-commerce nearly doubled from $174 billion to $320 billion. In terms of total sales, this represented an increase in electronic commerce from 7.3% to 11%. E-commerce was used more in the sales of medications, drug proprietaries, and druggists' sundries than any other product.

E-commerce and Retail

Retail sales consist of any product that is sold to an individual customer or company for use. Since the late 1990s, nearly every major retailer from AutoZone to Neiman-Marcus

to Wal-Mart has a created a Web site. Many offer a greater variety of merchandise online than is available in the store. The growth of such Web sites has allowed Americans to order just about anything and have it delivered to their front door within days. According to Lee Rainie in a Pew/Internet project memo released April 13, 2004, 65% of Internet users had bought something online. Figure 3.2 shows that e-commerce transactions accounted for 1.4% ($44 billion) of all retail sales in 2002. A U.S. Department of Commerce press release dated August 20, 2004, revealed that this number increased to 1.6% ($56 billion) in 2003 and again went up to 1.8% in the first six months of 2004.

Though these percentages may seem small, the amount of money made from electronic commerce in retail increased rapidly from the late 1990s. In 1998 e-commerce accounted for only $5 billion in retail sales. This number then tripled to $15 billion in 1999 and nearly doubled to $28 billion in 2000. As can be seen in Table 3.7, one big reason that e-commerce sales formed only a small percentage of total sales was that many of those items included in total sales, such as gasoline or building supplies, could not easily be purchased online. Of those retailing sectors that did sell merchandise online in 2002, non-store retailers and electronic shopping and mail-order houses topped the list in merchandise sold online. Motor vehicles and parts dealers came in third and electronics and appliances stores were fourth.

Table 3.8 focuses solely on the electronic shopping and mail-order house segment of retail. Many of the businesses in this category, such as Dell, sell their products almost exclusively online and through catalogs. Others are divisions of larger department stores, such as Nordstrom, created to sell the stores' products online. Online sales accounted for 28% of overall sales for electronic shopping and mail order businesses in 2002. That number had increased dramatically since 1999 when electronic commerce made up only 12% of sales of this sector of the retail community. As far as individual products sold, nearly half (46%) of the revenues from the sale of books and magazines came from online sales in 2002. This represented the highest percentage of online sales for any type of product in this retail segment. In terms of sheer sales volume, more computing hardware ($6 billion) was sold than any other type of product.

ONLINE AUCTIONS—A NEW SEGMENT OF THE ECONOMY. When e-commerce began back in the mid-1990s, many small business owners created modest commercial Web sites, hoping to sell their wares. However, Internet fraud and the propagation of distasteful Web sites made people reluctant to give personal information to unknown vendors on the Web. Smaller vendors and buyers needed a common marketplace with rules and regulations to trade goods.

In 1998 Pierre Omidyar, Jeff Skoll, and Meg Whitman, went public with eBay. The company, which was at

TABLE 3.5

Total and e-commerce value of manufacturing shipments*, 2001–02

[Estimates are based on data from the 2002 Annual Survey of Manufactures and 2002 Economic Census. Value of shipments estimates are shown in millions of dollars, consequently industry group estimates may not be additive.]

NAICS code	Description	Value of shipments 2002 Total	Value of shipments 2002 E-commerce	Value of shipments 2001 Total	Value of shipments 2001 Revised e-commerce	Y/Y percent change Total shipments	Y/Y percent change E-commerce shipments	E-commerce as percent of total shipments 2002	E-commerce as percent of total shipments 2001	Percent distribution of e-commerce shipments 2002	Percent distribution of e-commerce shipments 2001
	Total manufacturing	**3,840,319**	**751,985**	**3,970,500**	**724,228**	**−3.3**	**3.8**	**19.6**	**18.2**	**100.0**	**100.0**
311	Food products	469,031	51,094	451,386	53,556	3.9	−4.6	10.9	11.9	6.8	7.4
312	Beverage and tobacco	103,869	45,419	118,786	45,665	−12.6	−0.5	43.7	38.4	6.0	6.3
313	Textile mills	46,847	3,977	45,681	4,435	2.6	−10.3	8.5	9.7	0.5	0.6
314	Textile product mills	31,642	7,491	31,971	7,409	−1.0	1.1	23.7	23.2	1.0	1.0
315	Apparel	45,848	9,726	54,598	10,652	−16.0	−8.7	21.2	19.5	1.3	1.5
316	Leather and allied products	7,349	783	8,834	1,438	−16.8	−45.6	10.7	16.3	0.1	0.2
321	Wood products	88,492	4,567	87,250	4,919	1.4	−7.2	5.2	5.6	0.6	0.7
322	Paper	152,378	18,385	155,846	20,208	−2.2	−9.0	12.1	13.0	2.4	2.8
323	Printing and related support activites	95,735	4,725	100,792	5,885	−5.0	−19.7	4.9	5.8	0.6	0.8
324	Petroleum and coal products	215,663	25,523	219,075	16,312	−1.6	56.5	11.8	7.4	3.4	2.3
325	Chemicals	427,754	68,674	438,410	54,041	−2.4	27.1	16.1	12.3	9.1	7.5
326	Plastics and rubber products	166,089	23,953	170,717	27,324	−2.7	−12.3	14.4	16.0	3.2	3.8
327	Nonmetallic mineral products	94,391	7,144	94,861	7,887	−0.5	−9.4	7.6	8.3	1.0	1.1
331	Primary metals	136,971	12,828	138,245	14,274	−0.9	−10.1	9.4	10.3	1.7	2.0
332	Fabricated metal products	242,204	21,427	253,113	24,168	−4.3	−11.3	8.8	9.5	2.8	3.3
333	Machinery	241,406	30,390	266,553	35,670	−9.4	−14.8	12.6	13.4	4.0	4.9
334	Computer and electronic products	353,529	73,406	429,471	73,221	−17.7	0.3	20.8	17.0	9.8	10.1
335	Electrical equipment, appliances, and components	103,599	23,043	114,067	27,845	−9.2	−17.2	22.2	24.4	3.1	3.8
336	Transportation equipment	620,649	297,280	602,496	264,326	3.0	12.5	47.9	43.9	39.5	36.5
337	Furniture and related products	73,112	8,082	72,147	9,348	1.3	−13.5	11.1	13.0	1.1	1.3
339	Miscellaneous	123,761	14,068	116,201	15,644	6.5	−10.1	11.4	13.5	1.9	2.2

Note: Estimates are not adjusted for price changes. NAICS is North American Industry Classification System.
*Estimates include data only for businesses with paid employees and are subject to revision.

SOURCE: "Table 1. U.S. Manufacturing Shipments—Total and E-commerce Value: 2002 and 2001," in *United States Department of Commerce E-Stats*, U.S. Census Bureau, Economics and Statistics Administration, U.S. Department of Commerce, April 2004, http://www.census.gov/eos/www/papers/2002/2002finaltables.pdf (accessed November 11, 2004)

first an auction site for collectibles such as Beanie Babies, quickly attracted the attention of small business owners. For a modest insertion fee, people could list their products on eBay's Web site. Buyers then could bid on the objects, and when a sale was final, the seller paid eBay a commission of 1.25% to 5% of the item's sales price. The Web site included payment options that did not require the purchaser to provide credit card information, and they even offered protections against fraud.

The eBay Web site created a whole new economic outlet for small business owners and people who simply wanted to pawn off their used goods. No longer was someone who wanted to sell embroidered pillows relegated to local flea markets. Individual vendors from crafters to high-end car salesmen could reach out to a nationwide audience. Even people with used stuff suddenly had more options than simply giving it to charity or holding a garage sale. In a September 2004 standard quarterly presentation, eBay reported more than 114 million global registered users selling over $8 billion in merchandise. The report claimed that more than 430,000 people made their living full-time or part-time auctioning items on eBay, and noted that most businesses using eBay had five employees or less.

MMORPGS AND THE SALE OF VIRTUAL GOODS. One of the more unusual industries to sprout up, due in part to eBay, was the sale of virtual goods, including "gold" and characters from massive multiplayer online role-playing games (MMORPGs). Games such as Everquest and Star Wars Galaxies placed players in a virtual world with thousands of other people where they could kill monsters and collect gold and other valuable virtual artifacts. Some of these online games even gave the player the option to marry and build houses in this virtual world. Progressing far in these games and obtaining a high level, however, required hundreds of hours of playtime. As a result, an entire cottage industry sprouted up around the sale of virtual gold and characters on auction sites such as eBay. Typically, a player would buy the game, build up a character and gold and then sell their password to the game to a buyer on eBay, sometimes fetching hundreds of dollars. Such sales represented the first industry centered on completely virtual goods.

SERVICE INDUSTRIES. The service industry in the United States is enormous and encompasses everything from brokerage houses to real estate companies to travel agents to health care. Generally, any business that sells its

TABLE 3.6

Total and e-commerce wholesale trade sales*1998–2002

[Estimates are based on data from the Annual Trade Survey. Sales estimates are shown in millions of dollars, consequently industry group estimates may not be additive.]

	Description	Value of sales									
		2002		**2001 revised**		**2000 revised**		**1999 revised**		**1998 revised**	
		Total	E-commerce	Total	E-commerce	Total	E-commerce	Total	E-commerce	Total	E-commerce
42	**Total merchant wholesale trade**	**2,742,285**	**319,755**	**2,701,474**	**286,211**	**2,743,557**	**248,400**	**2,539,566**	**209,863**	**2,379,824**	**173,903**
421	**Durable goods**	**1,334,066**	**146,287**	**1,345,892**	**132,628**	**1,421,462**	**119,302**	**1,353,049**	**107,400**	**1,265,755**	**91,403**
4211	Motor vehicles and automotive equipment	215,437	53,348	205,605	47,933	199,522	41,097	195,724	38,269	173,239	35,914
4212	Furniture and home furnishings	43,611	4,690	44,862	3,940	46,725	2,851	42,792	2,672	40,423	2,284
4213	Lumber and other construction material	77,879	2,896	73,605	2,556	70,900	2,292	71,284	2,004	63,661	2,001
4214	Professional and commercial equipment and supplies	249,419	32,897	251,062	31,523	269,914	31,593	273,846	27,588	254,069	20,912
42143	Computer equipment and supplies	113,541	15,032	123,342	15,705	150,798	19,042	160,492	17,744	150,784	11,158
4215	Metals and minerals, excluding petroleum	89,811	(S)	92,792	(S)	102,717	(S)	94,813	(S)	97,108	(S)
4216	Electrical goods	204,350	19,263	212,924	15,160	240,362	11,754	208,355	9,578	186,721	7,973
4217	Hardware, plumbing and heating equipment	66,088	7,706	64,738	7,056	67,108	6,610	63,444	6,512	60,352	5,961
4218	Machinery, equipment and supplies	223,295	8,645	240,891	8,132	252,126	7,765	245,453	7,069	242,531	5,400
4219	Miscellaneous durable goods	164,176	15,752	159,413	15,314	172,088	14,508	157,338	12,942	147,651	10,435
422	**Nondurable goods**	**1,408,219**	**173,468**	**1,355,582**	**153,583**	**1,322,095**	**129,098**	**1,186,517**	**102,463**	**1,114,069**	**82,500**
4221	Paper and paper products	76,719	4,809	77,162	4,246	80,551	3,870	74,908	3,420	69,937	2,954
4222	Drugs, drug proprietaries and druggists' sundries	233,188	110,745	200,861	96,363	168,471	77,790	146,549	61,158	124,564	49,509
4223	Apparel, piece goods and notions	91,071	13,664	87,776	12,305	88,267	10,578	85,043	8,835	84,191	7,085
4224	Groceries and related products	402,691	21,357	389,731	18,056	383,882	13,321	361,928	10,815	344,437	8,828
4225	Farm-products raw materials	111,302	3,697	108,081	3,272	107,019	3,225	101,900	3,160	107,993	2,522
4226	Chemicals and allied products	60,446	(D)	59,633	(D)	59,044	(D)	55,270	(D)	55,073	(D)
4227	Petroleum and petroleum products	181,138	10,089	180,601	(D)	187,701	(D)	135,077	(D)	116,397	(D)
4228	Beer, wine, and distilled beverages	79,760	(D)	75,156	(D)	71,551	(D)	67,464	(D)	61,822	(D)
4229	Miscellaneous nondurable goods	171,904	5,614	176,581	5,071	175,609	4,986	158,378	4,481	149,655	4,526

(S) Estimate does not meet publication standards because of high sampling variability or poor response quality. Unpublished estimates derived from this table by subtraction are subject to these same limitations and should not be attributed to the U.S. Census Bureau.
(D) Estimate is withheld to avoid disclosing data of individual companies; these data are included in broader industry totals.
Note: Estimates are not adjusted for price changes. NAICS is North American Industry Classification System.
*Estimates include data only for businesses with paid employees.

SOURCE: "Table 2 Historical. U.S. Merchant Wholesale Trade Sales—Total and E-commerce: 1998–2002," in *United States Department of Commerce E-Stats*, U.S. Census Bureau, Economics and Statistics Administration, U.S. Department of Commerce, April 2004, http://www.census.gov/eos/www/historical/2002ht.pdf (accessed November 11, 2004)

TABLE 3.7

Total and e-commerce retail sales*, 1998–2002

[Estimates are based on data from the Annual Retail Trade Survey. Sales estimates are shown in millions of dollars, consequently industry group estimates may not be additive.]

NAICS code	Description	Value of sales									
		2002		2001 revised		2000 revised		1999 revised		1998 revised	
		Total	E-commerce	Total	E-commerce	Total	E-commerce	Total	E-commerce	Total	E-commerce
	Total retail trade	**3,230,122**	**44,287**	**3,156,754**	**34,263**	**3,070,186**	**28,000**	**2,878,914**	**14,667**	**2,644,785**	**4,926**
441	Motor vehicles and parts dealers	846,248	7,231	841,141	5,336	816,631	4,255	779,763	1,762	699,457	389
442	Furniture and home furnishing stores	93,689	(S)	91,442	(S)	91,662	(S)	85,218	(S)	78,574	(S)
443	Electronics and appliance stores	89,930	778	85,174	643	86,362	507	81,921	242	75,981	133
444	Building materials and garden equipment and supplies stores	299,893	603	287,233	527	275,996	447	263,205	339	243,490	31
445	Food and beverage stores	489,445	(S)	481,388	(S)	459,211	(S)	443,159	(S)	421,579	(S)
446	Health and personal care stores	181,111	(S)	168,050	(S)	156,861	(S)	143,610	(S)	130,228	(S)
447	Gasoline stations	244,796	(Z)	246,993	(Z)	247,160	(Z)	211,271	(Z)	191,749	(Z)
448	Clothing and clothing accessories stores	171,759	487	167,313	288	167,864	199	160,050	82	149,442	12
451	Sporting goods, hobby, book and music stores	80,222	662	79,818	506	78,056	400	74,045	261	69,456	52
452	General merchandise stores	451,365	(S)	430,095	(S)	406,204	(S)	381,403	(S)	351,706	(S)
453	Miscellaneous store retailers	104,400	684	105,097	516	108,477	383	105,782	242	99,803	116
454	Nonstore retailers	177,264	33,117	173,010	25,897	175,702	21,381	149,487	11,526	133,320	3,948
454110	Electronic shopping and mail-order houses	114,480	32,191	109,158	25,145	110,073	20,943	92,440	11,430	79,489	3,928

(S) Estimate does not meet publication standards because of high sampling variability or poor response quality. Unpublished estimates derived from this table by subtraction are subject to these same limitations and should not be attributed to the U.S. Census Bureau.

(Z) Sales estimate is less than $500,000 or percent estimate is less than 0.05%.

Note: Estimates are not adjusted for price changes.

*Estimates include data for businesses with or without paid employees.

SOURCE: "Table 5 Historical. U.S. Retail Sales—Total and E-commerce: 1998–2002," in *United States Department of Commerce E-Stats*, U.S. Census Bureau, Economics and Statistics Administration, U.S. Department of Commerce, April 2004, http://www.census.gov/eos/www/historical/2002ht.pdf (accessed November 11, 2004)

TABLE 3.8

Total and e-commerce sales of electronic shopping and mail-order houses, by merchandise line[1], 1999–2002

[Estimates are based on data from the Annual Retail Trade Survey. Sales estimates are shown in millions of dollars, consequently industry group estimates may not be additive.]

	Value of sales							
	2002		2001 revised		2000 revised		1999 revised	
Merchandise lines	Total	E-commerce	Total	E-commerce	Total	E-commerce	Total	E-commerce
Total electronic shopping and mail-order houses (NAICS 454110)	**114,480**	**32,191**	**109,158**	**25,145**	**110,073**	**20,943**	**92,440**	**11,430**
Books and magazines	4,017	1,848	3,825	1,691	4,093	1,775	3,407	1,436
Clothing and clothing accessories (includes footwear)	14,020	4,272	15,021	3,165	14,857	2,184	13,251	892
Computer hardware	21,203	5,873	22,653	5,506	27,113	5,988	23,383	4,094
Computer software	4,433	1,456	4,110	1,110	3,671	1,081	2,744	741
Drugs, health aids, and beauty aids	20,709	1,446	16,130	951	14,094	660	11,129	236
Electronics and appliances	4,419	2,030	3,877	1,508	3,356	1,055	2,631	485
Food, beer, and wine	1,869	639	1,901	487	1,870	557	1,405	227
Furniture and home furnishings	7,116	2,447	6,442	1,633	6,367	1,006	5,759	353
Music and videos	3,862	1,454	3,960	1,256	4,319	1,158	4,171	751
Office equipment and supplies	6,114	2,450	6,416	1,872	6,757	1,371	7,091	586
Sporting goods	2,687	910	1,718	502	1,706	396	NA	NA
Toys, hobby goods, and games	3,458	1,250	2,954	895	3,072	819	2,164	383
Other merchandise[2]	15,651	3,858	16,137	2,914	15,617	1,853	14,163	947
Nonmerchandise receipts[3]	4,922	2,258	4,014	1,655	3,181	1,040	1,142	299

NA Not applicable
Note: Estimates are not adjusted for price changes.
[1]Estimates include data for businesses with or without paid employees, are grouped according to merchandise categories used in the Annual Retail Trade Survey.
[2]Includes other merchandise such as collectibles, souvenirs, auto parts and accessories, hardware, lawn and garden equipment and supplies, and jewelry.
[3]Includes nonmerchandise receipts such as auction commissions, customer training, customer support, advertising, and shipping and handling.

SOURCE: "Table 6 Historical. U.S. Electronic Shopping and Mail-Order Houses (NAICS 454110)—Total and E-Commerce Sales by Merchandise Line: 1999–2002," in *United States Department of Commerce E-Stats,* U.S. Census Bureau, Economics and Statistics Administration, U.S. Department of Commerce, April 2004, http://www.census.gov/eos/www/historical/2002ht.pdf (accessed November 11, 2004)

services or some type of expertise belongs in this category. Of all the industries presented in Figure 3.2, e-commerce revenue made up the smallest percentage of total revenue for the service industries. In those areas of the service industry where e-commerce has broken through, however, it has created a deal of change. Probably no other type of business in the services sector has been affected more by the Internet than travel reservations services. Before the Internet, travelers had to either comb through travel books and call airlines, hotels, restaurants, and other venues one by one, or else hire a travel agent to do it for them. When the Internet became widely available, new businesses formed that essentially took over the role of traditional travel agents by consolidating information about airfare, hotels, and vacation packages and making it easily searchable online. Existing businesses, like the airlines, developed websites of their own. And so it became much easier for travelers to comparison shop and make travel plans on their own. As Table 3.9 shows, electronic commerce made up nearly a quarter (24%) of the travel arrangements and reservation services in 2001. According to marketing research firm PhoCusWright, thirty-five million Americans purchased travel reservations in 2003, which was a 17% increase over 2002. Within the next decade as many as 70% of all travel reservations could be made by individuals online.

Needless to say, many travel agencies have faced tough times since the late 1990s. In a 2001 report on trav-

el agency automation, the American Society of Travel Agents (ASTA) pointed out that airline ticket reservations were the main source of revenue for twentieth-century travel agents. Coincidentally, airline reservations have become the type of travel reservation made most often by online consumers. From 1998 to 2001, airline reservation sales by travel agents fell from 58% of total sales to 54%. As noted above, the number of travel agency jobs in the United States dropped by more than 18% between 1998 and 2003, and the U.S. Department of Labor estimates that by the year 2012 the number of working travel agents will likely shrink by another 14%. To avoid losing their jobs, many travel agents are beginning to focus on putting together more complex packages for travelers than can easily be arranged online.

Another service industry that experienced a great deal of change due to IT is the securities brokerage business. Since the early 1980s many of those who work in the industry have employed powerful computers and networking capabilities to track financial markets in real time and make financial transactions electronically. When the Internet became mainstream, large financial services organizations, such as Fidelity Investments and Charles Schwab, offered brokerage accounts to customers, allowing them to trade stocks online. Customers also had access to many of the research services only available to stockbrokers prior to the World Wide Web. An online 2001 *Wall Street Journal* fact sheet entitled "Trading

TABLE 3.9

Total and e-commerce revenue, selected services[1], 1998–2000

[Except where indicated, estimates are based on data from the Service Annual Survey. Revenue estimates are shown in millions of dollars, consequently industry group estimates may not be additive.]

NAICS code	Description	Value of revenue									
		2002		2001 revised		2000 revised		1999 revised		1998 revised	
		Total	E-commerce	Total	E-commerce	Total	E-commerce	Total	E-commerce	Total	E-commerce
	Total for selected service industries	4,862,961	41,463	4,756,317	36,045	4,639,947	36,022	4,264,199	24,182	3,929,669	14,463
	Selected transportation and warehousing[2]	237,485	3,429	235,659	2,810	237,782	2,555	221,967	1,959	207,535	1,641
484	Truck transportation	169,443	2,422	169,069	1,526	172,258	1,287	162,046	821	150,816	606
492	Couriers and messengers	53,101	913	53,317	1,192	52,738	1,188	47,368	1,082	44,890	981
493	Warehousing and storage	14,941	S	13,273	S	12,787	S	12,283	S	11,829	S
51	Information	876,984	11,059	870,684	10,438	845,266	9,303	767,261	5,212	687,991	2,577
511	Publishing Industries	230,916	5,362	231,714	4,941	232,069	4,745	218,124	3,065	200,576	1,544
513	Broadcasting and telecommunications	484,652	2,549	487,799	2,516	469,349	1,880	425,127	902	381,017	481
51419	Online Information services	31,842	1,823	32,347	1,850	31,438	1,997	20,121	1,020	11,866	431
	Selected finance[3]	256,879	4,191	288,417	3,754	331,497	5,976	285,317	3,996	239,802	2,259
5231	Securities and commodity contracts intermediation and brokerage	163,080	4,071	191,007	3,570	227,841	5,664	193,759	3,831	161,516	2,145
532	Rental and leasing services	100,507	S	99,126	S	101,188	S	93,605	S	85,002	S
	Selected professional, scientific, and technical services[4]	848,109	6,490	842,261	5,237	805,834	5,467	728,468	4,142	663,411	2,501
5415	Computer systems design and related services	162,175	4,267	174,367	3,526	175,338	3,444	154,286	2,869	131,481	1,644
	Administrative and support and waste management and remediation services[5]	421,107	10,463	409,984	9,612	408,315	9,674	372,054	6,989	336,298	4,815
5615	Travel arrangement and reservation services	26,545	6,385	26,487	6,269	26,611	6,181	25,069	5,263	23,092	4,196
62	Health care and social assistance services	1,203,447	S	1,110,231	S	1,027,870	S	971,892	S	931,520	S
71	Arts, entertainment, and recreation services	137,236	S	128,904	S	122,117	S	114,796	S	108,643	S
72	Accommodation and food services[6]	456,232	S	445,236	S	437,801	S	404,631	S	381,119	S
	Selected other services[7]	324,975	1,097	325,815	656	322,277	554	304,208	364	288,348	178
811	Repair and maintenance	131,205	254	130,482	214	125,012	256	119,478	115	114,753	107
813	Religious, grantmaking, civic, professional, and similar organizations	121,381	639	124,457	383	128,467	267	119,627	123	111,702	62

(S) Estimate does not meet publication standards because of high sampling variability or poor response quality. Unpublished estimates derived from this table by substraction are subject to these same limitations and should not be attributed to the U.S.Census Bureau.

Note: Estimates are not adjusted for price changes.

[1] Estimates are subject to revision and include data only for businesses with paid employees except for Accommodation and Food Services, which also includes business without paid employees.

[2] Excludes NAICS 481 (air transportation), 482 (rail transportation), 483 (water transportation), 485 (transit and ground passenger transportation), 486 (pipeline transportation), 487 (scenic and sightseeing transportation), 488 (support activities for transportation), and 491 (postal service).

[3] Excludes NAICS 521 (monetary authorities-central bank), 522 (credit intermediation and related activities), 5232 (securities and commodity exchanges), 52391 (miscellaneous intermediation), 52399 (all other financial investment activities), 524 (insurance carriers and related activities), and 525 (funds, trusts, and other financial vehicles).

[4] Excludes NAICS 54112 (offices of notaries) and 54132 (landscape architectural services).

[5] Excludes NAICS 56173 (landscaping services).

[6] Estimates are based on data from the 2002 Annual Retail Trade Survey.

[7] Excludes NAICS 81311 (religious organizations), 81393 (labor and similar organizations), 81394 (political organizations), and 814 (private households).

SOURCE: "Table 4 Historical. U.S. Selected Service Revenue—Total and E-Commerce: 1998–2000" in *United States Department of Commerce E-Stats,* U.S. Census Bureau, Economics and Statistics Administration, U.S. Department of Commerce, April 2004, http://www.census.gov/eos/www/historical/2002ht.pdf (accessed November 11, 2004)

Stocks Online" reported that in 1996 1.5 million brokerage accounts existed online. In 2001 that number shot up to twenty million despite the recession, and brokerage accounts were projected to continue growing for many years. In *America's Online Pursuits* (Washington, DC: Pew Internet & American Life Project, December 2003), researcher Mary Madden reported that some fourteen million online Americans said they bought and sold stock online. Despite the increase in self-service brokering, the U.S. Department of Labor reported in 2002 that the ranks of stockbrokers would continue to grow at the same pace as the national job rate. However, the number of brokerage clerks, who generally assist securities brokers in their jobs, was projected to decline 15% by 2012. One could surmise that while information technologies have not harmed brokers' business, IT has replaced many tasks once completed by brokerage clerks.

The real estate brokerage sector is another service industry that has undergone many changes due to the Internet. Before the Internet, people could only find real estate listings in the newspaper or at a real estate agency. Many Web sites, such as Realtor.com, started listing hundreds of houses for sale in every region of the country. These sites made it possible for people in Virginia, for instance, to get a feel for real estate and real estate prices in Alaska or Arizona. Monthly Internet statistics from Realtor.com show that Internet traffic on their site increased from 3.79 million unique visitors in June 2002 to 6.15 million unique visitors in June 2004. Due in part to a real estate boom that began around the turn of the twenty-first century, the number of real estate agents and brokers increased from 347,000 in 1998 to 407,000 by 2002, according to the U.S. Department of Labor. The Internet may or may not infringe on real estate brokerage job growth in the future as many realtors do not list all their homes on the Web. Many homebuyers also require assistance in the complex process of buying a house. In *Digital Economy 2003*, the U.S. Department of Commerce analyzed trends in housing price and buying behavior, and they found that the only discernible effect that the Internet had on the housing market was that online homebuyers tended to use the resource to make more personal visits to more houses.

IT AND CURRENCY

IT has not just changed how people pay for merchandise, but also how people make and receive payments in general. Credit cards, debit cards, electronic bank transfers, and online banking have eliminated much of the need to carry cash and personal checks. In *The Future of Banking in America: The Effect on U.S. Banking of Payment System Changes* (Washington, DC: FDIC, 2004), Neil B. Murphy reported that nearly 88% of households in the United States used some from of electronic payment. The advantages of a cashless system are undeniable. With credit cards and debit cards people always have buying power at their disposal, they can make purchases instantly, and they can access and transfer money online. Banks and businesses are no longer required to spend money moving paper bills and checks all over the country. Store owners do not have to worry about the security risks inherent with keeping large amounts of cash on hand.

Credit and Debit Cards

The most firmly established of these electronic payment methods is the credit card. The first general purpose credit card was issued in 1950 by Diners Club. This credit card allowed restaurant patrons in Manhattan to charge a meal at any restaurant that participated in the program. While credit card use has increased almost every year since then, credit card transactions took place entirely on paper at first, which kept some people away. In the 1980s a computerized, networked credit card system was put into place using modems and other networking technologies. Credit card use skyrocketed. In his report for the FDIC, Murphy estimated that in 2004 there were more than 1.2 billion credit cards in the United States. A little under half of these (552 million) were issued directly by retailers (for example, Banana Republic or J.C. Penney). The rest were issued by banks or as travel and entertainment cards. Murphy reported that between 1997 and 2001 the number of credit card transactions grew from 12.9 million to seventeen million.

A U.S. Census survey of credit card holders painted a slightly different picture. As can be seen in Table 3.10, the U.S. Census Bureau counted 1.4 billion credit cards in the United States in 2002. They projected that this number was likely to drop a little by 2005. As to annual spending, $1.6 trillion was spent using credit cards in 2002, and this number was projected to increase to $2 trillion by 2005. Table 3.11 shows credit card use by age and income, and provides information on median account charges, balances, and payments.

Since their introduction into the U.S. market in the early 1990s, debit cards have also become a very popular method of payment for most Americans. Debit cards, unlike credit cards, automatically remove existing money from a money market or bank account when used. The person paying does not owe money after the transaction. Debit cards grew out of the ATM system that became widespread in the early 1980s. Some ATM networks such as Cirrus, which were originally constructed to allow bank cards access to ATMs at multiple banks, expanded their networks to grocery stores and select mainstream retail stores such as Wal-Mart. Customers could then use their ATM cards to buy groceries or merchandise at the register without first having to get cash at a machine. When this debit card system appeared as if it might become widely used in many venues, VISA and Master-

TABLE 3.10

Credit card use, 2000 and 2002, and projections, 2005

[159 represents 159,000,000]

Type of credit card	Cardholders (mil.)			Number of cards (mil.)			Credit card spending (bil. dol.)			Credit card debt outstanding (bil. dol.)		
	2000	2002	2005, proj.	2000	2002	2005, proj.	2000	2002	2005, proj.	2000	2002	2005, proj.
Total[1]	**159**	**163**	**173**	**1,425**	**1,452**	**1,430**	**1,458**	**1,638**	**2,022**	**680**	**764**	**922**
Bank[2]	107	112	120	455	525	580	938	1,095	1,359	480	560	683
Phone	125	126	128	181	182	184	21	20	22	3	2	3
Store	114	115	118	597	547	464	120	127	147	92	91	97
Oil company	76	75	73	98	97	90	50	54	71	5	5	7
Other[3]	7	7	7	94	100	111	330	342	423	101	105	133

[1]Cardholders may hold more than one type of card.
[2]Visa and MasterCard credit cards. Excludes debit cards.
[3]Includes Universal Air Travel Plan (UATP), automobile rental, and miscellaneous cards. Except for cardholders, also includes Discover, American Express, and Diners Club.

SOURCE: "No. 1190. Credit Cards—Holders, Numbers, Spending, and Debt, 2000 and 2002, and Projections, 2005," in *Statistical Abstract of the United States: 2003,* U.S. Census Bureau, Economics and Statistics Administration, U.S. Department of Commerce, 2003, http://www.census.gov/prod/2004pubs/03statab/banking.pdf (accessed November 11, 2004)

TABLE 3.11

Use of general purpose credit cards by families, 1992–2001

[General purpose credit cards include Mastercard, Visa, Optima, and Discover cards. Excludes cards used only for business purposes. All dollar figures are given in constant 2001 dollars based on consumer price index data as published by U.S. Bureau of Labor Statistics. Families include one-person units.]

Age of family head and family income	Percent having a general purpose credit card	Median number of cards	Median new charges on last month's bills (dol.)	Percent having a balance after last month's bills	Median balance* (dol.)	Percent of cardholding families who—		
						Almost always pay off the balance	Sometimes pay off the balance	Hardly ever pay off the balance
1992, total	**62.4**	**2**	**100**	**52.6**	**1,200**	**53.0**	**19.6**	**27.4**
1995, total	**66.5**	**2**	**200**	**56.0**	**1,700**	**52.4**	**20.1**	**27.5**
1998, total	**67.5**	**2**	**200**	**54.7**	**2,000**	**53.8**	**19.3**	**26.9**
2001, total	**72.7**	**2**	**200**	**53.7**	**1,800**	**55.3**	**19.1**	**25.6**
Under 35 years old	64.2	2	100	68.2	1,800	40.6	24.1	35.4
35 to 44 years old	76.9	2	200	62.9	2,000	47.0	22.8	30.2
45 to 54 years old	80.0	2	200	57.3	2,000	54.3	19.3	26.4
55 to 64 years old	76.0	2	300	48.2	2,000	59.8	17.8	22.3
65 to 74 years old	76.5	2	200	30.0	1,100	75.8	11.0	13.2
75 years old and over	59.7	2	200	24.2	700	81.2	9.3.0	9.4
Less than $10,000	28.5	1	—	67.4	1,000	45.3	23.0	31.7
$10,000 to $24,999	56.1	2	100	57.0	1,000	49.5	19.9	30.6
$25,000 to $49,999	76.1	2	100	61.3	1,700	46.7	19.7	33.6
$50,000 to $99,999	87.9	2	200	53.9	2,000	55.2	20.8	24.0
$100,000 and more	95.8	2	1,000	36.1	3,000	75.2	13.9	10.9

— Represents zero.
*Among families having a balance.

SOURCE: "No. 1191. Usage of General Purpose Credit Cards by Families: 1992 to 2001," in *Statistical Abstract of the United States: 2003,* U.S. Census Bureau, Economics and Statistics Administration, U.S. Department of Commerce, 2003, http://www.census.gov/prod/2004pubs/03statab/banking.pdf (accessed November 11, 2004)

Card went into the business and opened up their extensive networks to banks and debit card users. Since 1995 the use of debit cards has grown at a rapid pace. According to Murphy in *The Future of Banking in America: The Effect on U.S. Banking of Payment System Changes*, from 1995 to 2001 the percentage of American households with a debit card grew from 17.6% to 47%. In 1995 there were 1.4 billion debit card transactions. Table 3.12 shows that this number jumped to 8.3 billion in 2000 and 13.3 billion by 2002. In 2005 the number of debit card transactions

was expected to be 22.7 billion, which was just two billion shy of the projections for credit card transactions.

Electronic Transfer of Money

Another type of paperless monetary transaction that has grown in popularity is the electronic transfer of money, formally known as the automated clearing house (ACH) system. Electronic transfer is an electronic form of the checking system. When making an ACH transaction,

TABLE 3.12

Consumer payment systems by method of payment, 2000 and 2002, and projections, 2005

[112.3 represents 112,300,000,000]

| | Transactions | | | | | Volume | | | | |
| | Number (bil.) | | | Percent distribution | | Amount (bil. dol.) | | | Percent distribution | |
Method of payment	2000	2002	2005, proj.	2000	2005, proj.	2000	2002	2005, proj.	2000	2005, proj.
Total	**112.3**	**120.7**	**132.4**	**100.0**	**100.0**	**5,183**	**5,660**	**6,465**	**100.0**	**100.0**
Paper	80.2	80.7	76.0	71.5	57.4	3,371	3,439	3,180	65.0	49.2
Direct check payments[1]	30.2	29.5	28.2	26.9	21.3	2,276	2,206	2,081	43.9	32.2
Cash	48.8	49.9	46.4	43.5	35.0	978	1,103	947	18.9	14.6
Money orders	0.9	1.0	1.1	0.8	0.9	82	94	114	1.6	1.8
Travelers cheques	0.2	0.2	0.2	0.2	0.1	13	12	12	0.3	0.2
Official checks[2]	0.1	0.1	0.1	0.1	0.1	22	23	26	0.4	0.4
Cards	30.0	37.0	50.2	26.7	37.9	1,593	1,904	2,570	30.7	39.7
Credit cards[3]	19.9	21.2	24.4	17.7	18.5	1,238	1,361	1,683	23.9	26.0
Debit cards[4]	8.3	13.3	22.7	7.4	7.1	309	477	801	6.0	12.4
Stored value cards[5]	1.3	1.8	2.0	1.1	1.5	31	48	59	0.6	0.9
EBT cards and food stamps[6]	0.6	0.7	1.0	0.5	0.8	15	18	27	0.3	0.4
Electronic	2.1	2.9	6.3	1.8	4.7	219	317	715	4.2	11.1
Preauthorized payments[7]	1.5	2.0	3.2	1.4	2.5	166	229	379	3.2	5.9
Remote payments[8]	0.5	0.9	3.0	0.5	2.3	53	88	337	1.0	5.2

[1]Excludes consumer check repayments and prepayments involving other payment systems as well as all commercial and government checks.
[2]Official checks include cashier's checks, teller checks, and certified checks purchased from financial institutions. Excludes those purchased by businesses.
[3]Credit cards include general purpose cards usable at all kinds of merchants and proprietary cards usable only at selected outlets. Includes some purchases on personal cards for government, commercial, and business-related spending. Cash advances are excluded.
[4]Debit cards include general purpose cards carrying the Visa or MasterCard brand, electronic funds transfer (EFT) brands of regional EFT systems, proprietary commercial cards issued by private firms to drivers in the long-haul trucking and business aviation industry, and proprietary consumer cards issued by supermarkets. Cash withdrawals at ATMs and cash back over the counter are excluded.
[5]Stored value cards are used primarily for gift certificates and telephone calls.
[6]Electronic benefits transfer cards are replacements for paper script food stamps.
[7]Preauthorized payments are handled electronically "end-to-end" through an automated clearing house.
[8]Remote payments are made using a telephone or a computer and include point-of-sale check conversions and utility-bill payments made at ATMs, self-service clerk-assisted electronic banking machines kiosks and clerk-assisted machines at supermarkets.

SOURCE: "No. 1187. Consumer Payment Systems by Method of Payment, 2000 and 2002, and Projections, 2005," in *Statistical Abstract of the United States: 2003*, U.S. Census Bureau, Economics and Statistics Administration, U.S. Department of Commerce, 2003, http://www.census.gov/prod/2004pubs/03statab/banking.pdf (accessed November 11, 2004).

the person or business with the checking account provides the account and routing number to another party along with the authorization to wire money directly into or out of an account. For the most part, large corporations employ this method of payment and receipt more extensively than individual households. In his FDIC report Murphy noted that 97% of large corporations use the ACH system extensively, largely for business-to-business transactions involving substantial amounts of money.

Most individual households typically use ACH to receive regular salary or Social Security payments and to make regular monthly payments. According to Murphy, 3.8 billion direct deposit payments were made into individual accounts in 2002, and the number of direct payments by consumers topped 2.8 billion, which was a 10.1% increase from 2001. Table 3.13 displays the percentage of households that took advantage of direct deposit and automatic bill paying in 1995 and 2001. Over those six years the percentage of households using direct deposit increased from 46.8% to 67.3%, and the percentage of households using ACH for paying bills increased from 21.8% to 40.3%. Many adults also receive their tax returns through an electronic payment method. In 2004 more than sixty million tax returns were filed over the Internet either from home or through a tax preparer such as H&R Block. When the tax return is sent via Internet, the Internal Revenue Service (IRS) provides the option of either paying taxes or receiving taxes directly through a personal bank account, using the Electronic Federal Tax Payment System (EFTPS).

Despite all the electronic transfers that take place in and out of bank accounts each year, Americans still write a staggering number of checks. Murphy reported in *The Future of Banking in America* that in 2001 144.6 checks were written per person in the United States, which amounts to 41.2 billion checks total. While this number decreased from 42.5 billion in 2000, Americans still wrote significantly more checks than other industrial nations. (France was second to the United States, with 71.2 checks per capita, but countries such as Belgium, Germany, Italy, the Netherlands, Sweden, and Switzerland counted fewer than ten checks per person in 2001.) Since the cost of creating, mailing, and handling so many paper checks is enormous, the U.S. government has made efforts to reduce the number of paper checks in the system. Early in 2003 the Federal Reserve reduced what it

TABLE 3.13

Households that use selected payment instruments, 1995 and 2001

[In percent. Based on Survey of Consumer Finance conducted by the Board of Governors of the Federal Reserve System.]

Age and education	Any of these instruments		ATM*		Debit card		Direct deposit		Automatic bill paying		Smart card*	
	1995	2001	1995	2001	1995	2001	1995	2001	1995	2001	1995	2001
All households	76.5	88.4	61.2	69.8	17.6	47.0	46.8	67.3	21.8	40.3	1.2	2.9
Under 30 years old	75.2	83.0	71.1	78.1	24.5	60.6	31.1	48.8	17.9	32.1	1.8	2.6
30 to 60 years old	77.4	89.3	67.2	76.8	19.7	53.4	42.9	64.8	24.5	44.1	1.5	3.3
61 years old and over	75.2	89.2	43.1	48.9	9.6	24.6	63.2	83.2	18.2	35.9	0.3	2.1
No college degree	69.8	84.7	52.8	63.7	14.3	42.3	40.4	61.8	18.2	33.7	0.8	2.4
College degree	91.5	95.6	80.1	81.6	25.2	56.2	61.0	78.0	30.1	53.2	2.1	3.8

*The questions on ATMs and smart cards asked whether any member of the household had an ATM card or a smart card, not whether the member used it. The other questions asked about usage.

SOURCE: "No 1186. Percent of U.S. Households That Use Selected Payment Instruments: 1995 and 2001," in *Statistical Abstract of the United States: 2003*, U.S. Census Bureau, Economics and Statistics Administration, U.S. Department of Commerce, 2003, http://www.census.gov/prod/2004pubs/03statab/banking.pdf (accessed November 11, 2004)

charges banks for processing electronic transfers (ACH) and raised the prices it charges banks for processing paper checks. Then on October 28, 2003, Congress passed and President George W. Bush signed the Check Truncation Act. The act, also known as Check21, went into effect on October 28, 2004. Under the Check Truncation Act banks were no longer required to hold onto the original paper checks they received. Instead, when a payee deposited a check in a bank, the bank made a digital copy of the check and shredded the original. The bank then simply wired the payer's bank for the money, avoiding the postage and processing involved in sending the actual check to the payer's bank. If the payer were to need a copy of the check in the future, the stored digital image would be printed.

ANTITRUST LITIGATION

Throughout American history, technological innovation has tended to give rise to the formation of monopolies. Those companies that create a widespread demand and a standard for new technologies often become the only producer of that technology, shutting down further competition in that industry. Since the passage of the Sherman Antitrust Act in 1890, companies in the private sector have been forbidden from blocking competitors from entering the market. If a company grows large enough and powerful enough to keep competitors out of the market and become a monopoly, then the U.S. Justice Department typically intervenes and either reaches a settlement with said company or files an antitrust suit and takes the company to court. The idea behind these laws is that monopolies reduce competition, which hinders economic progress and innovation. While this law may appear easy to understand, the courts and the Justice Department have to weigh a number of factors before breaking up a monopoly, including the negative affects the ruling may have on consumers.

In 1998 the Justice Department and the attorneys general of twenty states filed an antitrust suit against Microsoft. Along with other charges, the government claimed that Microsoft violated antitrust law when it integrated its Internet Explorer web browser software with Windows. At the time, Windows was the only operating system widely available for the PC. When Microsoft integrated Internet Explorer and Windows, other Web browsers such as Netscape could not compete. The Justice Department maintained that this act created unfair competition for those other companies who made browsers for PC systems. Microsoft claimed that the Internet Explorer was now part of Windows and that separating the two would destroy the most current versions of the operating system and years of development on their part.

On November 5, 1999, U.S. District Court Judge Thomas Penfield Jackson presented a preliminary ruling, which asserted that Microsoft did have a monopoly with their PC operating system and that the monopoly prevented fair competition among companies making software for personal computers. Five months later on April 3, 2000, the judge gave his final ruling, ordering that Microsoft should be split into two separate units—one that would produce the operating system and one that would produce other software components such as Internet Explorer. Microsoft immediately appealed, and the case went to the federal appeals court under Judge Colleen Kollar-Kotelly. In the midst of the judicial review, the White House administration changed, and the U.S. Justice Department, now led by John Ashcroft, came to an agreement with Microsoft that did not involve the breakup of the company. However, several of the states continued to battle the software giant in court. On November 1, 2002, Kollar-Kotelly decided that the company should not be broken up and should follow the agreement laid down by the Justice Department and accepted by the attorneys general of Illinois, Kentucky, Louisiana, Maryland, Michigan, New York, North Carolina, Ohio, and

Wisconsin. Additional remedies proposed by California, Connecticut, the District of Columbia, Iowa, Florida, Kansas, Massachusetts, Minnesota, Utah, and West Virginia were dismissed. The agreement required Microsoft to take a number of steps that would allow competitors to once again compete in the market. Among these provisions, Microsoft was required to give computer makers the option of removing Internet Explorer and other Microsoft programs that sit on top of the Windows operating system. Microsoft was also forced to reveal details about the Windows operating system that would allow makers of other software to better integrate software with Windows.

CHAPTER 4
TECHNOLOGY AND CRIME

New technologies introduce new problems into a society. Those technologies that became widespread in the 1980s and 1990s were no exception. Cell phones, the Internet, computers, and other forms of digital technology have fueled epidemics in identity theft, intellectual property theft, and other crimes that most people were hardly aware of in the 1970s. Brand new crimes related to advances in information technology, known as e-crimes, such as Internet auction fraud, computer hacking, and computer virus creation, have cost Americans many millions in money and wasted time. In *Fear of Online Crime* (Washington, DC: Pew Internet & American Life Project, April 2001), Susannah Fox reported findings from a survey conducted among more than 2,000 Americans on what they were most afraid of with regard to Internet crime. Table 4.1 shows that one-half of adult Americans feared Internet child pornography the most. Credit card theft (ID theft) and organizational terrorism came in second and third. Two percent of people were afraid of wide-scale fraud, and only 1% feared hackers attacking businesses.

Due to the nebulous nature of the Internet and high-tech crimes, comprehensive studies of e-crimes are hard to come by. Generally, the reports that are available can be contradictory and rarely include the effects of crime on both individuals and organizations. In addition, statutes are not uniform from jurisdiction to jurisdiction, meaning that criminal behavior that can result in prosecution in one country or state might be legal in another. Nevertheless, computer crime is increasingly being tracked and analyzed. According to its annual *Cybercrime Review*, the International Chamber of Commerce estimated that nearly two-thirds of all Internet crime in 2003 took place in the United States. Hacking and fraud were listed as the top offenses. Table 4.2, however, appears to confirm the fears of those surveyed by the Pew/Internet report. In 2001 child pornography transmission topped the list of e-crimes that resulted in criminal prosecution in the United States. Nationwide, nearly one-third (30%) of prosecutors' offices

TABLE 4.1

Most-feared Internet crimes, 2001

THE PERCENTAGE OF ALL AMERICANS WHO SAY THEY ARE MOST CONCERNED ABOUT...

Child pornography	50%
Credit card theft	10
Organized terrorism	10
Destructive computer viruses	5
Hackers attacking the government	5
Wide-scale fraud	2
Hackers attacking businesses	1
Another crime not listed as a choice	13

SOURCE: "Most-feared Internet Crimes," in *Fear of Online Crime*, Pew Internet and American Life Project, April 2, 2001, http://www.pewinternet.org/pdfs/PIP_Fear_of_crime.pdf (accessed November 12, 2004). Used by permission of the Pew Internet and American Life Project, which bears no responsibility for the interpretations presented or conclusions based on analysis of the data.

conducted cases against suspects accused of transmitting child pornography. This was followed closely by credit card fraud (identity theft) at 28% and bankcard fraud at 22.6%. Regardless of the differences suggested by various studies, all agree that crimes committed using computers and other forms of high technology will likely grow as the number of people using these technologies increases.

FRAUD AND THE INTERNET

The relative anonymity of the Internet combined with the proliferation of credit card and debit card accounts led to a dramatic increase in fraud around the turn of the twenty-first century. According to the Federal Trade Commission (FTC) in *National and State Trends in Fraud & Identity Theft: January–December 2003*, online fraud accounted for 55% of all fraud in the United States in 2003.

The most common type of fraud perpetrated in or outside of the virtual world was identity theft. Simply put, identity theft is the theft of an individual's personal infor-

TABLE 4.2

Computer-related crime prosecuted by prosecutors' offices, 2001

| Type of computer crime prosecuted | All offices | Full-time offices (population served) | | | Part-time |
		Large (1,000,000 or more)	Medium (250,000 to 999,999)	Small (under 250,000)	
Any computer-related crime	41.5%	97.0%	72.9%	44.2%	16.8%
Credit card fraud	27.4	93.5	61.2	28.2	7.4
Bank card fraud[1]	22.3	83.3	50.9	22.6	6.9
Computer forgery[2]	13.3	63.0	39.2	12.8	2.7
Computer sabotage[3]	4.6	53.6	14.4	3.8	0.5
Unauthorized access to computer[4]	9.6	60.7	28.8	8.8	2.3
Unauthorized copying or distribution of computer programs[5]	2.7	53.8	9.0	1.8	0.2
Cyberstalking[6]	16.3	76.7	47.8	15.1	4.5
Theft of intellectual property	3.2	40.7	13.4	2.3	0.5
Transmitting child pornography	30.0	87.1	67.1	30.4	10.8
Identity theft	18.2	80.0	51.9	17.2	4.5

Note: Data on prosecution of any computer related crime under their state's computer statutes were available for 2,151 prosecutors' offices. Data were available on credit card fraud for 1,995 prosecutors' offices, bank card fraud 1,956 offices, forgery 1,894 offices, sabotage 1,853 offices, unauthorized access to computer system 1,878 offices, unauthorized copying or distribution of computer programs 1,883 offices, cyberstalking 1,927 offices, theft of intellectual property 1,839 offices, transmitting child pornography 2,029 offices, and identity theft 1,927 offices.

[1] ATM or debit.
[2] Alteration of computerized documents.
[3] To hinder the normal function of a computer system through the introduction of worms, viruses, or logic bombs.
[4] Hacking.
[5] Software copyright infringement.
[6] The activity of users sending harassing or threatening e-mail to other users.

SOURCE: "Computer-related Crime Prosecuted by Prosecutors' Offices," in *Prosecutors in State Courts,* Bureau of Justice Statistics, Office of Justice Programs, U.S. Department of Justice, 2001, http://www.ojp.usdoj.gov/bjs/pub/pdf/psc01.pdf (accessed November 11, 2004)

mation such as a telephone number, address, a credit card number, or a Social Security number. Thieves use this information to buy things, set up false credit card and cell phone accounts, and even perpetrate crimes. With a victim's Social Security number, address, and phone number, for instance, a thief can apply for numerous credit cards in the victim's name and proceed to run up the limits on these cards. Such a crime leaves the victim's credit report in shambles, making it difficult to apply for loans or additional cards in the future.

In 1998 Congress gave the FTC the responsibility to track identity theft in the United States. As Figure 4.1 shows, reported cases of identity theft nearly tripled from 2001 to 2003, when they comprised 42% of all cases of fraud. Table 4.3 breaks down incidents of identity fraud by state. Arizona topped the list with the highest number of reported cases of ID fraud per capita, followed by Nevada, California, and Texas. North Dakota and South Dakota had the lowest number of victims of identity theft.

The cases reported to the FTC, however, did not necessarily paint a true picture of identity crime in the United States. In fact, most incidents were never reported. In 2003 the FTC also conducted a survey of random households to come up with a more complete understanding of how identity theft affected Americans. The resulting *Identity Theft Survey Report* (September 2003) revealed that most identity fraud involved the use of an existing account (both credit card and noncredit card) to purchase mer-

FIGURE 4.1

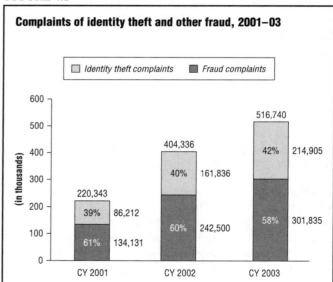

Complaints of identity theft and other fraud, 2001–03

Percentages are based on the total number of Sentinel complaints by calendar year. These figures exclude "Do not call" registry complaints.

SOURCE: "Sentinel Complaints by Calendar Year," in *National and State Trends in Fraud and Identity Theft,* Consumer Sentinel and Identity Theft Clearinghouse, U.S. Federal Trade Commission, January 22, 2004, http://www.consumer.gov/sentinel/pubs/Top10Fraud2003.pdf (accessed November 11, 2004)

chandise or services. Table 4.4 shows that 3.1% of Americans discovered that their existing accounts were being used by thieves in 2003. One-half that number of Americans (1.5%) reported that new accounts or loans were

TABLE 4.3

Indentity theft victims, by state, 2003

January 1–December 31, 2003

Rank	Consumer state	Complaints per 100,000 population	Number of complaints		Rank	Victim state	Victims per 100,000 population	Number of victims
1	Alaska	179.6	1,165		1	Arizona	122.4	6,832
2	Hawaii	131.0	1,647		2	Nevada	113.4	2,541
3	Wyoming	128.1	642		3	California	111.2	39,452
4	Washington	119.6	7,335		4	Texas	93.3	20,634
5	Colorado	114.3	5,200		5	Florida	83.0	14,119
6	Nevada	113.7	2,548		6	New York	82.4	15,821
7	New Hampshire	113.5	1,461		7	Oregon	81.7	2,909
8	Oregon	112.7	4,011		8	Colorado	81.3	3,698
9	Arizona	112.1	6,256		9	Illinois	77.4	9,792
10	Montana	111.5	1,023		10	Washington	77.3	4,741
11	Virginia	110.6	8,171		11	Maryland	74.9	4,124
12	Florida	108.2	18,419		12	Georgia	70.5	6,127
13	Maryland	107.7	5,931		13	New Mexico	70.3	1,317
14	California	104.9	37,221		14	New Jersey	68.9	5,948
15	Utah	104.1	2,447		15	North Carolina	65.9	5,537
16	New Jersey	97.8	8,451		16	Michigan	65.1	6,566
17	Delaware	97.4	796		17	Missouri	61.3	3,496
18	Connecticut	96.7	3,368		18	Indiana	59.1	3,660
19	Wisconsin	92.2	5,048		19	Virginia	58.2	4,297
20	Pennsylvania	91.9	11,358		20	Delaware	57.7	472
21	Missouri	90.8	5,179		21	Massachusetts	56.5	3,634
22	Kansas	90.5	2,465		22	Utah	56.4	1,326
23	Vermont	89.6	555		23	Connecticut	54.9	1,913
24	Rhode Island	89.5	963		24	Pennsylvania	52.9	6,545
25	Massachusetts	89.1	5,729		25	Hawaii	51.6	649
26	Idaho	88.9	1,215		26	Kansas	50.6	1,378
27	Indiana	88.0	5,455		27	Rhode Island	49.9	537
28	Nebraska	87.7	1,526		28	Minnesota	49.7	2,517
29	Ohio	87.6	10,020		29	Oklahoma	48.1	1,689
30	Maine	85.7	1,119		30	Ohio	48.0	5,494
31	Michigan	85.4	8,612		31	Tennessee	47.6	2,782
32	Illinois	84.4	10,681		32	Arkansas	47.5	1,294
33	New Mexico	84.3	1,580		33	South Carolina	45.7	1,895
34	New York	84.3	16,170		34	Nebraska	44.9	781
35	Minnesota	83.6	4,229		35	Wisconsin	42.5	2,325
36	North Dakota	81.7	518		36	Louisiana	41.7	1,875
37	Oklahoma	80.5	2,828		37	Alabama	40.5	1,823
38	South Dakota	79.9	611		38	New Hampshire	38.8	500
39	West Virginia	79.2	1,434		39	Mississippi	37.6	1,084
40	North Carolina	78.7	6,618		40	Idaho	36.1	493
41	Iowa	77.7	2,288		41	Alaska	35.6	231
42	Tennessee	76.7	4,479		42	Wyoming	34.3	172
43	Georgia	76.6	6,649		43	Kentucky	32.3	1,332
44	Texas	75.5	16,706		44	Montana	30.7	282
45	Kentucky	72.5	2,986		45	Iowa	30.6	900
46	Alabama	71.0	3,196		46	West Virginia	28.1	508
47	South Carolina	70.1	2,907		47	Maine	27.0	353
48	Louisiana	65.3	2,936		48	Vermont	25.7	159
49	Arkansas	62.8	1,712		49	North Dakota	20.0	127
50	Mississippi	52.2	1,503		50	South Dakota	19.6	150

Note: Per 100,000 unit of population estimates are based on the 2003 U.S. Census population estimates.
Numbers for the District of Columbia are: Fraud = 989 complaints and 175.5 complaints per 100,000 population; Identity Theft = 917 complaints and 162.8 victims per 100,000 population.

SOURCE: "Identity Theft Victims by State," in *National and State Trends in Fraud and Identity Theft*, Identity Theft Clearinghouse, U.S. Federal Trade Commission, January 22, 2004, http://www.consumer.gov/sentinel/pubs/Top10Fraud2003.pdf (accessed November 11, 2004)

taken out in their name in 2003. All told, an estimated ten million cases of identity fraud took place in the United States in 2003, affecting 4.6% of Americans. Banks and credit card companies, which typically assumed the cost of the merchandise purchased by identity thieves, lost an estimated $48 billion to identity theft. Victims of identity theft spent an average of thirty hours and nearly $500 of their own money dealing with the problem.

Figure 4.2 shows what types of accounts identity thieves opened after they obtained a victim's personal information. Nearly 8% of all identity victims reported that the thief opened up a credit card account in the victim's name. Five percent said their identity was used to take out a loan or subscribe to telephone service, and 3% claimed someone opened a checking/savings account in their name. Figure 4.3 displays which types of existing accounts thieves misused. By far, thieves stole credit card account numbers the most. Checking/savings accounts came in second at 19%, followed by telephone service at 9%, Internet at 3%, and insurance accounts at 2%.

TABLE 4.4

Cost of identity theft, 2002[1]

	New accounts & other frauds	Misuse of existing accounts (both credit card & non-credit card)	All ID theft
Victims in the last year			
Percent of population	1.5%	Credit card – 2.4% non credit card – 0.7%	4.6%
Number of persons[2]	3.23 million	6.68 million	9.91 million
Loss to businesses, inc. financial institutions			
Average per victim[1]	$10,200	$2,100	$4,800
Total	**$32.9 billion**	**$14.0 billion**	**$47.6 billion**
Loss to victims			
Average per victim	$1,180	$160	$500
Total	**$3.8 billion**	**$1.1 billion**	**$5.0 billion**
Hours victims spent resolving their problems			
Average per victim	60 hours	15 hours	30 hours
Total	**194 million hours**	**100 million hours**	**297 million hours**

[1]Totals by type of ID theft may not sum to the amount shown in the totals column due to rounding. "Average per victim" figures in the "All ID theft" column are a weighted average of the values for the different types of ID theft with the incidence in the past year used as weights.
[2]Based on U.S. population age 18 and over of 215.47 million as of July 1, 2002.

SOURCE: "Costs of Identity Theft in the Last Year," in *Federal Trade Commission—Identity Theft Survey Report*, U.S. Federal Trade Commission, September 2003, http://www.ftc.gov/os/2003/09/synovatereport.pdf (accessed November 11, 2004).

Identity Thieves

Identity thieves can operate alone or as a part of large crime organization. They can be someone the victim knows or a complete stranger. They gather personal information in various ways, stealing wallets and checkbooks or going through trash bins outside of homes and businesses to dig out credit card statements, old check books, and receipts. Some pilfer financial statements and other private information from open mailboxes. Since the mid-1990s, many thieves have turned to the Internet to steal information. In fact, the widespread use of the Internet coincided directly with the dramatic increase in identity theft nationwide.

There are a number of ways in which thieves use the Internet to retrieve personal information. Tech-savvy crooks will often take the direct method and hack into business and bank servers and make off with hundreds of credit card numbers. Most identity thieves, however, do not employ such sophisticated methods. According to Duncan Graham-Rowe in "Internet Fuels Boom in ID Theft" (*New Scientist*, March 13, 2003), one of the easiest ways to steal identities is simply to use a search engine such as Google. Many people naively post all manner of personal information on home and even office Web sites, including their Social Security number, date of birth, mother's maiden name, current address, and phone number. Simply typing "driver's license" or "passport" into

FIGURE 4.2

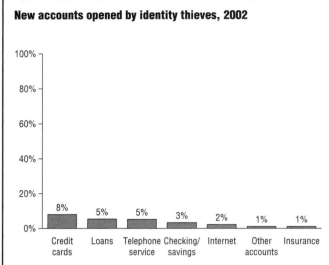

New accounts opened by identity thieves, 2002

SOURCE: "Q24/Q25/Q27—New Accounts Opened by Identity Thieves," in *Federal Trade Commission—Identity Theft Survey Report*, U.S. Federal Trade Commission, September 2003, http://www.ftc.gov/os/2003/09/synovatereport.pdf (accessed November 11, 2004).

the Google image search engine yields hundreds of photos of driver's licenses and passports from around the country. Businesses that keep lists of Social Security and credit card numbers sometimes inadvertently place the information in an insecure location. For a patient identity thief, the Internet is a treasure trove.

Another technique thieves use to acquire personal information is known as "phishing." Thieves will often send out bogus e-mails to scores of people. Typically, these e-mails will look like authentic e-mails from a prominent Internet service provider or bank. The e-mail will inform the receiver that there is something wrong with his or her account and that the problem can be fixed by clicking on a hyperlink. When the victim does click on the link, the victim is then taken to an official-looking site where he or she is asked to provide passwords, Social Security information, and even credit card information. The moment the victim types in their personal information, the thief has them. Once crooks have a credit card in another person's name, the Internet makes it easier to purchase items as well. No longer do crooks have to risk being caught using someone else's account in a shopping mall or grocery store.

Auction Fraud

Outside of identity fraud, the biggest fraud perpetrated in 2003 was auction fraud. (See Figure 4.4.) In 2003 the FTC received some 77,500 complaints of auction fraud. Internet auction fraud is usually very straightforward. Typically, a con artist advertises merchandise on an auction site such as eBay until a buyer is found. The buyer then sends a payment but receives no merchandise.

FIGURE 4.3

Existing accounts misused by identity thieves, 2002

```
100%

 80%
           67%
 60%

 40%

 20%                19%
                            9%
  0%                              3%       2%
       Existing  Checking/  Telephone  Internet  Insurance
       credit    savings    service
       card
```

SOURCE: "Q1/Q19/Q20—Existing Accounts Misused," in *Federal Trade Commission—Identity Theft Survey Report,* U.S. Federal Trade Commission, September 2003, http://www.ftc.gov/os/2003/09/ synovatereport.pdf (accessed November 11, 2004)

FIGURE 4.4

Top consumer complaint categories, 2003

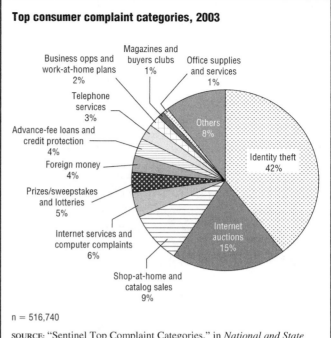

n = 516,740

SOURCE: "Sentinel Top Complaint Categories," in *National and State Trends in Fraud and Identity Theft,* Consumer Sentinel and Identity Theft Clearinghouse, U.S. Federal Trade Commission, January 22, 2004, http://www.consumer.gov/sentinel/pubs/Top10Fraud2003.pdf (accessed November 11, 2004)

The Internet Fraud Complaint Center (IFCC) annual report profiles several cases that they have helped solve each year. In one instance in 2002 a woman named Teresa Smith stole more than $800,000 from over three hundred people in an auction fraud involving computer sales. She operated out of an office in West Boylston, Massachusetts, where she put computers up for auction on eBay, receiving payments but not shipping the merchandise. When customers accused Smith of foul play, she gave them an excuse, often maintaining that the computer had been lost in the mail. Each time eBay shut down her account, she opened a new one under a different false name.

More elaborate auction frauds have also been set up to trick the seller. In a 2002 FTC case a con artist created a phony escrow company to avoid paying the seller. Legitimate escrow companies act as mediators; they hold onto the payment owed to a seller while the buyer has a chance to test the merchandise and see that it works. When the buyer gives approval, the escrow company sends the money to the seller. The phony escrow outfit in the FTC case, blandly named premier-escrow.com, was owned by a scam artist who bought items in auctions and then informed the sellers that he would like to use premier-escrow.com. The sellers, thinking the thief's money was secure in an escrow company, would send the merchandise to the thief.

Other Types of Online Fraud

While auction fraud and identity theft made up the vast majority of fraudulent activity on the Web, countless other frauds have been perpetrated over the years. These ranged from false merchandise advertised on a phony Web page to work-at-home e-mail schemes in which the victim was told to send in money as an initial investment. One of the more famous e-mail scams of the early twenty-first century was the Nigerian letter fraud scam, which had been circulating via traditional mail since the early 1980s. In its electronic form, an e-mail purportedly from a "Nigerian dignitary" informed the victim that he or she had the opportunity to receive vast sums of money currently being held in Nigeria. When the victim responded to the message, he or she was then told that the Nigerian dignitary required money in advance, usually to bribe government officials, so that the funds could be released and deposited in the victim's account. In 2002 the IFCC yearly report revealed that seventy-four U.S. individuals had sent money to perpetrators of this scam and lost a total of nearly $1.6 million.

Still other, more elaborate scams were designed to manipulate the stock market. Such scams were particularly effective in the late 1990s during the stock market bubble. The best known of these was the "pump-and-dump" scam. The criminals invested in a stock that was lightly traded and then tricked online investors into buying it. Typically, this involved posting fake documents and press releases on financial Web sites, telling investors that the company was either about to be bought out or had developed a new, money-making product. In other instances, scam artists bribed lesser-known stock pundits to tout the lifeless stock.

After the stock took off, the criminals simply sold their holdings, leaving other investors holding the bag.

VIRUSES

The common term "computer virus" is often used to refer to all malware (*mal*icious soft*ware*)—that is, programs such as viruses, worms, and Trojan horses that infect and destroy computer files. Technically speaking, viruses are self-replicating programs that insert themselves into other computer files. The virus is spread when the file is transferred to another computer via a disk or by way of the Internet. The first virus can be dated back to 1982 when fifteen-year-old Rich Skrenta wrote "Elk Cloner," a virus that attached itself to an Apple DOS 3.3 operating system and spread to other computers by floppy disk. The first computer worm to attract attention appeared six years later and was written by Robert Morris at the MIT Artificial Intelligence Laboratory. Worms are self-contained, self-replicating computer programs that spread through the Internet from computer to computer. Unlike viruses, they spread from computer to computer via the Internet under their own power and do not rely on people's actions or files to move from one machine to another. Like viruses, worms can destroy files and take advantage of vulnerabilities in computer programs or operating systems. A Trojan horse does not self-replicate and is typically disguised as something more innocent, such as an e-mail attachment. When the user opens the e-mail, malicious code is unleashed on the computer. As malware has become more advanced, the distinctions between types of malware have become less obvious. For instance, Trojan horses often contain viruses that replicate through computer files. For this reason the word "virus" will be used here to designate any type of malware, unless otherwise specified.

Viruses behave in a number of different ways. The Netsky virus, for instance, is typically hidden in an e-mail attachment and is launched when the user opened the attachment. Once active, Netsky set up its own e-mail protocol, looked for e-mail accounts on the hard drive, and mass-mailed itself to these accounts. Another virus named MSBlaster appeared on August 13th, 2003, and quickly wormed its way through the Internet, infecting hundreds of thousands of computers in a day through vulnerability in Windows operating systems. Once on a PC, the virus instructed the computer to take part in a Distributed Denial-of-Service (DDoS) attack on the windowsupdate.com Web site. (A DDoS attack occurs when hundreds of computers are used to access a single Web site, thus making it inaccessible.) Other viruses known as "bombs" lay dormant in a computer until a specific date was registered on the computer's clock. Still other viruses disabled any virus removal program on the computer, making the virus very difficult to remove.

People have all sorts of reasons for creating and sending viruses. Some viruses are written as pranks. Others are written by political activists or terrorists. Still other viruses are intended to injure specific corporations. According to McAfee, one of the largest makers of antivirus programs, in October 2004 more than 780,000 computers became infected with the top ten most prevalent viruses. WildList Organization International, an organization that tracks the number of computer viruses circulating around the world, reported that there were roughly 360 viruses in play in October 2004.

How Viruses Hurt American Businesses

Each year, ICSA Labs, a division of TruSecure Corporation, releases its "Computer Virus Prevalence Survey." In 2003 the survey cataloged computer virus trends and incidents in three hundred large organizations with a combined total of 962,278 desktops computers, servers, and perimeter gateways. The report revealed these organizations had 2.7 million encounters with viruses in 2003, which represented 201 encounters per one thousand machines per month. (An example of an encounter would be an employee receiving an e-mail attachment with a virus.) These encounters resulted in the infection of an average of 108 of the sites per month. Though the rate of infections appeared to plateau after the turn of the century, more infections occurred in 2003 than in any previous year. (See Figure 4.5.) The survey defined a virus disaster as an incident that affected more than twenty-five machines in an organization or caused significant damage within the organization. Nearly one-third (ninety-two) of all the organizations revealed they had experienced a virus disaster over the survey period. When asked if the virus problem in general was better or worse, a little more than half (154) of the organizations surveyed responded that it was "much worse."

Some viruses were encountered more than others. The viruses that the ICSA Labs survey respondents encountered the most was the Yaha virus, with thirty-two encounters per month. This was followed by the Klez virus, the Mimail virus, the BugBear virus, and the SirCam virus. Employees encountered more than 88% of the viruses in e-mail attachments. Internet downloads accounted for the second largest number of viruses (16%). Figure 4.6 is a chart showing how viruses were distributed from 1996 to 2003. As the graphic shows, viruses delivered through floppy disks have dropped dramatically since the mid-1990s, while viruses contracted by e-mail have skyrocketed. The viruses that do the most damage, however, are not necessarily the ones that were encountered most often. The survey participants reported that the viruses most responsible for their latest disasters were the Blaster worm, the Slammer worm, and the Sobig worm. Blaster alone infected 129,087 computers in twelve organizations, according to the survey.

Virus disasters have cost the companies involved in the ICSA survey a great deal of time and money. Eighty-

FIGURE 4.5

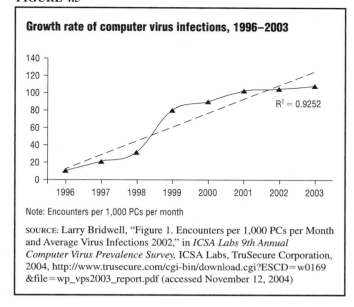

Growth rate of computer virus infections, 1996–2003

Note: Encounters per 1,000 PCs per month

SOURCE: Larry Bridwell, "Figure 1. Encounters per 1,000 PCs per Month and Average Virus Infections 2002," in *ICSA Labs 9th Annual Computer Virus Prevalence Survey,* ICSA Labs, TruSecure Corporation, 2004, http://www.trusecure.com/cgi-bin/download.cgi?ESCD=w0169 &file=wp_vps2003_report.pdf (accessed November 12, 2004)

FIGURE 4.6

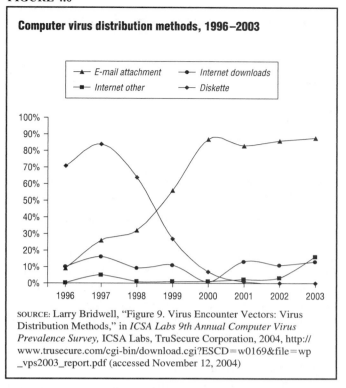

Computer virus distribution methods, 1996–2003

SOURCE: Larry Bridwell, "Figure 9. Virus Encounter Vectors: Virus Distribution Methods," in *ICSA Labs 9th Annual Computer Virus Prevalence Survey,* ICSA Labs, TruSecure Corporation, 2004, http://www.trusecure.com/cgi-bin/download.cgi?ESCD=w0169&file=wp _vps2003_report.pdf (accessed November 12, 2004)

two of the survey participants that reported virus disasters also reported that servers were involved in the disaster. Although the average downtime for a server was seventeen hours, five organizations reported that their servers were offline for more than one hundred hours. The 2003 respondents spent an average of eleven person-days and $99,000 to clean up a typical virus disaster, an amount that was $18,000 more than it had been 2002.

While the number of viral infections per year seemed to be leveling off in 2003, the viruses themselves were more damaging, in part because the new viruses spread faster. In the early 1990s file viruses sometimes took months to propagate via floppy disk. The Slammer virus, which was released on January 25, 2003, spread around the world in ten minutes, knocking out five of the thirteen Domain Name System (DNS) root servers and impacting everything from ATM systems to air traffic control systems. The quicker a virus moves, the less time the makers of antiviral software have to create a defense against it. Without a defense, the virus can attack computer systems unchecked.

Computer Emergency Response Team (CERT)

The Defense Advanced Research Projects Agency (DARPA, formerly ARPA) formed the Computer Emergency Response Team (CERT) in 1988 only two weeks after the Morris worm was let loose on the Internet. The headquarters for CERT, the CERT Coordination Center (CERT/CC), is located at Carnegie Mellon University in Pittsburgh, Pennsylvania. The purpose of the organization is to identify threats to the Internet as a whole. CERT/CC also coordinates the actions of the private and public sectors when major Internet incidents occur. In 2003 the US-CERT was formed by the Department of Homeland Security to work with the CERT Coordination Center in identifying threats to the Internet and U.S. national securi-

ty. While CERT does issue alerts on viruses that affect home users, CERT is more concerned with the big picture. They provide emergency incident response for network access ports (NAPs), root DNS servers, and other components that make up the Internet's infrastructure. They also coordinate responses to large automated attacks against the Internet, such as the Slammer virus, and monitor threats to U.S. government computers. The organization also analyzes virus code to come up with solutions to thwart them.

For years CERT has published a list of vulnerabilities and incidents reported to them. Most incidents were not garden-variety viral e-mail attachments, rather they were deliberate attacks by hackers and other criminals against computers at corporations, academic institutions, and government agencies. Table 1.2 in Chapter 1 shows the number of incidents reported to CERT between 1988 and 2003. Only six incidents were reported in 1988 when the organization was formed. The number of incidents had grown to 2,412 in 1995 and to 137,529 incidents in 2003. Incidents typically occur when vulnerabilities—weaknesses in computer software and systems—are exploited by cyber criminals. The MSBlaster worm exploited one such vulnerability in the Microsoft Windows program. The vulnerability enabled the creator of the worm to use other people's computers to launch a DDoS attack Microsoft's Web site. Table 4.5 displays the number of legitimate vulnerabilities reported to CERT from 1995 through the first three quarters of 2004. Between 1999 and 2002 the number of major vulnerabilities in Internet and computer systems shot up dramatically. In 2003, how-

TABLE 4.5

Computer security vulnerabilities reported, 1995–2004

1995–1999

Year	1995	1996	1997	1998	1999
Vulnerabilities	171	345	311	262	417

2000–2004

Year	2000	2001	2002	2003	2004
Vulnerabilities	1,090	2,437	4,129	3,784	3,780

Total vulnerabilities reported (1995–2004): 16,726

SOURCE: "Vulnerabilities Reported," in *Cert/CC Statistics 1988–2004,* CERT Coordination Center, Carnegie Mellon Software Engineering Institute, January 24, 2005, http://www.cert.org/stats/cert_stats.html#incidents (accessed February 18, 2005). Reproduced by special permission of the Carnegie Mellon Software Engineering Institute.

TABLE 4.6

Computer security threats organizations fear most, 2003

(base: 500)

Hackers	40%
Current employees	22%
Former employees	6%
Current service providers/contractors/consultants	3%
Customers	2%
Foreign entities	2%
Competitors	2%
Terrorists	1%
Former service providers/contractors/consultants	1%
Suppliers/business partners or information brokers	<1%
Don't know	20%

Note: percents may not sum to 100 due to rounding.

SOURCE: "Greatest Cyber Security Threat in 2003," in *2004 E–Crime Watch Survey,* CSO magazine/U.S. Secret Service/CERT Coordination Center, Carnegie Mellon Software Engineering Institute, May 25, 2004, http://www.cert.org/archive/pdf/2004eCrimeWatchSummary.pdf (accessed November 19, 2004). Reproduced by special permission of the Carnegie Mellon Software Engineering Institute.

TABLE 4.7

Types of electronic crimes reported, 2003

(base: 342)

Virus or other malicious code	77%
Denial of service attack	44%
Illegal generation of SPAM email	38%
Unauthorized access by an *insider*	36%
Phishing	31%
Unauthorized access by an *outsider*	27%
Fraud	22%
Theft of intellectual property	20%
Theft of other proprietary info	16%
Employee identity theft	12%
Sabotage by an *insider*	11%
Sabotage by an *outsider*	11%
Extortion by an *insider*	3%
Extortion by an *outsider*	3%
Other	11%
Don't know	8%

Note: percents may not sum to 100 due to rounding.

SOURCE: "Types of Electronic Crimes," in *2004 E–Crime Watch Survey,* CSO magazine/U.S. Secret Service/CERT Coordination Center, Carnegie Mellon Software Engineering Institute, May 25, 2004, http://www.cert.org/archive/pdf/2004eCrimeWatchSummary.pdf (accessed November 19, 2004). Reproduced by special permission of the Carnegie Mellon Software Engineering Institute.

ever, the number of vulnerabilities dropped by 8%, and they remained at about the same level in 2004. These numbers seemed to suggest that software designers and computer manufacturers were becoming better at catching vulnerabilities in 2003, although computer hackers and criminals were continuing their attacks.

E-crime Survey Results

In 2004 CERT began publishing an annual "E-crimes Survey Watch" to obtain a more detailed picture of how e-crimes affected companies in the United States. The survey polled five hundred organizations of all sizes and asked them about the problems they faced with regard to computer crimes in 2003. The CERT definition for an electronic crime is "any criminal violation in which electronic media is used in the commission of that crime." Over 30% of those surveyed reported security budgets of $1 million or more on computer systems security. Coincidentally, 30% said that they experienced no electronic crimes. Nearly 45% replied that they were victims of between one and fifty crimes, and the rest reported they experienced more than fifty crimes. Table 4.6 reveals that most organizations saw hackers and current and former employees as the biggest threat to their security. However, as can be seen in Table 4.7, the types of electronic crimes experienced the most by survey respondents were viruses and denial of service attacks. Unauthorized access to computers by insiders (current or former employees) came in fourth, with 36% of survey participants reporting the crime. Of those companies that reported e-crimes by insiders, 73% said the person was a current employee not in a management position. Unauthorized access by someone with little or no connection to the company was reported by 27% of respondents. The survey suggests that when it came to e-crime in 2003, companies had more to fear from current employees than from random computer hackers. With regard to preventive measures, Table 4.8 reveals that most organizations believed firewalls and encrypted data to be the most effective barriers to preventing e-crime. Manual patch management of system vulner-

abilities, wireless monitoring, and monitoring employees' keystrokes were considered the least effective.

The *Computer Crime and Security Survey,* conducted by the Computer Security Institute (CSI) and the Federal Bureau of Investigation (FBI) in 2004, presented similar findings to CERT's "E-crimes Survey Watch." One big difference between the two surveys was that the FBI survey included the theft of computer merchandise. Figure 4.7 lists multiple e-crimes that have plagued the respondents of the survey for the last five years. Viruses by far topped the list with 78% of respondents reporting a virus

TABLE 4.8

Technologies effective against e-crime, 2003

Technologies effectiveness (percents based on those with technology in use)	Very or extremely effective	Somewhat effective	Not effective	Don't know
Firewalls	71%[1]	22%	2%	4%
Encryption of critical data in transit	63%[2]	19%	5%	13%
Two factor authentication	56%[3-tie]	16%	8%	20%[4]
Encryption of critical data in storage	56%[3-tie]	21%	6%	17%[5]
Intrusion detection systems monitored by automated systems w/ built-in alarms	51%[4]	28%	8%	13%
Physical security systems	48%[5]	39%[1]	9%	4%
Intrusion detection systems monitored by person	45%	34%[4]	11%	10%
Role-based access control	44%	35%[3-tie]	9%	12%
Automated patch management	39%	32%[5]	14%[4]	16%
Information assurance technologies	35%	35%[3-tie]	13%[5]	16%
Anti-Fraud technologies working with ERP/account payable/billing systems	33%	30%	7%	30%[2]
Wireless monitoring	26%	31%	20%[2]	23%[3]
Manual patch management	26%	37%[2]	23%[1]	14%
Keystroke monitoring of individual users	24%	27%	16%[3]	33%[1]

Notes: Percents may not sum to 100 due to rounding.
The top five rankings for each column are provided (in parentheses).

SOURCE: "Technologies Effectiveness," in *2004 E–Crime Watch Survey,* CSO magazine/U.S. Secret Service/CERT Coordination Center, Carnegie Mellon Software Engineering Institute, May 25, 2004, http://www.cert.org/archive/pdf/2004eCrimeWatchSummary.pdf (accessed November 19, 2004). Reproduced by special permission of the Carnegie Mellon Software Engineering Institute.

attack in 2004. Insider abuse of Internet access came in second with 59%. Denial of service, which often involved the use of a virus, ranked sixth with 17%. Table 4.9 shows that the number of total incidents originating from the outside and the inside have been roughly equal during the five years the survey was taken. As to total dollar amount, Figure 4.8 displays how much each type of computer crime cost 269 of the survey participants (out of a total of 494). Viruses and denial of service topped the list in 2004 with $55 million and $26 million in losses. By comparison, insider Internet abuse cost these organizations only about $10 million. Overall, however, the cost of computer crimes to companies in the survey dropped from $201 million to $141 million between 2003 and the 2004 survey. The FBI's report concluded that the level of computer crimes dropped between 1999 and 2004. Interestingly, the CSI/FBI survey found that many respondents did not report e-crime incidents to law enforcement agencies. The most prominent reasons given were that they believed the associated negative publicity would be detrimental to the company's image or stock value (51%) or because they feared a competitor would use knowledge of the vulnerability against them (35%).

INTELLECTUAL PROPERTY THEFT

Intellectual property, which includes such copyrighted material as games, software, and movies, is a huge part of the U.S. economy. The industries that produced copyrighted material in 2002 contributed 6% ($626.6 billion) to the domestic economy of the United States and employed roughly 4% of the U.S. workforce, according to the *Report of the Department of Justice's Task Force on Intellectual Property* (October 2004). The task force further reported that between 1997 and 2002, the copyright industries added workers at an annual rate of 1.33%, which exceeded overall U.S. job growth by 27%. These industries are important to the American economy and to the people employed in them; financial profit is vital for those who create music, video games, books, or software.

Intellectual property theft has posed perhaps the greatest single threat to the copyright industries since the 1990s. In the mid-1980s, pirating software and entertainment media on a large enough scale to make a profit demanded a large initial investment and a huge time commitment. Pirating movies, for instance, required large banks of VCRs along with hundreds of blank tapes. Copies of the movie were typically of much lower quality than the original, and national copyright laws made storing, selling, and distributing the bulky tapes very difficult. As a result, most pirated copies of movies, music, games or software were copied and distributed overseas in countries where copyright law was nonexistent or not enforced. Technological advances in the 1990s put an end to many of the hassles faced by intellectual property thieves. The Internet, along with powerful computers and the conversion of nearly every type of media into digital form, made copying and distributing intellectual property very easy even in the United States. Once a thief found a way around the copyright protection that existed on the copyrighted material, the computer provided an easy way to store the material. Since digital media do not degrade when copied, the thief could produce perfect duplicates. FTP file sites and peer-to-peer networks allowed for easy distribution of the media over the Internet to any country in the world.

The Justice Department report revealed that in 2002, intellectual property theft worldwide cost American companies $250 billion. The Motion Picture Association of America (MPAA) estimated that the movie industry lost

FIGURE 4.7

Types of computer attacks reported, 1999–2004

(by percent)

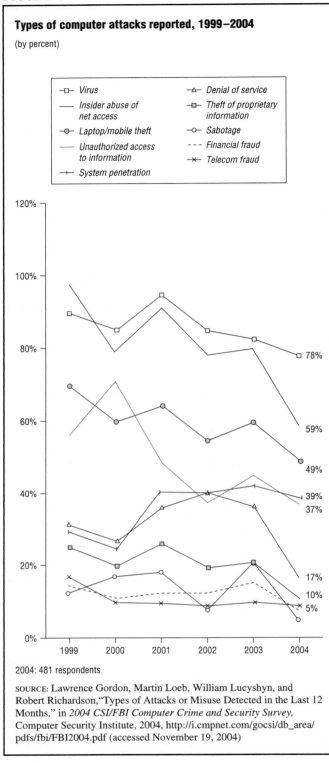

2004: 481 respondents

SOURCE: Lawrence Gordon, Martin Loeb, William Lucyshyn, and Robert Richardson, "Types of Attacks or Misuse Detected in the Last 12 Months," in *2004 CSI/FBI Computer Crime and Security Survey,* Computer Security Institute, 2004, http://i.cmpnet.com/gocsi/db_area/pdfs/fbi/FBI2004.pdf (accessed November 19, 2004)

TABLE 4.9

Computer crime incidents, outside and inside perpetrators, 1999–2004

HOW MANY INCIDENTS BY PERCENTAGE?

	1–5	6–10	>10	Don't know
2004	47%	20%	12%	22%
2003	38%	20%	16%	26%
2002	42%	20%	15%	23%
2001	33%	24%	11%	31%
2000	33%	23%	13%	31%
1999	34%	22%	14%	29%

HOW MANY INCIDENTS FROM THE OUTSIDE?

	1–5	6–10	>10	Don't know
2004	52%	9%	9%	30%
2003	46%	10%	13%	31%
2002	49%	14%	9%	27%
2001	41%	14%	7%	39%
2000	39%	11%	8%	42%
1999	43%	8%	9%	39%

HOW MANY INCIDENTS FROM THE INSIDE?

	1–5	6–10	>10	Don't know
2004	52%	6%	8%	34%
2003	45%	11%	12%	33%
2002	42%	13%	9%	35%
2001	40%	12%	7%	41%
2000	38%	16%	9%	37%
1999	37%	16%	12%	35%

280 respondents

SOURCE: Lawrence Gordon, Martin Loeb, William Lucyshyn, and Robert Richardson, "Figure 12. How many incidents? From outside? From inside?" in *2004 CSI/FBI Computer Crime and Security Survey,* Computer Security Institute, 2004, http://i.cmpnet.com/gocsi/db_area/pdfs/fbi/FBI2004.pdf (accessed November 19, 2004)

Creative Industries Fight Copyright Violators

One of the biggest threats to music industry profitability has been peer-to-peer networks. In the late 1990s, peer-to-peer networks were created that connected music lovers around the world. Napster was the largest of these with tens of millions of users at its peak. Napster, like all peer-to-peer networks, did not contain any music on its own Web site. Instead, Napster tracked the songs and albums its members had on their individual computers. By logging into the central server of the network owned by Napster, members could first locate what music files were available on the network and then proceed to download the music from another member's computer. From the industry point of view, the problem with peer-to-peer networks was that once an album made it on to the network, millions of people suddenly had access to it for free.

Less than a year after the Web site opened, the RIAA filed a case against Napster in Federal District Court on December 6, 1999. The RIAA represented most major recording labels and claimed the software maker infringed on these labels' copyrights. The court sided with RIAA. Napster appealed the ruling and in the end settled with RIAA and paid them $26 million for copyright infringement. Before the case was settled, Napster creator Shawn

$3.5 billion in 2004. The Recording Industry Association of America (RIAA) reported losses in the music industry of roughly $4.2 billion per year in 2004. The MPAA estimated that during each month of 2003, 2.6 billion songs, movies, and software programs were distributed illegally over the Internet, representing a 25% increase in the theft of intellectual property since 1997.

FIGURE 4.8

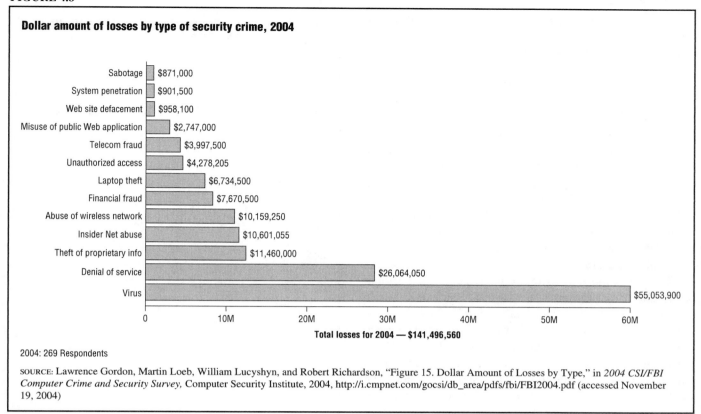

Dollar amount of losses by type of security crime, 2004

Type	Amount
Sabotage	$871,000
System penetration	$901,500
Web site defacement	$958,100
Misuse of public Web application	$2,747,000
Telecom fraud	$3,997,500
Unauthorized access	$4,278,205
Laptop theft	$6,734,500
Financial fraud	$7,670,500
Abuse of wireless network	$10,159,250
Insider Net abuse	$10,601,055
Theft of proprietary info	$11,460,000
Denial of service	$26,064,050
Virus	$55,053,900

Total losses for 2004 — $141,496,560

2004: 269 Respondents

SOURCE: Lawrence Gordon, Martin Loeb, William Lucyshyn, and Robert Richardson, "Figure 15. Dollar Amount of Losses by Type," in *2004 CSI/FBI Computer Crime and Security Survey,* Computer Security Institute, 2004, http://i.cmpnet.com/gocsi/db_area/pdfs/fbi/FBI2004.pdf (accessed November 19, 2004)

Fanning sold Napster to Bertelsmann, a huge German media conglomerate. Bertelsmann dismantled the file-sharing network and constructed a database of songs that could be downloaded for a fee, part of which goes to pay the record company royalties.

The court's ruling against the practice of open music file sharing meant that the RIAA and other organizations could continue to sue peer-to-peer networks that allowed the sharing of copyrighted material for free. While the RIAA was suing Napster, however, a new problem arose. Networks began to pop up that did not have a clearly defined center of operations. The Kazaa and Gnutella networks, for instance, had no central server to let members know who on the network had which songs. Instead, each member of the network installed a program that allowed him or her to see the individual music libraries of others on the network. According to the RIAA, music sales dropped from $40 billion to $26 billion between 2000 and 2002 even after the original Napster was shut down. In late 2003 RIAA began to go after individual file swappers. According to "Sharp Decline in Music File Swapping" (January 5, 2004) a press release from marketing research firm comScore Networks of Reston, Virginia, the RIAA filed 382 lawsuits in 2003 against individual illegal music file swappers, most of whom quickly settled their cases for between $2,500 to $10,000. Since then illegal downloading of music over the Internet has dropped. At the same time, more and more people have turned to downloading music from legitimate Internet music services, such as iTunes and MusicMatch. Nevertheless, on January 27, 2005, the RIAA announced 717 new law suits against individual file-swappers.

Inspired by the music industry's success, the Motion Picture Association of America also took steps to prevent piracy. Usually, the most damaging instances of piracy in the motion picture business occur when bootleggers digitally record a movie in a theater as they watch the film. The bootlegger then transfers the movie via the Internet to a buyer, who then offers the movie up on the Internet or makes copies on a DVD and sells them in a foreign country. According to Barry Fox in "It's Curtains for Video Pirates" (*New Scientist*, August 14, 2004), the Warner cinema chain began handing out night vision goggles to some employees in California to look for these bootleggers during premiers. In 2004 the MPAA began working with high-tech engineering firm Cinea in Reston, Virginia, to develop imaging techniques that would prevent digital camcorders from recordings movies in theaters. One technique involved altering the frame rate in movies so that the film would move out of sync with most digital camcorder's refresh rate, resulting in a copy of the movie that shudders when played. Finally, in November 2004 the MPAA announced that they too would be prosecuting individuals who used peer-to-peer networks to view movies.

Justice Department Begins to Crack Down

In the past most litigation over copyright law has been conducted in civil courts where individual citizens and organizations sue one another. If the defendant is found guilty, such as in the RIAA v. Napster case, then the defendant typically has to pay money to the plaintiff. In a criminal case, the defendant serves jail or probationary time if found guilty. The U.S. Department of Justice is in charge of prosecuting criminal cases against people and organizations that violate national copyright laws. The Justice Department also has specialized units based in cities where high-tech theft is common. These units are known as the Computer Hacking and Intellectual Property (CHIPS) units, and they identify and help prosecute intellectual property suspects. Figure 4.9 reveals that the Justice Department investigated a relatively small number of criminal intellectual property cases between 1994 and 2002. Most of these investigations involved international copyright crime organizations or individuals who made tens of thousands of dollars stealing intellectual property. For instance, in July 2004 a man was sentenced to a year in prison and fined over $120,000 for selling 11,000 illegal video and audio recordings of live music acts such as Kiss and Bob Dylan. Two months later in September 2004 the Justice Department seized over $56 million in counterfeit Microsoft software and charged eleven people with manufacturing counterfeit software and counterfeit packaging.

Responding to the new threats in intellectual property crime, U.S. Attorney General John Ashcroft created the Department of Justice's Task Force on Intellectual Property in March 2004. The task force was assigned to examine the entire range of intellectual property theft from counterfeit automotive parts to the theft of trade secrets to copyright infractions in the entertainment industry. In October 2004 the task force came out with its recommendations on how to address the rise in intellectual property theft. The report recommended that five more specialized CHIPS units be placed in areas rife with intellectual property theft and that more FBI agents be put on intellectual property theft cases. The task force also believed that more aggressive measures should be taken against crime organizations and individuals who infringe on copyrights. More specifically, the report recommended that Congress pass an act making it illegal for people to post copyrighted material they do not own on the Internet.

HIGH-TECH LAW ENFORCEMENT

Criminals have not been the only ones taking advantage of high technology. Since the 1980s new technologies have provided law enforcement with myriad resources to combat crime and protect citizens. Cameras have helped tremendously in identifying crooks that rob ATMs, banks, and convenience stores. Wiretaps and surveillance equipment have allowed law enforcement officials to catch

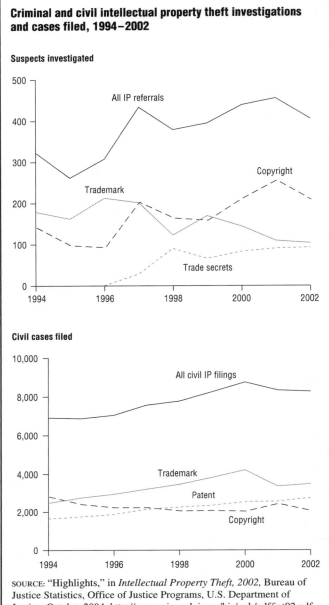

FIGURE 4.9

Criminal and civil intellectual property theft investigations and cases filed, 1994–2002

SOURCE: "Highlights," in *Intellectual Property Theft, 2002,* Bureau of Justice Statistics, Office of Justice Programs, U.S. Department of Justice, October 2004, http://www.ojp.usdoj.gov/bjs/pub/pdf/ipt02.pdf (accessed November 19, 2004)

criminals without putting themselves in harm's way. However, the biggest boon to law enforcement by far has been the increased access law enforcement officers have had to information. In the 1970s, for example, if a law enforcement officer in New York wanted the records of a criminal in California, he or she would have to call a police office in California and have the information read over the phone. Computer databases and communications technology have connected law enforcement offices and provided them easy access to criminal records across the country. Cell phone networks and portable computers have given the police the ability to access criminal records and information on license plates and license holders from within the patrol car. Electronic credit cards networks, bank

TABLE 4.10

AMBER alert progress, 1999–2004

Year	Number of recovered children	Number of statewide AMBER plans implemented
1999	8	1
2000	8	1
2001	2	2
2002	26	28
2003	72	14
2004 (to date)	38	2
Total	**155**	**49**

Note: AMBER is America's Missing: Broadcast Emergency Response.

SOURCE: "Amber Alert Progress 1999 to Date," in *Progress Report on the National AMBER Alert Strategy*, Office of Justice Programs, U.S. Department of Justice, September 2004, http://www.ojp.usdoj.gov/amberalert/docs/AMBERProgress0904.pdf (accessed November 19, 2004)

machines, debit card networks, and rental car records have all provided law enforcement with easily accessible, real-time information on where criminals have been or where they are going.

Communications technologies have also allowed law enforcement agencies to inform communities of terrorism, kidnapping, or other criminal activity in order to bring the perpetrators to justice. America's Missing: Broadcast Emergency Response (AMBER) plan is named after nine-year-old Amber Hagerman, who was kidnapped and brutally murdered in Arlington, Texas, in 1996. After her murder, Texas instituted the first statewide Amber Plan in 1999. Since then the program was introduced by the Justice Department into forty-eight other states. When an Amber Alert is issued, the regional Emergency Alert System (EAS) is utilized to tell the public about the missing child. Programs on television and radio stations are interrupted and followed by pertinent information on the abduction. All law enforcement officers are put on alert, and digital emergency signs above the highways tell anyone on the freeway where to receive more information on the abduction. As of August 31, 2004, more than 150 children had been recovered as a result of the plan. (See Table 4.10.) In one instance in Calhoun, Georgia, a motorist heard the alert on the radio, recognized the vehicle described in the alert and used a cell phone to call the police, who then stopped the car. In another instance in Lancaster, California, an animal control agent heard the alert and identified the abductor's car.

The speed at which information in the modern age can be retrieved has also aided the war on terrorism. Identifying the terrorists responsible for the horrifying events of 9/11 would have been an arduous if not impossible task were it not for electronic records of the terrorists' credit card and rental car use. The FBI was able to post a full list of the suspected terrorists within three days of the attacks, giving the White House the information it needed to plan retaliatory measures. Since 9/11 many new technologies have been designed to catch terrorists before they strike. By far the most controversial and perhaps powerful of the new technologies being developed in 2004 was data mining. Since 2001 the Department of Homeland security has spent a great deal of time and money trying to create a database and database searching techniques to allow authorities to view records of millions of citizens at once and determine if they have a link to terrorism. According to John Borland in "Homeland Security: A Global Assault on Anonymity?" (CNET News.com, October 20, 2004), the agency's latest attempt at such a system is called the Multistate Anti-Terrorism Information Exchange (MATRIX). The system contains the data from five state law enforcement centers as well as nationwide financial and commercial data of millions of Americans. If the Department of Homeland Security manages to get the database to work, it should be able to match criminal records with financial records to assess if a person is a terrorist threat. The database holds much more information than a typical criminal database, and could be used, for instance, to do a background check on someone applying for a license to drive hazardous materials across the country. Critics complain that the database constitutes an invasion of privacy and that it is apt to bring many innocent citizens under suspicion.

CHAPTER 5

ELECTRONICS, THE INTERNET, AND ENTERTAINMENT MEDIA

For many Americans, new technologies simply mean new toys. Nearly every advancement in consumer technology since the 1980s has in some way been tied to entertainment. Table 5.1 shows the amount of money Americans spent between 1998 and 2001 for media content, which included pay-TV subscriptions, video games, home video, and music. On average, most American adults spent $683.33 on all media in 2001, which was $113 more than they spent in 1998. This price tag does not seem unreasonable considering how much time Americans devoted to listening to music or immersing themselves in the virtual worlds of television and video games. Table 5.1 reveals that in 2001 the average American adult watched 1,661 hours of television. During 2001 Americans age twelve and over listened to an average 983 hours of radio programming and 238 hours of recorded music, according to the U.S. Census Bureau in *Statistical Abstract of the United States: 2003*; those twelve and over also spent an average seventy-eight hours playing video games.

While broadcast network television was still the media outlet of choice in 2001, Americans have rapidly been turning to new forms of entertainment made available by the Internet and other technologies. According to researcher Mary Madden in *America's Online Pursuits* (Washington, DC: Pew Internet & American Life Project, December 22, 2003), thirty-six million American adults downloaded music online as of October 2002. Representing 32% of American adults connected to the Internet, this number indicated an increase of 71% over the twenty-one million online users who had downloaded music in July 2000. With respect to online gaming, forty-two million people (37% of Internet users) played some type of online game as of July 2002, be it poker, EverQuest, or Warcraft, as opposed to only twenty-nine million people in March 2000. More people also seemed to be getting their gossip, sports, and news online as well. Nearly 44% of Internet users, for instance, checked sports scores or information online in 2002, versus only 35% two years before.

GAMING

Once considered the pastime of children and socially challenged adults, video and computer games now represent a major form of entertainment in America. Video games are played using a computer that is designed specifically to play a game or games. Consoles are video game machines designed to be hooked up to a television for display purposes and played at home. Arcade cabinet games are stand-alone machines dedicated to playing a particular video game or games. Computer games, by contrast, are just one type of program that can be run on standard personal computers. The difference between the two types of games is in how they are accessed, not necessarily in their contents. Many games can be played using either a video game system or a computer. Thus the terms video game and computer game are sometimes used interchangeably. As Table 5.1 shows, the amount of time American adults played video (and computer) games nearly doubled from forty-three hours in 1998 to seventy-eight hours in 2001. The table also reveals that the average adult in 2001 spent nearly $30 on these games—an increase of roughly $9 over the amount spent in 1998. The marketing research firm NPD Group reported that the video and computer gaming industry sold $11.7 billion in merchandise in 2002 and $11.2 billion in 2003. Of this, computer games accounted for $1.2 billion in 2003 and $1.4 billion in 2004.

Video games were becoming one of the more lucrative entertainment markets in America in 2004. According to Jose Antonio Vargas in "Halo 2 Ready to Run Rings around Video Game Industry" (*Washington Post*, November 9, 2004), the biggest retail launch in the history of the entertainment industry did not center around a movie, album release, or a television series. It took place November 9, 2004, and belonged to the video game Halo 2, developed by Bungie Studios for the Microsoft Xbox console. The game was expected to bring in more than $80 million on the day

TABLE 5.1

Media usage and consumer spending, 1998–2002

[Estimates of time spent were derived using rating data for television, cable and satellite television, and radio; survey research and consumer purchase data (units, admissions, access) for books, home video, Internet, interactive TV, magazines, movies in theaters, newspapers, recorded music, and video games. Adults 18 and older were the basis for estimates for television, cable & satellite television, daily newspapers, consumer books, consumer magazines, home video, and interactive TV. Persons 12 and older were the basis for estimates for radio, recorded music, movies in theaters, video games, and consumer Internet]

Item	1998	1999	2000	2001	2002, proj.	2003, proj.	2004, proj.	2005, proj.	2006, proj.
Hours per person per year									
Total	**3,347**	**3,469**	**3,519**	**3,570**	**3,623**	**3,661**	**3,715**	**3,750**	**3,785**
Television	1,551	1,588	1,640	1,661	1,661	1,656	1,669	1,672	1,679
Broadcast TV	884	867	865	815	810	798	796	790	787
Network stations[1]	710	706	805	753	749	736	735	729	726
Independent stations[1]	174	162	61	62	61	61	61	61	61
Cable & satellite TV	667	720	774	846	851	858	873	881	892
Basic cable and satellite TV[1]	565	617	638	692	698	706	720	729	726
Premium cable and satellite TV[1]	101	103	137	154	153	152	153	152	166
Radio	936	967	964	983	1,001	1,014	1,032	1,049	1,062
Box office	13	13	12	13	13	13	14	14	14
Home video[2]	36	39	46	56	77	96	109	120	126
Interactive TV[3]	—	2	2	2	2	3	3	5	6
Recorded music	283	290	264	238	228	219	211	203	195
Video games	43	61	75	78	84	90	95	101	106
Consumer Internet	54	82	106	134	157	174	189	199	213
Daily newspapers	185	183	179	177	175	173	172	170	169
Consumer books	120	121	111	109	107	106	105	104	103
Consumer magazines	125	124	121	119	117	116	115	113	112
Consumer spending per person per year (dol.)									
Total	**570.29**	**622.32**	**645.10**	**683.33**	**727.90**	**774.52**	**815.59**	**852.93**	**885.31**
Television	167.38	181.71	194.63	210.58	225.34	241.30	255.18	269.18	282.17
Broadcast TV	—	—	—	—	—	—	—	—	—
Cable and satellite TV	167.38	181.71	194.63	210.58	225.34	241.30	255.18	269.18	282.17
Basic cable & satellite networks	125.77	135.61	146.73	158.94	168.75	178.64	187.65	195.62	202.64
Premium cable & satellite services	41.61	46.10	47.90	51.64	56.58	62.66	67.54	73.56	79.53
Radio	—	—	—	—	—	—	—	—	—
Box office	31.23	33.11	33.40	36.57	39.79	41.86	44.33	45.82	48.88
Home video[2]	92.58	97.33	102.46	109.60	119.23	127.80	135.84	141.35	141.84
Interactive TV[3]	—	2.22	2.86	5.02	6.63	8.09	9.50	11.28	12.85
Recorded music	61.67	65.13	62.80	60.57	58.81	57.27	55.82	54.30	52.70
Video games	18.49	24.45	25.93	27.96	30.46	33.60	35.87	38.38	40.92
Consumer Internet	27.63	41.77	50.63	62.08	75.10	88.96	100.99	111.76	122.32
Newspapers	53.37	53.83	53.39	54.12	54.70	55.68	56.24	56.57	57.36
Consumer books	84.16	89.04	87.34	86.13	87.02	88.95	90.68	92.37	93.75
Consumer magazines	46.45	46.15	44.87	43.57	44.07	44.60	45.10	46.26	47.42

— Represents zero.

[1] UPN, WB, and PAX affiliates included in independent stations and pay-per-view included basic cable from 1998 to 1999. UPN, WB, and PAX affiliates moved to network-affiliated stations and pay-per-view moved to premium services in 2000.

[2] Playback of prerecorded tapes only.

[3] Video-on-demand (VOD) only. Personal video recorders (PVRs) included in total TV.

SOURCE: "No. 1125. Media Usage and Consumer Spending: 1998 to 2006," in *Statistical Abstract of the United States: 2003,* U.S. Census Bureau, Economics and Statistics Administration, U.S. Department of Commerce, 2003, http://www.census.gov/prod/2004pubs/03statab/inforcomm.pdf (accessed November 22, 2004)

of its release, far exceeding the leading one-day box office sales record of $44.8 million set by the movie *Shrek 2* on May 22, 2004. Instead, the game sold high above expectations, moving 2.4 million copies and grossing $125 million, according to Chris Morris in "Halo 2 Sales Top Grand Theft Auto" (CNN/Money.com, November 11, 2004).

The Rise of Video and Computer Games

Computer and video games are almost as old as computers. Many credit A. S. Douglas with creating the first graphics-based computer game at Cambridge University in England in 1952 as part of his doctoral research on human-computer interaction. The game was played on an enormous Electronic Delay Storage Automatic Calculator (EDSAC) computer, which was one of the first computers in existence and was made primarily from rows and rows of vacuum tubes. The EDSAC display screen was a 35 x 16 array of monochromatic dots. The name of Douglas's game was Noughts and Crosses, a human vs. machine version of tic-tac-toe in which the human player chose the first square. Ten years later, computer games were developed on mainframe computers and eventually on the ARPANET.

One of the more popular games that spread to computer mainframes across the United States during the

1960s was Spacewar. Spacewar was created in 1961 by Steve Russell and other researchers at the Massachusetts Institute of Technology (MIT) to test the capabilities of the $120,000 Digital Equipment Corporation PDP-1 computer. The game consisted of two low-resolution ships, one shaped like a needle and the other like a wedge, flying around a dot that represented a sun in the middle of the screen. The object was to destroy the other player's ship while maneuvering through the sun's gravitational pull.

In 1971 Nutting Associates released Computer Space, the first video game for the general public. Computer Space was a direct imitator of Spacewar set in a futuristic arcade-style cabinet. Most people considered the game too complicated at the time, so Nutting only made fifteen hundred copies and then stopped production. The next year, however, Atari released Pong. In this monochromatic game, a small cube was bounced back and forth between two slightly larger rods controlled by the player(s). The video game was a smash hit, and Atari sold over eight thousand arcade cabinets. A month earlier, Magnavox released the Odyssey, which was the first home console video game system that ran on a television set. The Odyssey, which sold for $100, had several different games installed on it, all of which involved hitting a pixilated square(s) on the screen with rectangles. The home version of Pong was released in 1975 and sold more than 150,000 units during the holiday season alone, according to the Atari Historical Society (www.atarimuseum.com).

The Golden Age of Video Games

Within a year after these initial offerings, video games quickly gained a foothold in the United States. A steady stream of fairly unremarkable cabinet games was released throughout the 1970s. For most of the decade, video games were novelties that sat next to pinball machines in bowling alleys, bars, and roller-skating rinks. With the arrival of Asteroids and Space Invaders in 1978, arcade video games came into their own. Space Invaders, a game in which the player shot row after row of advancing aliens, caused a nationwide coin shortage in Japan so severe the Japanese government had to more than double yen production. Namco introduced the first color game in 1979 with the arrival of Galaxian, and then in 1980 the company released Pac-Man. The original name of the game was Puckman, derived from the Japanese *pakupaku*, which means "flapping open and closed" (e.g., the character's mouth). Despite the game's simple concept of guiding a yellow, dot-eating ball around a maze, 100,000 arcade units sold in the United States. The game inspired an entire line of merchandise from lunch boxes to stuffed toys. Between 1980 and 1983 numerous colorful, engaging video games were released, including Defender, Donkey Kong, Centipede, Frogger, and Ms. Pac-Man, which still holds the record for the most arcade games sold at 115,000. Video arcades sprang up in every mall and town

in the United States. On January 18, 1982, the cover of *Time* magazine read "Gonk! Zap! Flash! Video Games Are Blitzing Our World." The cover story, "Games That Play People" by John Skow, revealed that in 1981 nearly $5 billion in quarters were spent playing arcade games. By comparison, the U.S. film industry took in $2.8 million that year.

At the same time, game consoles were gaining popularity in living rooms across America. In 1977 Atari launched the Atari VCS (later named the Atari 2600) for $200. By Christmas 1979, sales were brisk as people realized that the system could support more than just Pong. With the release of Space Invaders on the system the following year, units flew off the shelves at $150 a piece. According to a design case history on Atari by Tekla E. Perry and Paul Wallich published in the March 1983 issue of *IEEE Spectrum*, Atari sold over twelve million consoles between 1977 and 1983. More than two hundred games were made for the system. Other video systems such as Intellivision and Colecovision gained huge followings as well. The *Time* article stated that 600,000 Intellivision units were sold in 1981. Overall, in 1981 sales for home video games exceeded $1 billion dollars.

The Video Game Industry Stumbles

By 1984 the Commodore 64 home computer had debuted at $1,000, and the Apple IIc was introduced at the comparatively affordable price of $1,300. Such computers not only offered better graphics than the contemporary video game consoles, but they were also useful for such practical applications as spreadsheets and word processors. Consequently, people simply lost interest in video games and began buying home computers. In 1983, faced with a collapsing video game market, losses of the hundreds of millions of dollars, and far too much inventory, Atari loaded fourteen tractor-trailer trucks with thousands of unsold cartridges and pieces of hardware. They drove the surplus out to a landfill site in Alamogordo, New Mexico, and buried the inventory in a concrete bunker under the desert. The following year Warner Communications, the owner of Atari, sold the game and computer divisions of Atari to Jack Tramiel, the founder of Commodore. Mattel, the maker of Intellivision, also shed its electronics division, and in 1985 Coleco stopped producing its Colecovision products, eventually declaring bankruptcy in 1988. Hundreds of arcades closed as well.

For several years gaming was relegated to the computer. Prior to 1983, computer games were low on graphics and heavy on text, but by 1984 a number of colorful and entertaining games became available for home computers, including Ultima IV, Archon II: Adept, Impossible Mission, and the King's Quest series. However, toy and electronics manufacturers in the United States were wary of investing in video game consoles after the Atari disaster.

Japanese companies were not nearly as pessimistic and continued to pour money into video console development. Nintendo, a company that originally manufactured Japanese playing cards, surprised the entire gaming market in 1986 when it released the Nintendo Entertainment System (NES). The games looked better than most arcade games from the early 1980s and lasted as long as computer games. After two years on the market, the NES found its way into almost as many homes as the Atari 2600. According to Nintendo America, the sales of video games in 1988 once again reached $1 billion. Arcades at the time also enjoyed a brief revival with the advent of complex fighting games such as Mortal Kombat and Street Fighter II. Mortal Kombat, which eventually made it onto the NES, inspired a Congressional investigation into violence in video games and led to the establishment of the Entertainment Software Rating Board (ESRB), an industry self-regulatory organization that monitors the content of video games for depictions of violence, nudity, profanity, and other material that parents might find objectionable for young children.

The Present and Future of Gaming

Since the late 1980s, the electronic gaming market in the United States has continued a steady rise, with the lion's share of the gaming industry's sales coming from console systems and games. After the NES ran its course, the Sega Genesis became the hot video game system. This was followed by the Sony PlayStation, the Nintendo 64, the PlayStation 2, and finally the Microsoft Xbox. In the 1990s the computer game market split in two. Solitaire and countless other card and puzzle games found their way onto Windows desktops. Such games provided a brief escape from schoolwork or a job. At the same time, computers also became the platform for cutting edge strategy and shooting games. Such graphics-intensive games as Quake, Half Life, and Doom 3 often led to increased sales in computer components as gamers bought extra memory and bigger hard drives to boost computer performance in order to handle advanced graphic engines.

In the mid-1990s computer games began to go online. Hardcore fans of battle and quest adventures as well as card game fanatics could find competitors on the Web. As of 2001 the latest console systems also enabled gamers to go online and play against one another. According to Cade Metz in "The Future of Online Gaming" (*PC Magazine* March 27, 2003), online gaming traffic made up nearly 9% of the overall traffic along the Internet backbone in the United States in 2002. The fastest growing segment of online gaming appeared to be in the console game market. Xbox Live, an online service for the Xbox, gained 350,000 subscriptions at the beginning of 2003. By the end of 2004 the number of subscribers had more than quadrupled to 1.5 million. Metz reported that nearly 9% of all console gamers could be online by 2007, bringing in

$650 million annually for the big console makers. As of 2004, console makers had sold nearly one hundred million units worldwide, with Sony PlayStation 2 making up three-quarters of those units.

Gaming Addiction

Over the years games have grown exceedingly more complex and engaging. The Sims (2000) and the Sims 2 (2004) provided gamers with a real-life fantasy world where they could simulate alternate lives. Massive multiplayer online games, such as EverQuest, allowed players to freely roam and embark on quests in a virtual fantasy planet inhabited by other gamers.

As the complexity of games has grown, so too has the temptation for many to play video games in excess to escape their problems. Though still largely an unstudied phenomenon, gaming addiction appears to be more and more commonplace. Chris Richards reported in "Addicted Gamers Losing Their Way" (*Washington Post*, October 5, 2004) that the Web site of Online Gamers Anonymous (www.olganon.org) was receiving nearly three hundred visits per week at that time. The organization, one of the more prominent of its kind, was founded by Elizabeth Woolley after her son, a gaming addict, committed suicide in 2002. Many psychologists believe that games provide a means of escape for people with stressful lives or mental problems in much the same way as drugs and alcohol. Richards listed a number of symptoms that accompany gaming addition. These included failed attempts to stem gaming behavior, having a sense of well-being while playing games, craving more game time as well as feeling irritable when not playing, neglecting family and friends, and denying the adverse affects of too much gaming.

In "Evidence for Striatal Dopamine Release during a Video Game" (*Nature*, May 21, 1998), researchers at the Imperial College School in England reported that video games can cause secretions of the neurotransmitter dopamine in the brain. Neurotransmitters are chemicals that relay signals between brain cells. Dopamine is one of dozens of these chemicals and has been known to induce pleasure in the brain to reinforce behavior. Previous studies have shown that dopamine levels in hungry rats increased when they received food. In this case, the chemical reinforced the pleasure the hungry rat felt upon eating, so the next time the rat was hungry, it would be doubly motivated to eat and keep itself alive. Dopamine levels have also been associated with pleasure-producing drugs. In the *Nature* report, M. J. Koepp, R. N. Gunn, and others reported injecting human volunteers with a chemical that reacted to the brain's secretion of dopamine. The scientists then used an X-ray-like technique known as PET (positron emission tomography) to monitor the levels of dopamine in the brain as the volunteers steered a computer game tank through enemy territory picking up flags. The participants were awarded $10 for each level completed. The PET showed that dopamine levels shot up in the volunteers each time they finished blasting through a level. While the scientists said they were simply testing this technique of tracking dopamine and not gaming addiction, the possibility still existed that goal-oriented games elicit a pleasurable chemical response in the brain. Memory of such pleasure could cause addicted gamers to come back for more.

Online Gambling

There is no doubt inside or outside the scientific community that gambling can be addictive. One troubling development on the Internet in 2004 was the continued rise in online gambling. According to a Congressional statement by Deputy Assistant Attorney General John G. Malcolm dated April 29, 2003, seven hundred Internet gambling sites existed in 1999. By 2003, the U.S. Justice Department estimated that eighteen hundred gambling sites were in place, bringing in roughly $4.2 billion. Many of these sites, such as Party Poker, allowed gamblers to wire money from their checking accounts into a gambling account run by the casino. When the player wished to gamble, he or she simply went online and began a session. Since most of these big online gambling operations were based in foreign nations in the Caribbean or South America, the U.S. government could not regulate them. Malcolm pointed to instances where the online houses manipulated the software so that the odds of games such as blackjack were skewed heavily in the house's favor. Other fly-by-night gambling operations had simply run off with people's money. Even if the all these gambling houses were honest, Malcolm claimed they still pose a threat to society. Those with serious gambling addiction can log in and gamble unfettered for hours at a time from work or home. There is simply no one to monitor them as they lose hundreds or thousands of dollars.

Malcolm also addressed the issue of money laundering through online casinos. Criminals who made their money from such illegal activities as drugs have used online casino accounts to stash their profits. Once the money was in the casino, the crooks used the games themselves to transfer money to their associates. Some criminals have been known to set up private tables at online casino sites and then intentionally lose their money to business associates at the table. In other instances, the casino was part of the crime organization. All the criminal had to do in these cases was to lose money to the casino.

RECORDED MUSIC

The conversion from analog to digital music in the 1980s changed the way Americans listened to music. Humans talk and listen in analog. When people speak, they create vibrations in their throats that then travel through the air around them like ripples in a pond. A membrane in the ear, known as an eardrum, picks up these vibrations,

allowing people to hear. Patterns in these vibrations enable people to differentiate sounds from one another. Before compact discs (CDs) and MP3 files, all music was recorded in analog form. On a record player, the vibrations that create music are impressed in grooves on a vinyl disc. A needle passing over this impression vibrates in the same way, turning those vibrations into electrical waveforms that travel along a wire to an amplifier and into a speaker. With tape players, the analog waveforms are recorded in electronic form nearly verbatim on a magnetic tape.

The biggest problem with analog recordings is that each time the music is recorded or copied, the waveform degrades in quality much like a photocopy of an image. Digitizing the music resolves this problem of fidelity. To record and play music digitally, an analog-to-digital converter (ADC) and a digital-to-analog converter (DAC) are needed. In the recording process, the analog music is fed through the ADC, which samples the analog waveforms and then breaks them down into a series of binary numbers represented by zeros and ones. The numbers are then stored on a disc or a memory chip like any other type of digital information. To play the music back, these numbers are fed through a DAC. The DAC reads the numbers and reproduces the original analog waveform that then travels to headphones or speakers. Since the numbers always reproduce a high quality version of the original recording, no quality (fidelity) is lost, regardless of how many times the song is transferred or recorded.

The Compact Disc and Compact Disc Player

Digital music was first introduced into mainstream America in 1983 in the form of compact disc players and compact discs (CDs). Klass Compaan, a Dutch physicist, originally came up with the idea for the compact disc in 1969 and developed a glass prototype a year later at Philips Corporation. Over the next nine years both Philips and Sony worked on various prototypes of a CD player. In 1979 the two companies came together to create a final version and set the standards for the compact disc. The first disc players were sold in Japan and Europe in 1982 and then in the United States in 1983.

With a standard CD, music is recorded digitally on the surface of a polycarbonate plastic disc in a long spiral track 0.00002 inches wide that winds from the center of the disk to the outer edges. A space 0.00006 inches wide separates each ring of the spiral track from the one next to it. Tiny divots, or pits, a minimum of 0.00003 inches long, are engraved into the surface of the track. The polycarbonate disc is then covered by a layer of aluminum and a layer of clear acrylic. (See Figure 5.1.) As the disc spins in the disc drive, a laser follows this tiny track counterclockwise, and a light sensor, sitting next to the laser, tracks the changes in the laser light as it reflects off the CD. When the laser strikes a non-divoted section of track, the laser light bounces off of the aluminum and back to the light sensor uninterrupted. Each time the laser

TABLE 5.2

Manufacturers' shipments and value of recording media, 1982–2002

[577.4 represents 577,400,000. Based on reports of RIAA member companies who distributed about 84 percent of the prerecorded music in 2002. These data are supplemented by other sources. Minus sign (−) indicates returns greater than shipments]

Medium	1982	1985	1990	1995	1998	1999	2000	2001	2002
Unit shipments[1] (mil.)									
Total[2]	**577.4**	**653.0**	**865.7**	**1,112.7**	**1,123.9**	**1,160.6**	**1,079.2**	**968.5**	**859.7**
CDs	(X)	22.6	286.5	722.9	847.0	938.9	942.5	881.9	803.3
CD singles	(X)	(X)	1.1	21.5	56.0	55.9	34.2	17.3	4.5
Cassettes	182.3	339.1	442.2	272.6	158.5	123.6	76.0	45.0	31.1
Cassette singles	(X)	(X)	87.4	70.7	26.4	14.2	1.3	−1.5	−0.5
Albums—LPs and EPs	243.9	167.0	11.7	2.2	3.4	2.9	2.2	2.3	1.7
Vinyl singles	137.2	120.7	27.6	10.2	5.4	5.3	4.8	5.5	4.4
Music video	(X)	(X)	9.2	12.6	27.2	19.8	18.2	17.7	14.7
DVD video	(X)	(X)	(X)	(X)	0.5	2.5	3.3	7.9	10.7
DVD audio	(X)	(X)	(X)	(X)	(X)	(X)	(X)	0.3	0.4
Value (mil. dol.)									
Total[2]	**3,641.6**	**4,378.8**	**7,541.1**	**12,320.3**	**13,711.2**	**14,584.7**	**14,323.7**	**13,740.9**	**12,614.2**
CD's	(X)	389.5	3,451.6	9,377.4	11,416.0	12,816.3	13,214.5	12,909.4	12,044.1
CD singles	(X)	(X)	6.0	110.9	213.2	222.4	142.7	79.4	19.6
Cassettes	1,384.5	2,411.5	3,472.4	2,303.6	1,419.9	1,061.6	626.0	363.4	209.8
Cassette singles	(X)	(X)	257.9	236.3	94.4	48.0	4.6	−5.3	−1.6
Albums—LPs and EPs	1,925.1	1,280.5	86.5	25.1	34.0	31.8	27.7	27.4	20.5
Vinyl singles	283.0	281.0	94.4	46.7	25.7	27.9	26.3	31.4	24.9
Music video	(X)	(X)	172.3	220.3	508.0	376.7	281.9	329.2	288.4
DVD video	(X)	(X)	(X)	(X)	12.2	66.3	80.3	190.7	236.3
DVD audio	(X)	(X)	(X)	(X)	(X)	(X)	(X)	6.0	8.5

X Not applicable.
[1]Net units, after returns.
[2]Includes discontinued media.

SOURCE: "No. 1141. Recording Media—Manufacturers' Shipments and Value: 1982 to 2002," in *Statistical Abstract of the United States: 2003,* U.S. Census Bureau, Economics and Statistics Administration, U.S. Department of Commerce, 2003, http://www.census.gov/prod/2004pubs/03statab/inforcomm.pdf (accessed November 22, 2004)

hits one of the divots along the CD track, however, the light is scattered. These flashes of light represent the binary code that makes up the music. Electronics in the disc player read this code. The ones and zeros are then fed into a digital signal processor (DSP), which acts as a digital-to-analog converter, and the analog waveform for the music emerges to the delight of the listener.

When CD players were first released in the United States by both Sony and Philips, they ran close to $1,000 apiece. The CDs themselves, which occupied a very small section of the music store at the time, went for close to $20 a piece. Despite the high costs, 22.6 million CDs sold in 1985, according to U.S. Census figures. (See Table 5.2.) About 287 million compact discs were sold in 1990, and by 2002 this number reached 803 million. The Digital Electronics Association estimated that in 2000 fifty-four million CD players were produced. Over the years, CD players have become much more compact and have been equipped with many more features, often designed to increase sound quality. By 2005 personal CD players and CD boom boxes were widely available for less than $50.

The Rise of MP3

In 1985 the first compact disc read-only memory players (CD-ROMs) were released for computers, again by Sony

FIGURE 5.1

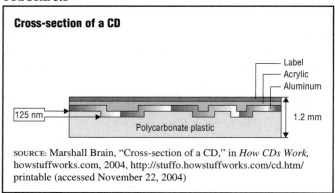

Cross-section of a CD

SOURCE: Marshall Brain, "Cross-section of a CD," in *How CDs Work,* howstuffworks.com, 2004, http://stuffo.howstuffworks.com/cd.htm/printable (accessed November 22, 2004)

and Philips. CD-ROM players could read computer data from CD-ROMs as well as music from CDs. While people with early CD-ROMs were able to listen to CD music, downloading it onto a computer was difficult. A three-minute song on a CD consisted roughly of thirty-two megabytes. (Each byte consists of a string of eight ones and zeros that can be used to represent binary numbers from zero to 255. In binary, which is base two number system, one is 00000001, two is 00000010, nineteen is 00010011, and 255 is 11111111.) During the late 1980s and early 1990s, most computer hard drives were only big enough to hold a few songs straight from an audio CD. In 1987 researchers at the Fraunhofer Institut Integrierte Schaltungen in Germany began to look into ways to compress digital video and sound data into smaller sizes for broadcasting purposes. Out of this work, the MP2 (MPEG-1 Audio Layer II) and then the MP3 (MPEG-1 Audio Layer III) audio file format emerged.

Using the MP3 format, digital songs can be compressed from thirty-two megabytes per song to roughly three megabytes per song. Compact disc recordings pick up any and every sound in a studio or concert. The MP3 compression system works by cutting out sounds in CD recordings that people do not pay attention to or do not hear. This may include sounds drowned out by louder instruments. In classical music, the MP3 might cut out a nearly indiscernible note from a flautist or the sound of a faint cough in the audience. MP3 encoders, such as XingMP3 from Real Networks or Apple Lossless from Apple Computer, can compress a typical CD track into an MP3 file only one-tenth the size of the original recording. When played back, MP3 files sound nearly as good as CD tracks and much better than tapes.

The first of the MP3 players on the market was the Rio PMP300 by Diamond Multimedia, released in February 1999. MP3 players consist of a hard drive, as large as sixty gigabytes in late 2004, and all the electronic circuitry necessary to transform an MP3 files into analog music. Using a USB cable, the device can be hooked up directly to a home computer. Once connected, the user can download thousands upon thousands of songs into the MP3 hard drive. When the user selects a song, a microprocessor in the MP3 player pulls the song from the hard drive. A built-in signal processor decompresses the MP3 file to CD format, converts the digital signal to an analog signal, and then sends the analog waveform to the headphones. Though MP3 files do not sound quite as good as a CD tracks, most people can place their entire music collection on an MP3 player.

According to the telecommunications research firm Juniper Research (www.juniperresearch.com), more than 1.7 million MP3 players were sold in 2002 and 3.5 million were sold in 2003. Sales were expected to increase by 50% a year for several years to follow.

MP3 and Peer-to-Peer File Sharing

The widespread use of MP3 files and the increased size of hard drives in the late 1990s caused a sea change in the music industry almost as big as the advent of digital music. People could now store entire music libraries on their computers and swap music for free over peer-to-peer file-sharing networks. According to Michael Gowan in "Requiem for Napster" (*PC World*, May 17, 2001), the Napster file-sharing service had approximately eighty million subscribers at its peak.

The availability of free music cut deeply into the recording industry's sales. Table 5.3 shows consumer expenditures for sound recordings from 1990 to 2002. Between 1999 and 2000 total expenditures fell from $14.6 billion to $14.3 billion, which represents a 2% decrease. This was followed by a 4% drop in 2001 and an 8% drop in 2002. Seeing diminishing profits, the Recording Industry Association of America (RIAA) sued Napster and the users of other peer-to-peer networks that shared music files. (See Chapter 4.) Some high-profile bands at the time, such as Metallica and Creed, joined the RIAA in its attempt to close down Napster. Other musicians, however, did not seem fazed by Internet file sharing. Radiohead released their album *Kid A* on the Internet three weeks before it was released in stores. The buzz generated by the Internet pre-release catapulted the album to number one in the United States after it hit record stores. Before *Kid A*, Radiohead had never had a number one album in the United States.

According to Madden in *Artists, Musicians, and the Internet* (Washington, DC: Pew Internet & American Life Project, December 5, 2004), musicians have mixed feelings about the impact of the Internet on the music business. They report favorable impact in such areas as creativity, ability to reach a wider audience, ability to connect with family, friends, and other musicians while traveling to performances, and ease of scheduling performances and travel arrangements. However, musicians are somewhat divided over the issue of online file sharing, according to the report. While 35% agreed that file-sharing services are "not bad" for musicians because the artist derives some promotional benefit from the download, 23% agreed that downloads "are bad" in that they allow people to obtain copyrighted material without paying for it. In the survey, 35% agreed to both statements, showing the ambivalence of artists themselves over the issue.

Regardless of what musicians thought, the lawsuits brought on by the RIAA succeeded in putting an end to much of the free file swapping on the Internet. The free Napster Web site shut down in May 2000 and reopened a year later as a pay music service where users could buy songs. After the RIAA began going after private citizens, traffic on many of the remaining peer-to-peer sites diminished greatly. As Figure 5.2 reveals, the number of people using the noncentralized Kazaa peer-to-peer network dropped precipitously after RIAA became litigious with file swappers in 2003. A memo released by Pew/Internet and comScore Media Metrix in April 2004 revealed that 38% of American adults who downloaded music from the Internet had cut back somewhat after the RIAA lawsuits began. The memo also revealed that 14% of online American adults who had ever downloaded music had stopped the practice as of spring 2004. At the same time, more people turned to pay music services, such as Musicmatch and iTunes. Over eleven million adult Americans visited the six major online music services in 2004. (See Table

TABLE 5.3

Profile of consumer expenditures for sound recordings, 1990–2002

[In percent, except total value (7,541.1 represents $7,541,100,000). Based on monthly telephone surveys of the population 10 years old and over]

Item	1990	1995	1997	1998	1999	2000	2001	2002
Total value (mil. dol.)	7,541.1	12,320.3	12,236.8	13,711.2	14,584.5	14,323.0	13,740.9	12,614.2
Percent distribution[1]								
Age:								
10 to 14 years	7.6	8.0	8.9	9.1	8.5	8.9	8.5	8.9
15 to 19 years	18.3	17.1	16.8	15.8	12.6	12.9	13.0	13.3
20 to 24 years	16.5	15.3	13.8	12.2	12.6	12.5	12.2	11.5
25 to 29 years	14.6	12.3	11.7	11.4	10.5	10.6	10.9	9.4
30 to 34 years	13.2	12.1	11.0	11.4	10.1	9.8	10.3	10.8
35 to 39 years	10.2	10.8	11.6	12.6	10.4	10.6	10.2	9.8
40 to 44 years	7.8	7.5	8.8	8.3	9.3	9.6	10.3	9.9
45 years and over	11.1	16.1	16.5	18.1	24.7	23.8	23.7	25.5
Sex:								
Male	54.4	53.0	48.6	48.7	50.3	50.6	48.8	49.4
Female	45.6	47.0	51.4	51.3	49.7	49.4	51.2	50.6
Sales outlet:								
Record store	69.8	52.0	51.8	50.8	44.5	42.4	42.5	36.8
Other store	18.5	28.2	31.9	34.4	38.3	40.8	42.4	50.7
Music club	8.9	14.3	11.6	9.0	7.9	7.6	6.1	4.0
Ad or 800 number	2.5	4.0	2.7	2.9	2.5	2.4	3.0	2.0
Internet[2]	(NA)	(NA)	0.3	1.1	2.4	3.2	2.9	3.4
Music type:[3]								
Rock	36.1	33.5	32.5	25.7	25.2	24.8	24.4	24.7
Pop	13.7	10.1	9.4	10.0	10.3	11.0	12.1	9.0
Rap/Hip Hop	8.5	6.7	10.1	9.7	10.8	12.9	11.4	13.8
R&B/Urban	11.6	11.3	11.2	12.8	10.5	9.7	10.6	11.2
Country	9.6	16.7	14.4	14.1	10.8	10.7	10.5	10.7
Religious	2.5	3.1	4.5	6.3	5.1	4.8	6.7	6.7
Jazz	4.8	3.0	2.8	1.9	3.0	2.9	3.4	3.2
Classical	3.1	2.9	2.8	3.3	3.5	2.7	3.2	3.1
Soundtracks	0.8	0.9	1.2	1.7	0.8	0.7	1.4	1.1
New age	1.1	0.7	0.8	0.6	0.5	0.5	1.0	0.5
Oldies	0.8	1.0	0.8	0.7	0.7	0.9	0.8	0.9
Children's	0.5	0.5	0.9	0.4	0.4	0.6	0.5	0.4
Other	5.6	7.0	5.7	7.9	9.1	8.3	7.9	8.1
Media type: CDs	31.1	65.0	70.2	74.8	83.2	89.3	89.2	90.5
Cassettes	54.7	25.1	18.2	14.8	8.0	4.9	3.4	2.4
Singles (all types)	8.7	7.5	9.3	6.8	5.4	2.5	2.4	1.9
Music video[4]	(NA)	0.9	0.6	1.0	0.9	0.8	1.1	0.7
DVD audio	(NA)	(NA)	(NA)	(NA)	(NA)	(NA)	1.1	1.3
Digital download	(NA)	(NA)	(NA)	(NA)	(NA)	(NA)	0.2	0.5
Vinyl LPs	4.7	0.5	0.7	0.7	0.5	0.5	0.6	0.7

NA Not available.

[1] Percent distributions exclude nonresponses and responses of don't know.
[2] Excludes record club purchases over the Internet.
[3] As classified by respondent.
[4] Beginning 2001 includes video DVDs.

SOURCE: "No. 1142. Profile of Consumer Expenditures for Sound Recordings: 1990 to 2002," in *Statistical Abstract of the United States: 2003*, U.S. Census Bureau, Economics and Statistics Administration, U.S. Department of Commerce, 2003, http://www.census.gov/prod/2004pubs/03statab/inforcomm.pdf (accessed November 22, 2004)

5.4.) Between October 2003 and March 2004, iTunes had added nearly one million unique visitors to its site.

TELEVISION

Since the 1970s steady advances in cable, satellite, and digital technology have changed the way Americans watch television. As Table 5.5 shows, cable television was installed in 6.7% of American households with a TV in 1970 (about four million homes). This percentage rose dramatically through the early 1990s, leveling out at roughly two-thirds (68%) of American households by the late 1990s.

Cable television began in 1948 in Mahanoy City, Pennsylvania. John Walson, the owner of an electronics shop, began selling TVs in 1947. However, few customers in the local area wanted to buy a television due to the bad reception caused by the surrounding mountains. To increase sales potential, Walson erected an antenna on a nearby mountaintop, ran a cable from the antenna to his store, and connected it to his television. He then agreed to attach cables to the houses of those who bought TVs from him. From then until the early 1970s, cable networks were generally only used in rural or mountainous areas. At

FIGURE 5.2

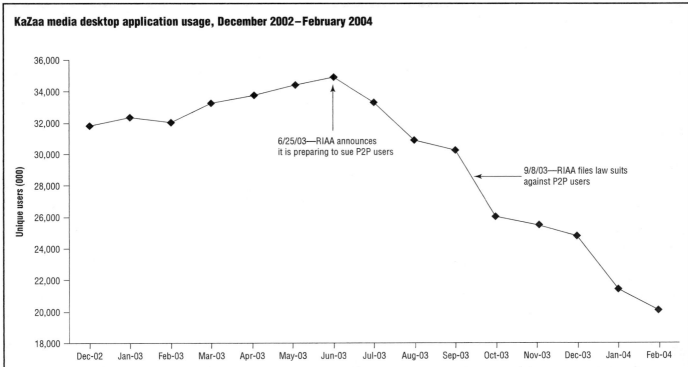

KaZaa media desktop application usage, December 2002–February 2004

SOURCE: Lee Rainie, Mary Madden, Dan Hess, and Graham Mudd, "KaZaa Media Desktop Application Usage," in *Pew Internet Project and comScore Media Metrix Data Memo: The State of Downloading and File-Sharing Online,* Pew Internet and American Life Project, April 2004, http://www.pewinternet.org/pdfs/PIP_Filesharing_April_04.pdf (accessed November 22, 2004). Used by permission of the Pew Internet and American Life Project, which bears no responsibility for the interpretations presented or conclusions reached based on analysis of the data.

TABLE 5.4

Visitors to selected online music services, March 2004

	Unique visitors (000)
Total visitors to selected music services	**11,249**
MUSICMATCH.COM	5,335
Roxio, Inc (Napster)	2,567
ITunes	2,333
Listen.com sites	1,387
Walmart Music Store	535
LIQUID.COM	169

SOURCE: Lee Rainie, Mary Madden, Dan Hess, and Graham Mudd, "Unique Visitors to Selected Online Music Services March 2004," in *Pew Internet Project and comScore Media Metrix Data Memo,* Pew Internet and American Life Project, April 2004, http://www.pewinternet.org/pdfs/PIP_Filesharing_April_04.pdf (accessed November 22, 2004). Used by permission of the Pew Internet and American Life Project, which bears no responsibility for the interpretations presented or conclusions reached based on analysis of the data.

most, early cable television programming included local broadcasts and a broadcast or two from a nearby region.

As early as 1965 the U.S. government and various contractors began putting up a communications satellite network. A satellite network remedied the biggest obstacle faced by broadcasters in the 1960s, which was the curvature of the earth. If the earth were flat, TVs could receive broadcast signals from thousands of miles away.

Due to the curvature of the earth, these broadcast signals escape into space after traveling a hundred miles or so. With a satellite system in place, a transmitter on the East Coast was able to beam a signal to a satellite above Kansas. The satellite then relayed the signal to the West Coast without interruption.

Home Box Office (HBO) became the first pay cable station in 1972 and was the first television broadcaster to take advantage of a satellite communications network. HBO began in Wilkes-Barre, Pennsylvania, and broadcast its movies and shows to a limited number of cable networks in and around the state. In 1975, in order to expand the subscription television market, HBO leased the right to use one of the uplinks on RCA's Satcom I communications satellite. Once HBO was on the satellite network, any cable network provider around the United States could buy a large, three-meter satellite dish and provide HBO for any house on the network. By 1978 HBO had one million customers. Ted Turner, who put his WTBS station in Atlanta on the satellite network in 1976, created the Cable News Network (CNN) in 1980. This was followed by the Music Television Network (MTV) and a slew of other stations in 1981.

The early 1980s also saw the emergence of VCRs. As can be seen in Table 5.5, only 1.1% of households had a VCR in 1980. The percentage of households with VCRs

TABLE 5.5

Utilization of selected media, 1970–2001

[62.0 represents 62,000,000]

Item	Unit	1970	1980	1990	1995	1996	1997	1998	1999	2000	2001
Households with—											
Telephone service[1]	Percent	87.0	93.0	93.3	93.9	93.8	93.9	94.1	94.0	94.6	94.6
Radio[2]	Millions	62.0	78.6	94.4	98.0	98.0	98.0	(NA)	(NA)	(NA)	(NA)
Percent of total households	Percent	98.6	99.0	99.0	99.0	99.0	99.0	99.0	99.0	99.0	99.0
Average number of sets	Number	5.1	5.5	5.6	5.6	5.6	5.6	5.6	5.6	5.6	5.6
Television[3]	Millions	59	76	92	95	96	97	98	99	101	102
Percent of total households	Percent	95.3	97.9	98.2	98.3	98.3	98.4	98.3	98.2	98.2	98.2
Television sets in homes	Millions	81	128	193	217	223	229	235	240	245	248
Average number of sets per home	Number	1.4	1.7	2.1	2.3	2.3	2.4	2.4	2.4	2.4	2.4
Color set households	Millions	21	63	90	94	95	97	98	99	101	102
Cable television[4]	Millions	4	15	52	60	63	64	66	67	69	69
Percent of TV households	Percent	6.7	19.9	56.4	63.4	65.3	66.5	67.2	67.5	68.0	68.0
VCRs[4]	Millions	(NA)	1	63	77	79	82	83	84	86	88
Percent of TV households	Percent	(NA)	1.1	68.6	81.0	82.2	84.2	84.6	84.6	85.1	86.2
Commercial radio stations:[2]											
AM	Number	4,323	4,589	4,987	4,909	4,857	4,762	4,793	4,783	4,685	4,727
FM	Number	2,196	3,282	4,392	5,296	5,419	5,542	5,662	5,766	5,892	6,051
Television stations:[5] Total	Number	862	1,011	1,442	1,532	1,533	1,564	1,589	1,615	1,663	1,686
Commercial	Number	677	734	1,092	1,161	1,174	1,195	1,221	1,243	1,288	1,309
VHF	Number	501	516	547	562	554	555	561	561	567	572
UHF	Number	176	218	545	599	620	640	660	682	721	737
Cable television:											
Systems[5]	Number	2,490	4,225	9,575	11,218	11,119	10,950	10,845	10,700	10,243	9,926
Households served	Millions	4.5	17.7	54.9	63.0	64.6	65.9	67.0	68.5	69.3	73.0
Daily newspaper circulation[6]	Millions	62.1	62.2	62.3	58.2	57.0	56.7	56.2	56.0	55.8	55.6

NA Not available.
[1]For occupied housing units. 1970 and 1980 as of April 1; all other years as of March.
[2]1980–1995 as of December 31, except as noted.
[3]1970, as of September of prior year; all other years as of January of year shown. Excludes Alaska and Hawaii.
[4]As of February. Excludes Alaska and Hawaii.
[5]As of January[1].
[6]As of September 30.

SOURCE: "No. 1126. Utilization of Selected Media: 1970 to 2001," in *Statistical Abstract of the United States: 2003,* U.S. Census Bureau, Economics and Statistics Administration, U.S. Department of Commerce, 2003, http://www.census.gov/prod/2004pubs/03statab/inforcomm.pdf (accessed November 22, 2004)

in 1997 jumped to 84.2%, but then slowed down and leveled off at around 86% of households by 2001.

Closed Captioning and the V-Chip

By the mid-1970s, television had become the predominant medium not just for entertainment but for news and emergency information. Recognizing this, the Federal Communications Commission set aside part of the television broadcast spectrum for closed captioning for the hearing impaired. Closed captioning consists of scrolling text at the bottom of a TV screen that spells out what is being said on television. Four years after the FCC action, ABC, PBS and NBC ran their first closed captioned programs, which included the *Wonderful World of Disney* and the *ABC Sunday Night Movie*. At first closed captioning was scripted, but then the National Captioning Institute developed a keyboard interface that could be used to create captioning for live sports, television shows, and newscasts. A stenographer listened to the audio portion of a broadcast and typed it into the broadcast in real time. In 1990 Congress required that all television receivers contain decoders that display closed captioning, and in the 1996 Telecommunications Act, Congress insisted that closed captioning be included in all shows by the turn of the century.

As part of this act, Congress also requested that broadcasters rate their shows. The industry heeded the request and developed the "TV Parental Guidelines." At the beginning of every television show, a rating is shown in the corner of the screen for fifteen seconds. TV-G designated general audiences, while TV-MA warned of content not suitable for anyone under seventeen. Even with the ratings system in place, parents across the country found they still could not monitor all the shows on cable as well as broadcast television. According to a statement delivered to Congress by FCC Commissioner Gloria Tristani on March 12, 1998, the average child spent twenty-five hours a week in front of the television. In response, in 2000, the FCC insisted that all television sets thirteen inches or larger contain a "V-chip." The V-chip worked in conjunction with the ratings system. If a parent set the V-chip to allow only TV-G shows, the microchip would simply block every show not rated TV-G.

Advances in Television in the 1990s

In 1994 a new way of broadcasting movie and television shows became available when RCA released its

TABLE 5.6

Digital television standards

Analog	DTV	HDTV
Broadcasts at least through 2006, and most likely longer. Consumers will always be able to connect an inexpensive receiver, a set top box, to their existing analog TV to decode DTV broadcast signals. Set top boxes will not convert your analog TV to high-definition. Analog TVs will continue to work with cable, satellite, VCRs, DVD players, camcorders, video games consoles and other devices for many years.	Digital cable or digital satellite does not mean a program is in high-definition. Digital pictures will be free from the "ghosts" and "snow" that can affect analog transmissions. Multicasting is available. HDTV is available. Data streaming is available.	High-definition broadcasts offered. Best available picture resolution, clarity and color. Dolby theatre surround-sound. Dolby surround-sound. Wide screen "movie-like" format.

SOURCE: "What is DTV?" Federal Communications Commission, http://www.dtv.gov/whatisdtv.html (accessed November 22, 2004)

Direct Satellite System (DSS). The DSS was the first affordable satellite receiver available to the American public. By installing an eighteen-inch satellite dish on their houses, Americans could receive nearly two hundred channels in their living rooms. To squeeze so many channels into a stream of data small enough to travel to space and back, the direct broadcasting satellite provider had to use a form of digital compression known as MPEG-1. The MPEG-1 compression format works much like an MP3 format. (The MP3 format in fact was developed from the audio portion of MPEG-1 format.) In order to employ the MPEG-1 format, all television shows recorded in analog must first be transformed by analog-to-digital converters into a digital format. MPEG-1 encoders, owned by the direct broadcasting satellite provider, then compress the digital data largely by removing redundant scenery between frames. For example, if a character's face is the only discernable movement between two frames in a movie, then the background from the first frame is applied to both frames, cutting out the redundant information in the second frame. The compressed signal is then beamed to the satellite network. Upon receiving the signal, the satellite network broadcasts the signal to homes all across the country. A DSS box in the home decompresses the signal and delivers it to the viewer.

Several years after the first direct broadcast satellites were released, cable companies introduced digital cable. Digital cable works in much the same way as direct broadcast satellites, but uses a slightly more advanced MPEG-2 format for compression. By digitally compressing their programming, cable providers found they could transmit ten times more television stations than before along their cables. Many cable providers added music stations, pay-per-view movies, and multiple movie channels to their services. The only drawback with both systems was that the decoder could only work on one television at a time, and it was very bulky.

In terms of television accessories, the big development in the late 1990s was the DVD. Since its release in 1997, the DVD quickly rose to become the preferred format for watching recorded movies. Looking at Table 5.5, the intro-

duction of the DVD coincides precisely with a slowdown in VCR sales. According to the research-marketing firm Digital Entertainment Group, some 110 million DVDs were sold by 2004. DVDs work almost exactly in the same way as CDs, but the standard DVD can hold up to seven times more information per disc, which allows the DVD to carry the data needed for a much larger video files. DVDs are recorded in the MPEG-2 format as well.

Digital TV

Many confuse the concept of digital cable with digital TV. Digital cable simply uses digital technology to compress the size of broadcasts so that the customer has more channels. Most of the programming fed through the digital cable systems is not digitally recorded. Digital television, however, is digital from start to finish. Digital cameras are used to record the broadcast; digital cables, satellite systems, and broadcast towers send a digital signal; and digital televisions play the broadcast. The result is a television picture that more closely resembles an image on a computer monitor than an image on a television set. The FCC has established a number of standards for digital television, which are shown in Table 5.6. Standard definition TV (SDTV) has the resolution of an analog TV, which is roughly 480 x 440 dots per inch (dpi) or 210,000 pixels total. The next step up in visual quality is the enhanced definition TV (EDTV), which generally has the same overall resolution as a standard TV but features a wider screen. Finally, high definition television (HDTV) is the highest quality television format with resolutions up to 1,920 dpi horizontally and 1,080 dpi vertically. Overall, the HDTV has more than two million pixels to display each image, which provides the viewer with ten times the detail of standard TV. For a television to earn the HDTV name, it has to have the ability to play the latest versions of Dolby stereo as well.

The digital TV standards were adopted by the FCC after Congress passed the 1996 Telecommunications Act. The act called for a full conversion to digital television across America by 2006. By that time every television station serving every market in the United States was

TABLE 5.7

Estimated revenue, printing expenses, and inventories for newspaper, periodical, database, and directory publishers, 1999–2001

[In millions of dollars (48,414 represents $48,414,000,000). For taxable and tax-exempt employer firms. Estimates have not been adjusted to the results of the 1997 Economic Census. Based on the North American Industry Classification System, 1997.]

Item	Newspaper publishers (NAICS 51111)			Periodical publishers (NAICS 51112)			Database and directory publishers (NAICS 51114)		
	1999	2000	2001	1999	2000	2001	1999	2000	2001
Revenue*	48,414	51,507	47,277	37,901	39,834	39,266	15,433	16,657	17,469
Print	(NA)	(NA)	42,367	(NA)	(NA)	31,714	(NA)	(NA)	11,730
Subscription and sales	(NA)	(NA)	9,394	(NA)	(NA)	13,816	(NA)	(NA)	594
Advertising	(NA)	(NA)	32,973	(NA)	(NA)	17,898	(NA)	(NA)	11,136
Internet	(NA)	(NA)	433	(NA)	(NA)	1,150	(NA)	(NA)	1,010
Subscription and sales	(NA)	(NA)	(S)	(NA)	(NA)	856	(NA)	(NA)	603
Advertising	(NA)	(NA)	324	(NA)	(NA)	293	(NA)	(NA)	407
Contract printing	(NA)	(NA)	1,788	(NA)	(NA)	934	(NA)	(NA)	144
Distribution of flyers, inserts, etc.	(NA)	(NA)	977	(NA)	(NA)	110	(NA)	(NA)	(NA)
Graphic design services	(NA)	(NA)	42	(NA)	(NA)	44	(NA)	(NA)	(NA)
Sales or licensing of rights of content	(NA)	(NA)	75	(NA)	(NA)	231	(NA)	(NA)	121
Rental or sales of mailing lists	(NA)	(NA)	14	(NA)	(NA)	161	(NA)	(NA)	1,253
Publishing services for others	(NA)	(NA)	12	(NA)	(NA)	369	(NA)	(NA)	31
Expenses: purchased printing	3,427	3,352	3,121	4,287	4,981	4,426	1,198	1,112	1,238
Inventories at end of year	737	786	748	1,258	1,340	1,185	408	398	376
Finished goods and work-in-process	43	51	63	877	879	773	383	370	355
Materials, supplies, fuel, etc.	694	736	685	381	462	413	(S)	(S)	22

NA Not available.
S Data do not meet publication standards.
*Includes other sources of revenue, not shown separately.

SOURCE: "No. 1129. Newspaper, Periodical, Database, and Directory Publishers—Estimated Revenue, Printing Expenses, and Inventories: 1999 to 2001," in *Statistical Abstract of the United States: 2003,* U.S. Census Bureau, Economics and Statistics Administration, U.S. Department of Commerce, 2003, http://www.census.gov/prod/2004pubs/03statab/inforcomm.pdf (accessed November 22, 2004)

required to air digital programming in one of the formats described in Table 5.6. In addition, broadcasters no longer had to air analog content. Americans with an analog TV set would be required to either buy a digital television or a $50 to $100 analog-to-digital conversion device in order to watch TV. At the close of 2004, however, only a very small percentage of Americans had HDTV or even EDTV. Fortunately, the Congress placed a clause in the act that allowed for a postponement of the deadline should most households not be ready for the transition.

JOURNALISM AND NEW MEDIA

The Internet has made getting news much more convenient. No longer do Americans have to rustle through a newspaper or patiently wait in front of the TV for the evening news. With the Internet, hundreds of magazines and news sites can be accessed in seconds. According to Madden in *America's Online Pursuits*, the number of online Americans who visited news sites daily grew from nineteen million people in March 2000 to twenty-nine million people in December 2002. A press release issued by comScore Media Metrix (July 8, 2002) revealed that unique visitors to local news Web sites in many major metropolitan areas in 2002 far exceeded the growth in online population in those areas. From December 2001 to May 2002, for instance, the number of Internet users in the New York metropolitan area expanded by 3%, where-

as the number of unique visitors to the *New York Post* Web site (www.nydailynews.com) grew by 23%. Online periodicals have also been bringing in serious revenue. As Table 5.7 shows, online periodical publishers generated $856 million from Internet subscriptions and $293 million from online advertisers.

Needless to say, such online news sources have led to the continued erosion of newspaper circulation. Cable and broadcast news started the trend in the late 1960s. Most big cities that once had two newspapers could support only one by the turn of the century. As Table 5.5 reveals, the number of newspapers circulated daily dropped from 62.1 million papers to 55.6 million nationwide between 1970 and 2001. According to the U.S. Census Bureau, the U.S. population over this period grew from 205 million people to 280 million people. Table 5.1 reveals a slightly different trend for books and magazines. Generally, books are difficult to read online, and magazine publishers have been careful not to provide people with free magazine content on the Web. According to the Census Bureau in *Statistical Abstract of the United States: 2003*, from 1998 to 2001 consumer expenditures for books actually increased by $2 per person. The amount of hours people spent reading books each year, however, declined by eleven hours from 120 hours to 109 hours. The time Americans devoted to magazines dropped six hours during the same period.

High technology has not only changed how newspapers are sold, but also how reporters and writers do their jobs. With the Internet, anyone can feasibly start a publication or web log (blog) and begin reporting on current events or writing commentary. No longer do reporters and writers have to work for a large publishing house or magazine to build a name for themselves. Matt Drudge, for instance, began the *Drudge Report* Web site in 1997 to report on current events. He was largely responsible for breaking the story of President Clinton's relationship with former White House intern Monica Lewinsky in 1998. In the year ending January 27, 2005, the *Drudge Report* Web site counted more than 3.2 billion visits. Advanced communications and video technology have also allowed reporters with established organizations to report from anywhere in the world in real time. Embedded television reporters played a big part at the beginning of the Iraq War in March 2003. Armed with night-vision cameras and portable satellite transmitters, they were able to give viewers at home an idea of how the war was progressing as it unfolded.

CHAPTER 6
THE INTERNET AND EDUCATION

Knowing how to use an Internet browser has become as important a skill in modern life as knowing multiplication tables. Internet illiteracy restricts a person's access to job listings, e-mail communication, online information sources, and dozens of convenient, efficient tools that make work and life easier. Aware of this, high schools and colleges in the late 1990s increased efforts to expose students to the Internet before graduation. Most secondary and elementary schools installed computers with Internet access in classrooms and libraries. College administrations provided widespread broadband access to students on campus, and many professors began requiring the use of the Internet in college courses.

Due in part to these actions, high school students and college students were among the most Internet-savvy Americans at the turn of the century. According to Steve Jones in *The Internet Goes to College* (Washington, DC: Pew Internet & American Life Project, September 15, 2002), nearly 86% of the 14.5 million college students in 2002 had been online. A similar report released in 2001 by Pew/Internet reported that 73% of young people aged twelve through seventeen had gone online. The percentage of Internet users in both demographics were well above the overall percentage of adult Americans who had been online at the time.

Providing students with access to the Internet, however, has not been without problems. Not only did the Internet provide a great deal of distraction for many young people, but it also opened up an avenue for plagiarism. Largely because of the Internet, academic cheating and plagiarism skyrocketed around the turn of the millennium. Students appeared to have no qualms about copying text from the Internet and pasting it verbatim into reports and papers. A 2003 study conducted by Donald McCabe of Rutgers University in conjunction with the Center for Academic Integrity at Duke University revealed that 38% of students had used the cut-and-paste technique, and 44% regarded the practice as "trivial or not cheating at all."

ELEMENTARY AND SECONDARY SCHOOLS

On February 8, 1996, President Bill Clinton signed the Telecommunications Act into law. This legislation ushered in the E-rate program, which provides elementary and secondary public schools with discounts of 20% to 90% when purchasing computers for libraries and classrooms. The program had a tremendous impact on computer and Internet accessibility in public schools. The National Center for Education Statistics (NCES) surveyed a cross section of elementary and secondary U.S. public schools of all sizes and in all states and published the results in *Internet Access in U.S. Public Schools and Classrooms: 1994–2002* (October 2003). As Table 6.1 shows, almost all public schools had Internet access by 2002. The availability of the Internet in public schools grew rapidly in the late 1990s and then leveled off. Only 35% of public schools were wired in 1994. By 1997 nearly 78% had Internet access, and in 1999, 95% were connected to the Internet. Though private schools generally have the reputation for maintaining better facilities than public schools, Table 6.2 reveals that private schools lagged behind in terms of Internet access. Of all private schools surveyed, only 67% had access to the Web in 1999. More Catholic schools were wired in 1999 (83%) than other types of private schools.

As to the type of Internet connection found in public schools, the NCES survey found that in 2002, 94% of public schools had always-on broadband connections as opposed to dial-up. (See Table 6.3.) This was a huge increase from 1996 when a full 74% of schools still used dial-up connections. Wireless connections were also on the rise. Some 23% of public schools had wireless connections in 2002. Larger schools were more likely to have a wireless connection. Only 17% of smaller schools (three hundred students or fewer) had wireless Internet connections as opposed to 37% of larger schools (one thousand students or more).

Internet Use in the Classroom

Table 6.4 reveals that in 2002, 92% of public school classrooms had Internet access. The number of wired

TABLE 6.1

Public schools with Internet access, 1994–2002

School characteristic	Public schools with internet access								
	1994	1995	1996	1997	1998	1999	2000	2001	2002
All public schools	35	50	65	78	89	95	98	99	99
Instructional level[1]									
Elementary	30	46	61	75	88	94	97	99	99
Secondary	49	65	77	89	94	98	100[2]	100[2]	100[2]
School size									
Less than 300	30	39	57	75	87	96	96	99	96
300 to 999	35	52	66	78	89	94	98	99	100
1,000 or more	58	69	80	89	95	96	99	100	100
Locale									
City	40	47	64	74	92	93	96	97	99
Urban fringe	38	59	75	78	85	96	98	99	100
Town	29	47	61	84	90	94	98	100	98
Rural	35	48	60	79	92	96	99	100[2]	98
Percent minority enrollment[3]									
Less than 6 percent	38	52	65	84	91	95	98	99	97
6 to 20 percent	38	58	72	87	93	97	100	100	100
21 to 49 percent	38	55	65	73	91	96	98	100	99
50 percent or more	27	39	56	63	82	92	96	98	99
Percent of students eligible for free or reduced-price lunch[4]									
Less than 35 percent	39	60	74	86	92	95	99	99	98
35 to 49 percent	35	48	59	81	93	98	99	100	100
50 to 74 percent	32	41	53	71	88	96	97	99	100
75 percent or more	18	31	53	62	79	89	94	97	99

[1]Data for combined schools are included in the totals and in analyses by other school characteristics but are not shown separately.
[2]The estimate fell between 99.5 percent and 100 percent and therefore was rounded to 100 percent.
[3]Percent minority enrollment was not available for some schools. In 1994, this information was missing for 100 schools. In subsequent years, the missing information ranged from 0 schools to 46 schools. In 2002, this information was missing for 15 schools. The weighted response rate was 98.6 percent.
[4]Percent of students eligible for free or reduced-price lunch was not available for some schools. In the 1994 survey, free and reduced-price lunch data came from the Common Core of Data (CCD) only and were missing for 430 schools. In reports prior to 1998, free and reduced-price lunch data were not reported for 1994. In 1998, a decision was made to include the data for 1994 for comparison purposes. In subsequent years, free and reduced-price lunch information was obtained on the questionnaire, supplemented, if necessary, with CCD data. Missing data ranged from 0 schools (2002) to 10 schools (1999).
Note: All of the estimates in this report were recalculated from raw data files using the same computational algorithms. Consequently, some estimates presented here may differ trivially (i.e., 1 percent) from results published prior to 2001.

SOURCE: Anne Kleiner, Laurie Lewis, and Bernard Greene, "Table 1. Percent of Public Schools with Internet Access, by School Characteristics: 1994–2002," in *Internet Access in U.S. Public Schools and Classrooms: 1994–2002,* National Center for Education Statistics, Institute of Education Sciences, U.S. Department of Education, October 2003, http://www.nces.ed.gov/surveys/frss/publications/2004011/tables.asp (accessed November 22, 2004)

classrooms had increased fairly steadily since 1994 when only 3% of classrooms had Internet access. The more minorities and impoverished students the school had, the less likely the school was to have classrooms with Internet access. City schools were also less likely to have wired classrooms than rural or suburban schools.

Counting the number of instructional rooms with Internet access, however, does not necessarily render an accurate picture of how much exposure children had to the Internet during class. A better yardstick for student exposure is the ratio of students to instructional (classroom) computers with Internet connections. As Figure 6.1 shows, the number of students per instructional computer with Web access in 2002 was 4.8—a substantial decrease from 1998 when the ratio was 12.1 to 1. Table 6.5 is a breakdown of students to Internet accessible computers by minority enrollment, school size, school locale, and other factors. Surprisingly, rural area schools had more instructional computers with Internet access per student than city, urban, or town schools in 2002. In rural areas,

one Internet-equipped computer was present for every four students. In the city, only one Internet-equipped computer was present for every 5.5 students. Schools with 50% minority enrollment had roughly one instructional, Internet-ready computer for every 5.1 students, whereas schools with less than 6% minority enrollment had four students for each computer. Smaller schools and schools with more impoverished students also tended to have fewer classroom computers with Internet access.

According to the NCES in *Internet Access in U.S. Public Schools and Classrooms: 1994–2002*, one-half of teachers reported that they used the Internet for instruction during class time in 1999. Only one-third of teachers, however, felt they were adequately prepared to use the Internet to teach classes. To improve this situation, schools began offering their teachers Internet training courses. By 2002, 87% of schools with Internet access reported that their school or school district offered teachers professional instruction on ways to integrate the use of the Internet into the classroom curriculum.

TABLE 6.2

Advanced telecommunications in private schools, 1995 and 1999

[For fall 1995 and school year 1998–99. Based on the Fast Response Survey System.]

Characteristic	Number of students per computer		Internet access (percent)						Percent of schools without access that plan to have access in the future, 1999	Percent of teachers using computers for teaching, 1999*
			Schools with access		Instructional rooms with access		Students enrolled in schools with access			
	1995	1999	1995	1999	1995	1999	1995	1999		
All private schools	9	6	25	67	5	25	41	81	46	45
Affiliation:										
Catholic	10	7	35	83	4	27	43	86	74	48
Other religious	9	7	16	54	2	18	30	72	41	41
Nonsectarian	6	4	32	66	13	41	59	84	38	49
Instructional level:										
Elementary	9	7	23	64	3	21	32	77	46	45
Secondary	7	5	57	90	6	32	70	97	31	47
Combined	8	5	19	64	8	28	41	80	46	44
Size of enrollment:										
Less than 150	7	5	13	48	2	16	16	60	38	41
150 to 299	9	7	27	77	3	17	28	77	60	43
300 or more	9	6	50	85	8	34	56	87	77	47
Minority enrollment:										
Less than 6 percent	9	7	24	59	3	28	38	83	13	41
6 to 20 percent	7	6	29	75	9	27	51	86	71	46
21 to 49 percent	8	6	29	76	3	32	44	85	59	45
50 percent or more	11	8	18	52	2	10	24	59	59	47

*Percent of teachers using computers or advanced telecommunications (e.g. networked computers and interactive television) for teaching.

SOURCE: "No. 257. Advanced Telecommunications in Private Schools: 1995 and 1999," in *Statistical Abstract of the United States: 2003,* U.S. Census Bureau, Economics and Statistics Administration, U.S. Department of Commerce, 2003, http://www.census.gov/prod/2004pubs/03statab/educ.pdf (accessed November 22, 2004)

Access to Inappropriate Material

In 1996 Congress established the Children's Internet Protection Act (CIPA). Under CIPA schools that could not prove that they use filtering or blocking technology to keep children from viewing pornographic or sexually explicit Web sites were no longer eligible for the E-rate program. Consequently, almost all schools (99%) with Internet access in 2002 used some type of technology or procedure to control the access students had to content on the Internet. The types of controls various schools used can be seen in Table 6.6. Ninety-six percent of schools in 2002 employed Internet content filtering or blocking software. Teachers or staff monitored students' activities online in 91% of schools with Internet access. Some 82% of schools required written contracts from the parents, and 77% required written contracts from students. Monitoring software, which tracks the Web pages that individual student's visit, was used in 52% of schools.

Computers at Home and at School

Table 6.7 displays the percentage of American children who had computer and Internet access available to them at home in 1999. Sixty-five percent of children had access to a home computer, and 30.4% had Internet access at home. To level the playing field between kids who had access to Internet and those who did not, many public schools began allowing children access to school comput-

ers before and after regular school hours. Table 6.8 reveals that 53% of wired public schools allowed students to log onto the Internet outside of regular hours. Of these, most (96%) permitted access after hours, three-quarters (74%) let students come in before school, and a small number (6%) granted students use of the Internet on the weekends.

The NCES reported in *Internet Access in U.S. Public Schools and Classrooms: 1994–2002* that in 2002 8% of public schools surveyed provided laptop computers for their students to use as well. Only seven laptops, however, were available on average at these schools. Of the schools that provided laptops to students, 59% reported they typically lent laptops to students for less than one week. Nineteen percent said they lent students laptops between one week and a month, and 16% of these schools offered use of the laptops to students for the entire school year. Seven percent of schools that did not offer laptops in 2002 planned to do so during the 2003–04 school year.

School Web Sites

According to the NCES in *Internet Access in U.S. Public Schools and Classrooms: 1994–2002,* 86% of all public schools had created a Web site by 2002, an increase from 75% the year before. (See Table 6.9.) Ninety-four percent of large schools (one thousand or more students) and 84% of small schools (three hundred students or fewer) had a Web site. The percentage of Web sites maintained by rural schools

TABLE 6.3

Public schools with broadband access, 2000–02

School characteristic	Use broadband connections			
	2000[1]	2001[1]	2002[2]	Percentage change 2000–2002[3]
All public schools	80	85	94	+17
Instructional level[4]				
Elementary	77	83	93	+20
Secondary	89	94	98	+10
School size				
Less than 300	67	72	90	+35
300 to 999	83	89	94	+13
1,000 or more	90	96	100	+11
Locale				
City	80	88	97	+22
Urban fringe	85	88	92	+9
Town	79	83	97	+23
Rural	75	82	91	+21
Percent minority enrollment[5]				
Less than 6 percent	76	81	92	+21
6 to 20 percent	82	85	91	+11
21 to 49 percent	84	85	96	+14
50 percent or more	81	93	95	+18
Percent of students eligible for free or reduced-price lunch[6]				
Less than 35 percent	81	84	93	+14
35 to 49 percent	82	86	96	+16
50 to 74 percent	79	84	93	+17
75 percent or more	75	90	95	+27

[1]Respondents were instructed to circle as many types of connections as there were in the school. The data were then combined to show the percentage of schools using broadband connections. Percentages include schools using only broadband connections, as well as schools using both broadband and narrowband connections. They do not include schools using narrowband connections exclusively. Broadband connections include T3/DS3, fractional T3, T1/DS1, fractional T1, and cable modem connections. In 2001, they also included DSL connections, which had not been on the 2000 questionnaire.
[2]The 2002 questionnaire directly asked whether the schools used broadband and narrowband connections. Broadband connections include T3/DS3, fractional T3, T1/DS1, fractional T1, cable modem, and DSL connections.
[3]This percentage was calculated as follows: [(e2001-e2000)/e2000] × 100, where "e" stands for "estimate."
[4]Data for combined schools are included in the totals and in analyses by other school characteristics but are not shown separately.
[5]Percent minority enrollment was not available for 9 schools in 2000 and 31 schools in 2001. In 2002, this information was missing for 15 schools. The weighted response rate was 98.6 percent.
[6]Percent of students eligible for free or reduced-price lunch was not available for 2 schools in 2000 and 2001. This information was available for all schools in 2002.
Note: Percentages are based on the percent of public schools with Internet access: 98 percent in 2000 and 99 percent in 2001 and 2002.

SOURCE: Anne Kleiner, Laurie Lewis, and Bernard Greene, "Table 3. Percent of Public Schools with Internet Access Using Broadband Connections, by School Characteristics: 2000–2002," in *Internet Access in U.S. Public Schools and Classrooms: 1994–2002,* National Center for Education Statistics, Institute of Education Sciences, U.S. Department of Education, October 2003, http://www.nces.ed.gov/surveys/frss/publications/2004011/tables.asp (accessed November 22, 2004)

FIGURE 6.1

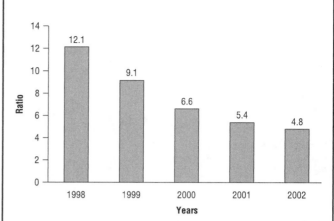

Ratio of public school students to instructional computers with Internet access, 1998–2002

Note: Ratios are based on all public schools. All of the estimates in this report were recalculated from raw data files using the same computational algorithms. Consequently, some estimates presented here may differ trivially (i.e., 1 percent) from results published prior to 2001.

SOURCE: Anne Kleiner, Laurie Lewis, and Bernard Greene, "Figure 3. Ratio of Public School Computers to Instructional Computers with Internet Access: 1998–2002," in *Internet Access in U.S. Public Schools and Classrooms: 1994–2002,* National Center for Education Statistics, Institute of Education Sciences, U.S. Department of Education, October 2003, http://www.nces.ed.gov/surveys/frss/publications/2004011/6.asp (accessed November 22, 2004)

one-third (29%) of the Web sites were administered by a teacher or other staff member as part of their responsibilities. Eighteen percent of school Web sites were managed by teachers or staff members on a voluntary basis.

Internet Use among Teens

The Pew Internet & American Life Project (Pew/Internet) estimated in *Teenage Life Online* (Washington, DC: 2001) that seventeen million (73%) young people aged twelve through seventeen had used the Internet sometime in their life. Of these, 11% (1.9 million) primarily accessed the Internet through the computers provided at school. (See Table 6.10.) Sixty-four percent of online students said they went online at school occasionally. The survey found that those students dependent on school computers were more likely to come from single-parent households, low-income families, and families that do not use the Internet. Most online teenagers replied they used the Internet primarily at home. In fact, nearly 83% (fourteen million) reported they go online most often at home, which was a much higher percentage than that reported by the U.S. Census Bureau in 1999. (See Table 6.7.) The Pew/Internet study also found that 3% of students used a friend's house most often, 1% used the public library, and 1% went someplace else such as a cyber café for access.

Fully 94% of online students logged on to the Internet to do research for school. When asked where they retrieved

and suburban schools was much higher than for schools in urban areas. Schools were also less likely to have a Web site if they had a high enrollment of minority students.

Of schools in the NCES survey that reported having a Web site, 68% updated their site at least monthly; 32% updated their site less often than once a month. In addition, only 2% of all Web sites were student run. Nearly

TABLE 6.4

Public school instructional rooms with Internet access, by school characteristics, 1994–2002

School characteristic	Instructional rooms with Internet access								
	1994	1995	1996	1997	1998	1999	2000	2001	2002
All public schools	3	8	14	27	51	64	77	87	92
Instructional level[1]									
Elementary	3	8	13	24	51	62	76	86	92
Secondary	4	8	16	32	52	67	79	88	91
School size									
Less than 300	3	9	15	27	54	71	83	87	91
300 to 999	3	8	13	28	53	64	78	87	93
1,000 or more	3	4	16	25	45	58	70	86	89
Locale									
City	4	6	12	20	47	52	66	82	88
Urban fringe	4	8	16	29	50	67	78	87	92
Town	3	8	14	34	55	72	87	91	96
Rural	3	8	14	30	57	71	85	89	93
Percent minority enrollment[2]									
Less than 6 percent	4	9	18	37	57	74	85	88	93
6 to 20 percent	4	10	18	35	59	78	83	90	94
21 to 49 percent	4	9	12	22	52	64	79	89	91
50 percent or more	2	3	5	13	37	43	64	81	89
Percent of students eligible for free or reduced-price lunch[3]									
Less than 35 percent	3	10	17	33	57	73	82	90	93
35 to 49 percent	2	6	12	33	60	69	81	89	90
50 to 74 percent	4	6	11	20	41	61	77	87	91
75 percent or more	2	3	5	14	38	38	60	79	89

[1]Data for combined schools are included in the totals and in analyses by other school characteristics but are not shown separately.
[2]Percent minority enrollment was not available for some schools. In 1994, this information was missing for 100 schools. In subsequent years, the missing information ranged from 0 schools to 46 schools. In 2002, this information was missing for 15 schools. The weighted response rate was 98.6 percent.
[3]Percent of students eligible for free or reduced-price lunch was not available for some schools. In the 1994 survey, free and reduced-price lunch data came from the Common Core of Data (CCD) only and were missing for 430 schools. In reports prior to 1998, free and reduced-price lunch data were not reported for 1994. In 1998, a decision was made to include the data for 1994 for comparison purposes. In subsequent years, free and reduced-price lunch information was obtained on the questionnaire, supplemented, if necessary, with CCD data. Missing data ranged from 0 schools (2002) to 10 schools (1999).
Note: Percentages are based on all schools. All of the estimates in this report were recalculated from raw data files using the same computational algorithms. Consequently, some estimates presented here may differ trivially (i.e., 1 percent) from results published prior to 2001.

SOURCE: Anne Kleiner, Laurie Lewis, and Bernard Greene, "Table 2. Percent of Public School Instructional Rooms with Internet Access, by School Characteristics: 1994–2002," in *Internet Access in U.S. Public Schools and Classrooms: 1994–2002,* National Center for Education Statistics, Institute of Education Sciences, U.S. Department of Education, October 2003, http://www.nces.ed.gov/surveys/frss/publications/2004011/tables.asp (accessed November 22, 2004)

information for their last major report, 71% of online teens said they primarily relied on the Internet, 24% responded that they used library resources, and 4% said they utilized both equally. Students felt that conducting research for classes using the library was more difficult than surfing the Internet. When asked about the validity of information on the Internet, many teenagers replied that they did not trust everything on the Web and instinctively knew which Web sites provided accurate information.

As Table 6.11 shows, teens used the Internet most to send and receive e-mail and instant messages. Of daily teenage Internet users, almost all (99%) used e-mail, roughly nine-tenths (89%) sent instant messages, and three-quarters (73%) downloaded music online. There were a number of activities that teenagers engage in online much more than adults, as Table 6.12 reveals. Seventy-four percent of teens used instant messaging, as opposed to only 44% of adults. A similar discrepancy existed between the percentage of online teenagers who played

or downloaded games (66%) and online adults who partook in these activities (34%). Teenagers also listened to more music online, visited more chat rooms, downloaded more music, and checked sports scores more often than adults.

COLLEGES AND UNIVERSITIES

No group was more wired in 2002 than college students. According to Jones in *The Internet Goes to College*, nearly 86% of the 14.5 million college students in 2002 had been online. (See Table 6.13.) Surprisingly, many students first started using the Web regularly only in college. Roughly half (49%) of online college students first became Internet users in college, while the other half (47%) had used the Internet before college. All college students had used a computer by the time they were nineteen, and 20% had used a computer before the age of nine.

As to time spent on the Internet per week, 75% of online college students were online four or more hours a

TABLE 6.5

Ratio of public school students to instructional computers with Internet access, by school characteristics, 1998–2002

School characteristic	Ratio of students to instructional computers with Internet access				
	1998	1999	2000	2001	2002
All public schools	12.1	9.1	6.6	5.4	4.8
Instructional level[1]					
Elementary	13.6	10.6	7.8	6.1	5.2
Secondary	9.9	7.0	5.2	4.3	4.1
School size					
Less than 300	9.1	5.7	3.9	4.1	3.1
300 to 999	12.3	9.4	7.0	5.6	5.0
1,000 or more	13.0	10.0	7.2	5.4	5.1
Locale					
City	14.1	11.4	8.2	5.9	5.5
Urban fringe	12.4	9.1	6.6	5.7	4.9
Town	12.2	8.2	6.2	5.0	4.4
Rural	8.6	6.6	5.0	4.6	4.0
Percent minority enrollment[2]					
Less than 6 percent	10.1	7.0	5.7	4.7	4.0
6 to 20 percent	10.4	7.8	5.9	4.9	4.6
21 to 49 percent	12.1	9.5	7.2	5.5	5.2
50 percent or more	17.2	13.3	8.1	6.4	5.1
Percent of students eligible for free or reduced-price lunch[3]					
Less than 35 percent	10.6	7.6	6.0	4.9	4.6
35 to 49 percent	10.9	9.0	6.3	5.2	4.5
50 to 74 percent	15.8	10.0	7.2	5.6	4.7
75 percent or more	16.8	16.8	9.1	6.8	5.5

[1]Data for combined schools are included in the totals and in analyses by other school characteristics but are not shown separately.
[2]Percent minority enrollment was not available for some schools. Over the years, the missing information ranged from 0 schools (1999) to 31 schools (2001). In 2002, this information was missing for 15 schools.
[3]Percent of students eligible for free or reduced-price lunch was not available for some schools. Over the years, the missing information ranged from 0 schools (2002) to 10 schools (1999).
Note: Ratios are based on all public schools. All of the estimates in this report were recalculated from raw data files using the same computational algorithms. Consequently, some estimates presented here may differ trivially (i.e., 1 percent) from results published prior to 2001.

SOURCE: Anne Kleiner, Laurie Lewis, and Bernard Greene, "Table 7. Ratio of Public School Students to Instructional Computers with Internet Access, by School Characteristics: 1998–2002," in *Internet Access in U.S. Public Schools and Classrooms: 1994–2002,* National Center for Education Statistics, Institute of Education Sciences, U.S. Department of Education, October 2003, http://www.nces.ed.gov/surveys/frss/publications/2004011/tables.asp (accessed November 22, 2004)

week. Nineteen percent were hardcore users, devoting twelve hours or more to the Internet. Although 85% of college students owned a computer, 33% reported that they used a campus computer more often than their own. In terms of demographics, Table 6.13 reveals that slightly more men (87%) were online in 2002 than women (85%). Some 90% of white college students were online, versus 82% of Hispanic students, and 74% of African-American students.

As can be seen in Table 6.14, the most popular Internet activity among college students was communicating socially, which was also the most popular activity for teenagers. Forty-two percent of college students used the Internet to e-mail and instant message friends more often than they used it for any other activity. Engaging in work for classes came in a close second at 38%. Only 10% of college students used the Internet for entertainment more than they used it for any other purpose. Based on statistics from the marketing research firm comScore Media Metrix, Table 6.15 displays a list of twenty Web sites in 2002 where a disproportionate amount of hits came from college students. The list generally reflects the activities noted in Table 6.14. The number one Web site on the list is Live-Journal (www.livejournal.com). Combining entertainment with communication, this Web site allows people to create an online journal (blog) for others to read. While most of the other Web sites are related to gaming and music, a few are linked to academic and cultural endeavors. FastWeb (fastweb.monster.com) is a search engine for those looking for scholarships, and DueNow.com (www.duenow.com) is a homework resource center for students.

College Students and Communication

In *The Internet Goes to College* Jones concluded that the most popular Internet activity for students was social communication with others. Some 85% of college students believed the Internet to be a convenient way to interact with others. Table 6.16 lists the people college students communicated with the most via the Internet. Friends topped the chart (72%), followed by family (10%), and professors (7%). Only a small fraction (6%) of college students communicated most with their romantic partners, and fewer still (5%) primarily communicated with work colleagues. Sixty-nine percent of undergraduates replied, however, that they still liked to use the phone more than the Internet to talk to people. Many students simply saw the Internet as a way to touch base with people or set up a time to talk on the phone or in person at a later date. Fully 19% of college students said they had dealt with someone first online before meeting them in person. Forwarding jokes and other messages to friends and family was the most popular online social activity among wired college students.

E-mail was by far the favorite online communications tool used by online undergraduates in 2002. (See Table 6.17.) Twice as many students preferred e-mail over instant messaging as their primary method of keeping in touch with others online. Online college students, however, used instant messaging far more than the general population of Internet users. (Only half of all adult Internet users in 2002 used instant messaging, as opposed to three-quarters of undergraduates.) The third favorite communications tool employed by college students was Web boards, followed by chat rooms, and finally newsgroups. As to the time spent communicating, 25% of all college students reported that they interact socially online three or more hours a week.

College Students and Academics

Though the two are not mutually exclusive, the Internet appeared to occupy as much time as homework for

TABLE 6.6

Public schools using procedures to prevent student access to inappropriate material on the Internet, 2001–02

School characteristic	Monitoring by teachers or other staff		Blocking/ filtering software		Written contract that parents have to sign		Written contract that students have to sign		Monitoring software		Honor code for students		Intranet	
	2001	2002	2001	2002	2001	2002	2001	2002	2001	2002	2001	2002	2001	2002
All public schools	91	91	87	96	80	82	75	77	46	52	44	41	26	32
Instructional level[1]														
Elementary	90	91	85	95	78	82	72	74	43	51	44	41	24	34
Secondary	93	92	93	98	87	82	87	84	52	57	45	43	33	28
School size														
Less than 300	88	90	81	97	73	82	69	78	42	51	38	40	17	19
300 to 999	92	91	88	95	82	82	76	75	47	52	46	42	29	37
1,000 or more	93	95	93	99	86	81	84	81	48	59	46	43	32	33
Locale														
City	90	88	83	91	78	78	72	74	49	45	51	38	29	38
Urban fringe	91	92	88	96	80	79	76	69	44	53	43	44	29	37
Town	84	93	87	99	79	84	76	85	37	65	39	40	19	24
Rural	95	91	87	98	82	87	78	83	49	51	42	42	24	26
Percent minority enrollment[2]														
Less than 6 percent	92	92	86	96	82	83	77	81	47	51	41	39	21	20
6 to 20 percent	93	92	86	96	80	82	75	73	44	57	45	41	30	37
21 to 49 percent	91	94	86	96	79	83	77	77	46	53	46	50	29	41
50 percent or more	88	87	87	95	78	80	72	75	45	48	44	39	27	35
Percent of students eligible for free or reduced-price lunch[3]														
Less than 35 percent	92	95	87	95	82	82	77	75	45	54	48	44	29	34
35 to 49 percent	94	89	86	98	83	86	78	80	40	47	38	42	23	28
50 to 74 percent	90	90	86	97	81	83	79	81	51	53	40	40	22	30
75 percent or more	87	86	86	95	73	76	64	71	46	52	45	37	28	35

[1]Data for combined schools are included in the totals and in analyses by other school characteristics but are not shown separately.
[2]Percent minority enrollment was not available for 31 schools in 2001. In 2002, this information was missing for 15 schools. The weighted response rate was 98.6 percent.
[3]Percent of students eligible for free or reduced-price lunch was not available for 2 schools in 2001.
Note: Percentages are based on 95 percent of public schools (99 percent with Internet access times 96 percent using technologies/procedures to prevent student access to inappropriate material on the Internet) in 2001, and 98 percent of public schools (99 percent with Internet access times 99 percent using technologies/procedures to prevent student access to inappropriate material on the Internet) in 2002.

SOURCE: Anne Kleiner, Laurie Lewis, and Bernard Greene, "Table 18. Percent of Public Schools with Internet Access Using Various Technologies or Procedures to Prevent Student Access to Inappropriate Material on the Internet, by School Characteristic: 2001–02," in *Internet Access in U.S. Public Schools and Classrooms: 1994–2002,* National Center for Education Statistics, Institute of Education Sciences, U.S. Department of Education, October 2003, http://www.nces.ed.gov/surveys/frss/publications/2004011/tables.asp (accessed November 22, 2004)

most students, according to Jones in *The Internet Goes to College*. Only 14% of students said they studied twelve hours or more a week. Two thirds (62%) claimed they studied for less than seven hours per week. Despite the potential distraction posed by the Internet, 79% of college students believed the Internet impacted their academic experience favorably.

E-mail has greatly affected the relationship between student and professor. About 47% of all college student said their professor required them to use e-mail as part of a class. Professors tended to use e-mail the most to notify the entire class of changes to homework assignments or to make general announcements such as class cancellations. Eighty-two percent of undergraduates reported receiving assignment information via e-mail during their college career. This student-professor relationship, however, was generally a one-way affair. Half (51%) of online college students rarely e-mailed their professors, and only roughly one-tenth (11%) contacted their professor once or more a week via e-mail. The rest were somewhere in between.

In terms of what students e-mailed professors about, three quarters (75%) of college students said they had used e-mail to contact a professor sometime in their college career to ask about an assignment. Almost two-thirds (62%) of students had used email to arrange a time to meet, and roughly the same amount (58%) had e-mailed a professor to discuss grades. E-mails also allowed students to express their views and opinions to professors. The Pew/Internet study on college life reported that in 2002 nearly 46% of online college students agreed that e-mail was useful in articulating ideas that they did not feel comfortable verbalizing in class. A quarter (25%) of online students used e-mail to tell professors they were unable to finish an assignment, and two-thirds (65%) notified their professors of absences via e-mail. Overall, half of online students believed in 2002 that e-mail improved their interaction with their professor.

The Internet also gave students who lived on and off campus the ability to collaborate with one another on coursework without having to leave their rooms. Sixty-

TABLE 6.7

Children's access to home computer and use of the Internet at home, 2000

[As of August. For children 3 to 17 years old. (60,635 represents 60,635,000). Based on the Current Population Survey and subject to sampling error.]

Characteristic	Home computer access			Use of the Internet at home	
	Children (1,000)	Number (1,000)	Percent	Number (1,000)	Percent
Total	60,635	39,430	65.0	18,437	30.4
Age:					
3 to 5 years	11,915	6,905	58.0	864	7.3
6 to 11 years	24,837	15,924	64.1	6,135	24.7
12 to 17 years	23,884	16,600	69.5	11,439	47.9
Sex:					
Male	31,055	20,273	65.3	9,392	30.2
Female	29,580	19,156	64.8	9,045	30.6
Race and Hispanic origin:					
White	47,433	33,062	69.7	15,940	33.6
White non-Hispanic	38,438	29,731	77.3	14,773	38.4
Black	9,779	4,161	42.5	1,441	14.7
Asian and Pacific Islander	2,581	1,855	71.9	909	35.2
Hispanic*	9,568	3,546	37.1	1,229	12.8
Householder's educational attainment:					
Less than high school diploma	10,159	3,060	30.1	1,126	11.1
High school diploma/GED	18,915	10,559	55.8	4,600	24.3
Some college	16,994	12,712	74.8	5,926	34.9
Bachelor's degree or more	14,567	13,098	89.9	6,786	46.6
Household type:					
Family households	60,012	39,119	65.2	18,284	30.5
Married-couple household	42,936	31,593	73.6	15,050	35.1
Male householder	3,092	1,508	48.8	740	23.9
Female householder	13,984	6,017	43.0	2,493	17.8
Nonfamily household	620	310	50.0	154	24.8
Family income:					
Total children in families	59,288	38,729	65.3	18,139	30.6
Under $15,000	7,480	2,041	27.3	578	7.7
15,000 to 19,999	2,896	1,044	36.0	373	12.9
20,000 to 24,999	3,596	1,507	41.9	547	15.2
25,000 to 34,999	6,967	3,755	53.9	1,463	21.0
35,000 to 49,999	8,463	6,044	71.4	2,694	31.8
50,000 to 74,999	10,374	8,574	82.6	4,142	39.9
75,000 and over	12,115	11,294	93.2	6,263	51.7
Not reported	7,395	4,470	60.4	2,079	28.1

*Persons of Hispanic origin may be of any race.

SOURCE: "No. 260. Children's Access to Home Computer and Use of the Internet at Home: 2000," in *Statistical Abstract of the United States: 2003*, U.S. Census Bureau, Economics and Statistics Administration, U.S. Department of Commerce, 2003, http://www.census.gov/prod/2004pubs/03statab/educ.pdf (accessed November 22, 2004)

nine percent of undergraduates felt that e-mail was a good way to maintain contact with classmates regarding class. Seventy-five percent said they used the Internet to confer with classmates about a group project, and 31% reported that they e-mailed classmates once a week or more.

The Internet has also become a primary resource of information for school reports and papers. According to statistics published on the Web site of the Association of Research Libraries (www.arl.org), reference queries at university libraries have fallen sharply since the late 1990s when Internet use became widespread. In *The Internet Goes to College*, Jones found that in 2002, 73% of college students used the Internet more than the library when searching for information. Only 9% of students said they used the library more than the Internet. Like high school students, college students felt that using the library was much more difficult than surfing the Web. Jones's Pew/Internet report on college life further revealed that when students were observed using school library computers, they were typically looking for information on commercial Web browsers rather than the library's Web sites. Many professors and librarians worried that the Internet has made students less adept at finding credible resources when researching a topic. These educators feared that college students were more interested in a quick fix than in sound research techniques.

College Students and Entertainment

College students use the Internet to entertain themselves much more than the general population. According to Jones in *The Internet Goes to College*, a little over three-quarters (78%) of college students went online for fun in 2002, versus only roughly two-thirds (64%) of the general online adult

TABLE 6.8

Public schools allowing student access to the Internet outside of school hours, 2001–02

| School characteristic | Internet available to students outside of regular school hours[1] | | Time of availability[2] | | | | | |
| | | | After school | | Before school | | On weekends | |
	2001	2002	2001	2002	2001	2002	2001	2002
All public schools	51	53	95	96	74	74	6	6
Instructional level[3]								
Elementary	42	47	94	95	69	69	4	6
Secondary	78	73	97	98	85	83	8	8
School size								
Less than 300	47	49	91	93	79	79	9	7
300 to 999	47	50	96	96	71	69	4	5
1000 or more	82	79	98	98	82	84	7	8
Locale								
City	49	55	96	99	64	62	4	9
Urban fringe	45	51	94	97	78	76	4	6
Town	52	50	97	98	78	76	3	7
Rural	58	54	95	92	76	79	8	4
Percent minority enrollment[4]								
Less than 6 percent	50	52	95	95	84	78	6	6
6 to 20 percent	45	50	97	96	74	80	9	2
21 to 49 percent	52	54	95	96	74	77	2	6
50 percent or more	56	54	96	97	66	62	6	10
Percent of students eligible for free or reduced-price lunch[5]								
Less than 35 percent	52	52	98	96	79	82	6	6
35 to 49 percent	50	54	94	95	77	75	4	5
50 to 74 percent	50	50	91	97	73	71	8	5
75 percent or more	49	56	95	95	61	57	3	10

[1]Percentages are based on the 99 percent of public schools with Internet access.
[2]Percentages are based on 50 percent of public schools (99 percent with Internet access times 51 percent allowing students to access the Internet outside of regular school hours) in 2001, and on 52 percent of public schools (99 percent with Internet access times 53 percent allowing students access to the Internet outside of regular school hours) in 2002.
[3]Data for combined schools are included in the totals and in analyses by other school characteristics but are not shown separately.
[4]Percent minority enrollment was not available for 31 schools in 2001. In 2002, this information was missing for 15 schools. The weighted response rate was 98.6 percent.
[5]Percent of students eligible for free or reduced-price lunch was not available for 2 schools in 2001.

SOURCE: Anne Kleiner, Laurie Lewis, and Bernard Greene, "Table 8. Percent of Public Schools Allowing Students to Access the Internet Outside of Regular School Hours, by School Characteristic: 2001–02," in *Internet Access in U.S. Public Schools and Classrooms:1994–2002,* National Center for Education Statistics, Institute of Education Sciences, U.S. Department of Education, October 2003, http://www.nces.ed.gov/surveys/frss/publications/2004011/tables.asp (accessed November 22, 2004)

population. In no area was this more apparent than with music. According Jones, 59% of online college students listened to streaming music on the Internet, as opposed to 39% of online adult Americans. Students were twice as likely to download music over the Internet than the general adult population. Only 28% of adults downloaded music in 2002, compared to 60% of college students. A full 44% of online college students took part in a file-sharing networks and shared files from their own computers. Only 26% of the general adult population took part in music file sharing.

In July 2003 Pew/Internet released another study by Steve Jones, *Let the Games Begin,* a survey conducted on the gaming habits of college students. The survey found that about 70% of college students played computer, video, or online games once in a while. Table 6.18 is a breakdown of what types of games college students played most. Some 71% said they played computer games. Video games and online games followed at 59% and 56%, respectively. The study speculates that these numbers had to do with accessibility of computer games. Computer games, such as Solitaire or Tetris variants, could be played on a laptop in class, in a computer lab, or wherever there was a computer. As to gender, men generally preferred to play video games, but a higher percentage of women played online and computer games. Roughly 60% of women played online and computer games, as opposed to 40% of men. The Pew/Internet report suggests that women enjoyed nonaction card and puzzle games, and these games could be found on a computer. Online games provided the benefit of anonymity, and many online gaming sites catered to women's interests and tastes. Video games, on the other hand, were often violent, and when they did feature female characters, the characters often had oversized breasts and were scantily clad. Of all those college students who did play games, most believed the experience to be a positive one. Half of the gamers, however, said that they used video games as a way of avoiding their studies.

DISTANCE LEARNING

Jones's September 2002 Pew/Internet report on the Internet and college revealed that distance learning was

TABLE 6.9

Percent of public schools with a Web site or Web page, 2001–02

School characteristic	2001	2002
All public schools	75	86
Instructional level[1]		
Elementary	73	85
Secondary	83	93
School size		
Less than 300	63	84
300 to 999	78	86
1,000 or more	87	94
Locale		
City	73	76
Urban fringe	79	91
Town	80	84
Rural	70	91
Percent minority enrollment[2]		
Less than 6 percent	78	92
6 to 20 percent	80	87
21 to 49 percent	78	91
50 percent or more	65	76
Percent of students eligible for free or reduced-price lunch[3]		
Less than 35 percent	83	94
35 to 49 percent	77	89
50 to 74 percent	71	86
75 percent or more	59	66

[1]Data for combined schools are included in the totals and in analyses by other school characteristics but are not shown separately.
[2]Percent minority enrollment was not available for 31 schools in 2001. In 2002, this information was missing for 15 schools. The weighted response rate was 98.6 percent.
[3]Percent of students eligible for free or reduced-price lunch was not available for 2 schools in 2001.
Note: Percentages are based on the 99 percent of public schools with Internet access. In 2001, the questionnaire asked about the school's "web site." In 2002, the wording was changed to "web site or web page."

SOURCE: Anne Kleiner, Laurie Lewis, and Bernard Greene, "Table 14. Percent of Public Schools with a Web Site or Web Page, by School Characteristics: 2001–02," in *Internet Access in U.S. Public Schools and Classrooms: 1994–2002,* National Center for Education Statistics, Institute of Education Sciences, U.S. Department of Education, October 2003, http://www.nces.ed.gov/surveys/frss/publications/2004011/tables.asp (accessed November 22, 2004)

TABLE 6.10

Where teens logged on, 2000

	Ever[1]	Most often[2]
Home	90%	83%
School	64%	11%
A friend's house	64%	3%
Library	36%	1%
Someplace else, like work or a cyber cafe	8%	1%

[1]n = 754.
[2]n = 659; teens who go online from multiple locations.

SOURCE: Amanda Lenhart, Lee Rainie, and Oliver Lewis, "Where Teens Log On," in *Teenage Life Online,* Pew Internet and American Life Project, June 20, 2001, http://www.pewinternet.org/pdfs/PIP_Teens_Report.pdf (accessed November 22, 2004). Used by permission of the Pew Internet and American Life Project, which bears no responsibility for the interpretations presented or conclusions reached based on analysis of the data.

TABLE 6.11

What teens did online, 2000

	Daily users	Less often
Send or receive email	99%	87%
Send instant messages	89%	64%
Research products online	74%	60%
Download music	73%	40%
Listen to music online	70%	52%
Visit a chat room	62%	50%
Buy products online	39%	26%
Create a Web page	34%	16%

SOURCE: Amanda Lenhart, Lee Rainie, and Oliver Lewis, "Teens Online Every Day Compared to Teens Online Less Often," in *Teenage Life Online,* Pew Internet and American Life Project, June 20, 2001, http://www.pewinternet.org/pdfs/PIP_Teens_Report.pdf (accessed November 22, 2004). Used by permission of the Pew Internet and American Life Project, which bears no responsibility for the interpretations presented or conclusions reached based on analysis of the data.

not very popular among college students in 2002. Roughly 6% of students surveyed had taken online courses for credit, and only half of these students believed the courses were worthwhile. Despite how undergraduates felt about distance learning, the number of people enrolled in distance learning courses offered by postsecondary (i.e., following high school) institutions nearly doubled between the 1997–98 and 2000–01 school years. (See Figure 6.2.) According to Tiffany Waits and Laurie Lewis in *Distance Education at Degree-Granting Postsecondary Institutions: 2000–2001* (Washington, DC: National Center for Education Statistics, July 2003), 3.1 million students were enrolled in distance learning classes. Of these, 2.9 million people were in college-level, credit-granting courses. As Figure 6.2 reveals, in 2000–01 public two-year institutions, such as community colleges, had the highest enrollment in distance education classes, followed by public four-year institutions, and private four-year institutions.

The widespread use of the Internet and personal computers largely explains the growth in distance learning. E-mail allows for affordable, convenient day-to-day communication between teachers and students. CD-ROMs and the Internet provide the possibility for completely interactive course modules and timed tests. A full 90% of institutions surveyed in the NCES study offered Internet courses where the students could review the course material on their own timetable (in other words, not in sync with everyone else in the class). Forty-three percent of institutions offered synchronous Internet courses where all students in the class were required go on the Internet at the same time to receive instruction or take tests. Nearly a third (29%) of the schools delivered the course material to students via CD-ROM. In 2003 this growth in high-tech distance learning appeared as if it would continue. Nearly 88% of institutions said they planned on increasing or introducing Internet courses into their distance learning programs in the next three years, and 39% planned to use CD-ROMs more as well.

TABLE 6.12

Teen Internet use compared to adult Internet use, 2000

	Teens	Adults
Go online for fun	84%	63%
Look for info about movies or other leisure activities	83%	65%
Use instant messaging	74%	44%
Play or download games	66%	34%
Listen to music online	59%	40%
Visit a chat room	55%	26%
Download music	53%	29%
Check sports scores online	47%	38%
Some activities show a negligible difference between teens and adults:		
Send or receive email	92%	93%
Get news	68%	66%
And there are some activities favored by adults:		
Research a purchase or new product	66%	73%
Buy a product	31%	53%
Look for health information	26%	57%

SOURCE: Amanda Lenhart, Lee Rainie, and Oliver Lewis, "Teens' Internet Use Compared to Adults," in *Teenage Life Online,* Pew Internet and American Life Project, June 20, 2001, http://www.pewinternet.org/pdfs/PIP _Teens_Report.pdf (accessed November 22, 2004). Used by permission of the Pew Internet and American Life Project, which bears no responsibility for the interpretations presented or conclusions reached based on analysis of the data.

CHEATING

Cheating is one of the biggest problems facing academia today and includes any instance in which a student breaks the rules for an assignment or test to gain an advantage over fellow classmates. A specific type of cheating known as plagiarism occurs when a student submits someone else's work as his or her own. Plagiarism itself has several forms, including purchasing a previously written paper, copying sentences or ideas from an original source document without proper attribution, or paying someone else to complete the work. In 1999 Donald L. McCabe, founder and president for the Center for Academic Integrity (CAI), conducted a survey of 2,100 college students at twenty-one campuses across the country. The survey results, which are posted in part on the CAI Web site (www.academicintegri-ty.org), revealed that a full three-quarters of all college students cheated. Of those who admitted cheating in 1999, one-third said they had cheated seriously on a test and half said they had cheated seriously on written assignment. A 2001 survey involving 4,500 high school students at twenty-five schools demonstrated that the problem was perhaps worse in high school. Seventy-four percent of high school students admitted cheating on a test in a serious manner, and 72% said they cheated on a written assignment in a serious manner. In "Colleges Clamp Down on Cheaters" (Karen Thomas, *USA Today*, June 20, 2001), McCabe noted that academic cheating will continue to escalate unless schools impose stricter policies because high school students have "defined their own rules and will take them to college." Many students cheat because they believe others are getting away with it, and they want to stay competitive.

TABLE 6.13

College students who had ever gone online compared to general population online experience, 2002

	College students (n)	General population (N)
All respondents	86%	59%
Men	87%	62%
Women	85%	56%
Whites	90%	61%
Blacks	74%	45%
Hispanics	82%	60%

N = 2,501
n = 1,092

SOURCE: Steve Jones and Mary Madden, "Table 1. Have you ever gone online?" in *The Internet Goes to College* Pew Internet and American Life Project, September 15, 2002, http://www.pewinternet.org/pdfs/PIP_College _Report.pdf (accessed November 22, 2004). Used by permission of the Pew Internet and American Life Project, which bears no responsibility for the interpretations presented or conclusions reached based on analysis of the data.

TABLE 6.14

How college students described their use of the Internet, 2002

Communicate socially	42%
Engage in work for classes	38%
Be entertained	10%
Communicate professionally	7%
Not sure/Don't know	2%

n = 1,021

SOURCE: Steve Jones and Mary Madden, "Table 2. Students use the Internet MOST OFTEN to:" in *The Internet Goes to College* Pew Internet and American Life Project, September 15, 2002, http://www.pewinternet.org/ pdfs/PIP_College_Report.pdf (accessed November 22, 2004). Used by permission of the Pew Internet and American Life Project, which bears no responsibility for the interpretations presented or conclusions reached based on analysis of the data.

The Internet and other information technologies have only served to fuel American's cheating epidemic. Phones with instant messaging allow students the opportunity to communicate with outsiders or others in class during a test. Companies that specialize in writing papers for students, commonly known as "paper mills," can now deliver papers discreetly to students via e-mail. The Internet in general provides an endless source of documents and papers from which students might copy material. Catching plagiarism on the Web, however, involves combing through countless articles and Web sites. The issue of plagiarism on the Internet is further complicated by the fact that the Internet has obscured the distinction between what information requires attribution and what information is public knowledge. According to McCabe's research, 10% of college students admitted to cut-and-paste online plagiarism in 1999. Only two years later, nearly 41% of students admitted to using the Internet to plagiarize, and as many as 68% of students did not think this type of plagiarism was a big deal. Of high school students in 2001, more than 50% admitted to using the Internet to plagiarize.

TABLE 6.15

Web sites* that received a disproportionate number of hits from college campuses, 2002

Web site	The primary activity that takes place at the site	The proportion of site traffic that comes from college PCs (August 2002)
livejournal.com	Online journal posting service	20.1%
audiogalaxy.com	Peer-to-peer file-sharing service	18.1
billboard.com	Online music magazine	17.7
mircx.com	Provides access to IRC and related downloads	17.3
imesh.com	Peer-to-peer file-sharing service	17.1
fastweb.com	College and scholarship search engine	17.1
hotornot.com	Entertainment site for rating individuals' appearances	17.0
thespark.com	Entertainment and humor site	16.7
duenow.com	Online homework resources for students	16.5
azlyrics.com	Resource for song lyrics	16.4
winamp.com	Entertainment site with free Winamp downloads	15.7
astraweb.com	Portal to MP3 and song lyrics search engines	15.5
badassbuddy.com	Source for Instant Messenger buddy icons	15.5
blizzard.com	Online gaming site	15.1
fileplanet.com	Online gaming site	15.0
abercrombie.com	Retail site for Abercrombie and Fitch apparel	14.9
picturetrail.com	Online photo album services	14.6
lyrics.com	Song lyric search engine	14.6
blackplanet.com	Online community for African Americans	14.4
gamefaqs.com	Gaming information site	14.4

*Defined as sites with more than 1 million total U.S. home, work and college visitors in August 2002

SOURCE: Steve Jones and Mary Madden, "20 Large Web Sites Where the Proportion of Traffic from College Students is Particularly High," in *Pew Internet and American Life Project Data Memo: College Students and the Web,* "Pew Internet and American Life Project, September 2002, http://www.pewinternet.org/pdfs/ PIP_College_Memo.pdf (accessed November 22, 2004). Used by permission of the Pew Internet and American Life Project, which bears no responsibility for the interpretations presented or conclusions reached based on analysis of the data.

The CAI Web site suggested that one of the more effective ways to control cheating is to set up an honor code. Honor codes place the responsibility not to cheat on the student. Teachers monitor students less and rely on other students to turn in cheating classmates. Since the cheater has been made aware of the rules, penalties in honor code schools can be very stiff. According to the CAI Web site, honor codes typically reduced cheating on tests by one-third to one-half of normal levels. To catch plagiarizers some schools are also using high-tech online services. In her *USA Today* article, Thomas reported that the service teachers relied on most in 2002 was Turnitin.com. This online service receives papers from teachers and scans them into a database. The papers then are checked against more than two billion Web sites, a quarter of a million previously submitted student papers, and a number of books and encyclopedias. The site handled nearly six thousand papers daily in 2002. Of these, more than 30% of papers typically turned out to be fakes (i.e., from a paper mill), and 75% contained plagiarized text from the Internet.

FIGURE 6.2

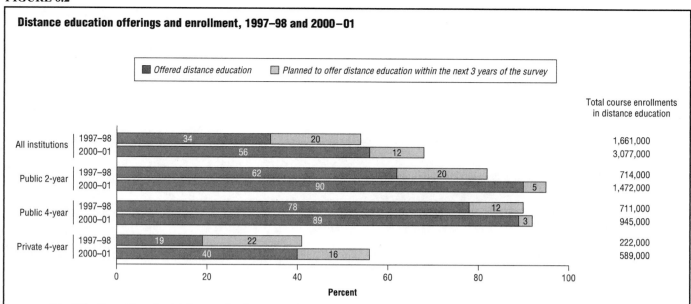

Distance education offerings and enrollment, 1997–98 and 2000–01

■ *Offered distance education* ☐ *Planned to offer distance education within the next 3 years of the survey*

				Total course enrollments in distance education
All institutions	1997–98	34	20	1,661,000
	2000–01	56	12	3,077,000
Public 2-year	1997–98	62	20	714,000
	2000–01	90	5	1,472,000
Public 4-year	1997–98	78	12	711,000
	2000–01	89	3	945,000
Private 4-year	1997–98	19	22	222,000
	2000–01	40	16	589,000

Percent (0, 20, 40, 60, 80, 100)

SOURCE: John Wirt, Susan Choy, Patrick Rooney, Stephen Provasnik, Anindita Sen, Richard Tobin, Barbara Kridl, and Andrea Livingston, "Distance Education Offerings and Enrollment: Percentage of 2-year and 4-year Postsecondary Institutions Offering Distance Education Courses or Planning to Offer Them Within the Next 3 Years of the Survey and Total Course Enrollments, by Type of Institution: 1997–98 and 2000–01," in *The Condition of Education 2004,* National Center for Education Statistics, Institute of Education Sciences, U.S. Department of Education, June 2004, http://www.nces.ed.gov/pubs2004/2004077.pdf (accessed November 22, 2004)

TABLE 6.16

Internet communication habits of college students, 2002

Friends	72%
Family	10%
Professors	7%
Romantic partners	6%
Work colleagues	5%

n = 1,021

SOURCE: Steve Jones and Mary Madden, "Table 6. With Whom Do Students Communicate Most While Using the Internet?" in *The Internet Goes to College,* Pew Internet and American Life Project, September 15, 2002, http://www.pewinternet.org/pdfs/PIP_College_Report.pdf (accessed November 22, 2004). Used by permission of the Pew Internet and American Life Project, which bears no responsibility for the interpretations presented or conclusions reached based on analysis of the data.

TABLE 6.17

Online communication tools used by college students, 2002

Email	62%
Instant messaging	29%
Web boards	5%
Chat rooms	2%
Newsgroups	1%

n = 1,021

SOURCE: Steve Jones and Mary Madden, "Table 7. Internet Communications Tools Used Most by College Students," in *The Internet Goes to College,* Pew Internet and American Life Project, September 15, 2002, http://www.pewinternet.org/pdfs/PIP_College_Report.pdf (accessed November 22, 2004). Used by permission of the Pew Internet and American Life Project, which bears no responsibility for the interpretations presented or conclusions reached based on analysis of the data.

TABLE 6.18

Types of electronic games played by college students, 2002

Play computer games	71%
Play video games	59%
Play online games	56%

n = 1,162

SOURCE: Steve Jones, "Table 2. Do you ever:" in *Let the Games Begin,* Pew Internet and American Life Project, July 6, 2003, http://www.pewinternet.org/pdfs/PIP_College_Gaming_Reporta.pdf (accessed November 22, 2004). Used by permission of the Pew Internet and American Life Project, which bears no responsibility for the interpretations presented or conclusions reached based on analysis of the data.

CHAPTER 7

INFORMATION TECHNOLOGY AND GOVERNMENT

Since the 1990s, government bodies in the United States at the local, state, and federal level have made a concerted effort to use the Internet and other information technologies to streamline their operations and their dealings with the public. Much of this effort has been focused on making information available via the Internet. Local and municipal governments began posting meeting minutes and agendas online. Many states erected Web sites that allowed citizens to renew registrations and obtain licenses online. The federal government brought myriad services and information to the Web, allowing Americans to do everything from applying for a patent online to reviewing the holdings of the Smithsonian Institution. Even politicians began to campaign and raise money online. The American public has taken advantage of these services. According to John B. Horrigan in *How Americans Get in Touch with Government*, a May 2004 Pew Internet & American Life Project (Pew/Internet) report, nearly eighty-three million people said they had looked for information on a federal Web site in 2003, which represents an increase of seventeen million people from the year before.

Various government entities have employed other forms of information technology to streamline services outside of cyberspace. After the hotly contested presidential race of 2000, state election commissions replaced many of the aging voting systems with electronic touch-screen and optical scanning systems. These systems made the voting booth accessible for many disabled people and presumably led to more accurate ballot totals in elections. Advances in communications and detection systems have also given rise to networks along American highways that monitor traffic and weather conditions on a real-time basis. In 1999 the federal government designated 511 as the universal phone number by which people could access these systems to obtain details on traffic and weather in their area. As of fall 2004, the 511 system serviced more than seventy-one million people in twenty-four cities.

TABLE 7.1

Reasons for contacting the government, 2003

	All government patrons	Government patrons with very urgent reason	Government patrons with very complicated reason
Transaction	30%	26%	22%
Specific question	25	23	19
Express opinion	19	16	24
Solving a problem	11	23	19
Some other purpose	7	7	8
Combination of above	5	5	5

n = 1,657

SOURCE: John Horrigan, "Reason for Last Contact with Government," in *How Americans Get in Touch with Government,* Pew Internet and American Life Project, May 24, 2004, http://www.pewinternet.org/pdfs/PIP_E-Gov _Report_0504.pdf (accessed December 11, 2004). Used by permission of the Pew Internet and American Life Project, which bears no responsibility for the interpretations presented or conclusions reached based on analysis of the data.

COMMUNICATING WITH GOVERNMENT

American citizens are constantly interacting with their government. According to Horrigan in *How Americans Get in Touch with Government*, some sixty-eight million American adults (54%) said they contacted the government yearly by electronic or other means. (These numbers do not include the filing of taxes.) As Table 7.1 shows, many of those Americans (30%) who dealt with the government in 2003 did so to complete a transaction, which included obtaining a license or getting a loan. Other Americans (25%) wanted specific questions answered. Still others felt the need to express an opinion (19%) about topics including the environment, the war in Iraq, and transportation issues.

Some 42% of the Americans surveyed by Pew/Internet for *How Americans Get in Touch with Government* said they contacted the government by telephone, versus 47% who reached the government electronically by e-mail or Web site. (See Table 7.2.) Perhaps due to the lack of consistency and quality associated with government Web sites, more people preferred to reach the government by phone. According to Horrigan, 40% of Americans reported that the phone was the best way to contact the government, while 24% believed the Internet was better. Even among Internet users who contacted the government, traditional means of reaching the government won out over electronic means. Fifty-five percent of Internet users said they were more likely to turn to the telephone or write a traditional letter; 53% said they preferred to e-mail or visit a Web site. Typically, Americans were more likely to call a government office if the matter was urgent or complex, such as if a passport needed to be renewed on short notice. People used the Internet more frequently to take care of government transactions (e.g., car registration renewal) and to obtain information. (See Table 7.3.)

Having Internet service at home or work increased the likelihood that respondents had contacted the government, according to *How Americans Get in Touch with Government*. In fact, 72% of Internet users said they had contacted the government sometime in the previous year. Only 23% of offline Americans did so. Part of this trend had to do with the fact that wealthier, highly educated people both used the Internet more and contacted the government more regularly than people with lower incomes and less education.

Why Americans Contact the Government

Table 7.4, taken from *How Americans Get in Touch with Government*, illustrates the ways Internet users accessed information on government Web sites as of 2003. By far, the most popular activity was searching for information. Two-thirds (66%) of all Internet users reported looking for information from a local, state, or federal Web site in 2003, which represented an increase of 10% (seventeen million people) from 2002. This included searching for everything from a NASA launch timetable to a brochure on local burning laws. Researching official

documents, such as U.S. Census statistics, came in second, with 41% of Internet users partaking in this activity. Obtaining recreational or tourist information on such destinations as national parks and monuments was the third most popular activity. Not all experiences with government Web sites, however, were positive. (See Table 7.5.) Of those who used a Web site to contact the government, 33% said that the last time they tried, the government site did not contain the information they needed. Twenty percent felt that site was difficult to navigate, and 18% said they had trouble figuring out where to go on the site.

The Internet has also lent itself to those who want to express their opinions to government officials. Roughly one-third (30%) of Internet users surveyed for *How Americans Get in Touch with Government* said they had used e-mail to try to change a policy or a politician's vote in 2003. This represented a dramatic increase from 2001, when only 19% of people surveyed had contacted a government official or politician to express a personal opinion. Nearly 15% of those who contacted the government about an issue of policy in 2003 did so because of an environmental issue. Eleven percent said that their message involved education, and another 11% cited tax issues. The

TABLE 7.2

How people contacted government officials, 2003

	Method of last contact	Preferred means of contact
Telephone	42%	40%
Web site	29	24
In person	20	13
Email	18	11
Letter	17	10

n = 1,657

SOURCE: John Horrigan, "Means of Contacting Government," in *How Americans Get in Touch with Government,* Pew Internet and American Life Project, May 24, 2004, http://www.pewinternet.org/pdfs/PIP_E-Gov_Report _0504.pdf (accessed December 11, 2004). Used by permission of the Pew Internet and American Life Project, which bears no responsibility for the interpretations presented or conclusions reached based on analysis of the data.

TABLE 7.3

Preferred means of contacting the government, by reason for contact, 2003

	Problem was very complex or urgent	Contacted government to solve problem	Contacted government for transaction	Contacted government to get information
Telephone	46%	47%	40%	41%
Web site	14	17	30	33
In person	16	15	15	10
Email	10	9	6	10
Letter	11	9	7	4

n = 1,657

SOURCE: John Horrigan, "Preferred Means of Contacting the Government by Reason for Contact," in *How Americans Get in Touch with Government,* Pew Internet and American Life Project, May 24, 2004, http://www.pewinternet.org/pdfs/PIP_E-Gov_Report_0504.pdf (accessed December 11, 2004). Used by permission of the Pew Internet and American Life Project, which bears no responsibility for the interpretations presented or conclusions reached based on analysis of the data.

TABLE 7.4

How Internet users accessed government information, 2003

Look for information from a local, state, or federal government Web site	66%
Research official government documents or statistics	41
Get recreational or tourist information	34
Get advice or information from a government agency about a health or safety issue	28
Send email to local, state, or federal government	27
Get information about or apply for government benefits	23

N = 1,899

SOURCE: John Horrigan, "Percent of Internet Users Who Have Ever Done the Following Things Online," in *How Americans Get in Touch with Government*, Pew Internet and American Life Project, May 24, 2004, http://www.pewinternet.org/pdfs/PIP_E-Gov_Report_0504.pdf (accessed December 11, 2004). Used by permission of the Pew Internet and American Life Project, which bears no responsibility for the interpretations presented or conclusions reached based on analysis of the data.

TABLE 7.5

Problems encountered with government Web sites, 2003

	Yes	No
Web site didn't have information needed	33%	65%
Web site was difficult to navigate or figure out	20	79
Had difficulty figuring out what site to go to	18	83
Site had bad or outdated links	16	85
Experienced difficulty downloading forms or instructions	13	86

n = 480

SOURCE: John Horrigan, "Problems Encountered at Government Web Sites," in *How Americans Get in Touch with Government*, Pew Internet and American Life Project,May 24,2004,http://www.pewinternet.org/pdfs/PIP_E-Gov_Report_0504.pdf (accessed December 11, 2004). Used by permission of the Pew Internet and American Life Project, which bears no responsibility for the interpretations presented or conclusions reached based onanalysis of the data.

TABLE 7.6

Features found on municipal Web sites, 2002

Featured on site	Percent
City staff directory	78%
Meeting agendas with minutes	71%
Information on receiving municipal services	71%
Calendars for meetings/events	70%
City staff directory with email links	61%
Access to zoning/city planning information	54%
Budget/tax information	41%
Municipal forms and applications	40%
Voting information	34%
Information for citizen lobbying	18%

N = 520.

SOURCE: Elana Lawson and Lee Rainie, "The Features on Municipal Web Sites," in *Digital Town Hall*, Pew Internet and American Life Project, October 2, 2004, http://www.pewinternet.org/pdfs/PIP_Digital_Town_Hall.pdf (accessed December 11, 2004). Used by permission of the Pew Internet and American Life Project, which bears no responsibility for the interpretations presented or conclusions reached based on analysis of the data.

Iraq war, health care, and civil rights issues were each the subject of 10% of personal opinion messages.

Online Contacts with State and Local Government

According to Horrigan in *How Americans Get in Touch with Government*, adults went online more frequently to contact their state government than their local governments or the federal government. Twenty-three percent of those surveyed said that they had been in touch with their local government online, and 37% said they had contacted their state government. As of late 2004, every state government and the District of Columbia had a Web site that contained information on various government agencies, policies, and procedures. Many states allowed residents to complete a few administrative tasks online such as renewing a vehicle registration or obtaining a fishing license. Some states even conducted more complex transactions online. In Washington State, for example, residents could file a formal consumer fraud complaint on the attorney general's Web site. In Washington, D.C., residents or visitors could pay a parking ticket online.

Despite the relatively low number of people contacting municipal governments via the Internet, 80% of local governments had a Web site in 2002, according to Elena Larsen and Lee Rainie in *Digital Town Hall* (Washington, DC: Pew Internet & American Life Project, October 2, 2002). Table 7.6 lists the information presented most on these municipal Web sites. A city staff directory appeared on nearly 78% of municipal Web sites. Seventy-one percent of local government Web sites reported listing both meeting agendas with minutes and city services information.

For municipal governments, e-mail appeared to play a bigger role than the Web. Unlike federal or even state government politicians, many local government leaders have time to answer e-mail personally. In fact, some 82% of online municipal government officials (e.g., mayors and city council members) replied that they used e-mail to communicate with citizens in the October 2002 Pew/Internet report. Of these, roughly two-thirds (60%) did so on a weekly basis, and one-fifth (21%) did so on a daily basis. Some of these officials employed e-mail to actively gain insight into what their constituents thought. Twenty-one percent utilized e-mail to get feedback on a community issue, and 13% reported using e-mail to float new ideas among citizens. For the most part, city officials believed that e-mails from their constituents did have an impact on local government. Seventy-three percent replied that they had a better understanding of community opinion by reading e-mails sent by residents, and 61% agreed that e-mail facilitates the discussion of complex issues. Opinions were mixed among politicians with regards to mass e-mail campaigns designed to sway their opinion on an issue. Roughly 35% of officials surveyed had been the target of mass mailings, and of these, 48% said the mass mailings had not had any persuasive power.

THE FEDERAL GOVERNMENT AND INTERNET TECHNOLOGIES

Since the early 1990s, hundreds of federal government Web sites have sprung up on the Internet. In the beginning, each agency or division developed its Web site in a unique way, offering varying levels of accessibility to the user. Some were useful and informative. For instance, in 1994, the U.S. Census Bureau launched the first U.S. government World Wide Web portal. From the start, hundreds of U.S. Census records from decades past could be easily viewed on the Web site. The Internal Revenue Service (IRS) also maintained a useful site. In 1997 the IRS allowed people to download tax forms and file their taxes electronically. Nearly one million tax returns were filed from home computers in 1997. However, many other government Web sites, such as many of the National Oceanic and Atmospheric Administration (NOAA) Web sites, offered citizens very little in the way of practical information or accessibility. Overall, by the late 1990s, profit-driven commercial Web sites far outshone government Web sites in terms of both appearance and functionality. Seeing the untapped potential of numerous government Web sites, the Congress and the White House put through a series of initiatives and laws to make federal government Web sites and services more accessible to the American people.

Government Paperwork Elimination Act (GPEA)

One of the first major Congressional acts designed to improve the functionality of government Web sites was the Government Paperwork Elimination Act (GPEA) of 1998. GPEA required that by October 2003 each government agency should provide people, wherever possible, with the option of submitting information or transacting business electronically. The act mandated that forms and documents involved in government transactions be placed online and that electronic signature systems be put in place to replace paper signatures. Companies, for instance, that made electronic components for NASA projects would have the option to bid for NASA contracts, complete all paperwork with regard to sale of the merchandise, and receive payment without having to use paper. Similarly, individuals would have the option to apply for a patent online or to fill out a U.S. Census survey on the Internet.

FedForms.gov

FedForms.gov (www.fedforms.gov) was created as a portal to all electronic forms available from all federal government agencies. Table 7.7, published by the White House Office of Budget and Management, shows the percentage of government transactions that were compliant to GPEA standards as of the October 2003 deadline. Though over half (56%) of government transactions could be performed electronically, roughly one-tenth (12%) of transactions for one reason or another did not meet the deadline and were expected to be completed after 2003. A

TABLE 7.7

Compliance of government agencies to the Government Paper Elimination Act (GPEA), December 2003

	Percentage	Number of transactions
Transactions compliant as of October 21, 2003	56%	4,040
Transactions compliant after October 21, 2003*	12%	898
Transactions that will not be completed	32%	2,249
Total transactions reported		**7,187**

*Agencies provided an expected date of completion of 2004 and beyond

SOURCE: "Table 1. Summary of Federal Government Compliance," in *FY 2003 Report to Congress on Implementation of the E-Government Act*, Office of Management and Budget, Executive Office of the President of the United States, March 8, 2004, http://www.whitehouse.gov/omb/egov/downloads/2003egov_report.pdf (accessed December 11, 2004)

full 32% of government transactions, however, were not deemed suitable for electronic transactions. These included transactions such as customs forms, which are typically filled out in paper on an airplane approaching a U.S. airport, on a ship as it nears a U.S. port, or at an entry point along the border with Canada or Mexico.

E-government Act of 2002

In 2001 President Bush initiated the President's Management Agenda, which contained a number of initiatives intended to expand the role of the Internet in the federal government beyond the scope of GPEA. Many of these initiatives were made law in 2002 when the Congress passed the E-government Act of 2002. The E-government Act was a broad-reaching act designed to streamline government Web sites and to provide a wide range of services to the American people via the Internet. The act established an E-government Fund to provide money for agencies that could not afford Information Technology (IT) and Web site development. According to the *FY 2003 Report to Congress on Implementation of the E-government Act* (Washington, DC: Office of Management and Budget, March 8, 2004), for instance, $200,000 of the fund was given to the Federal Emergency Management Agency in 2003 to set up DisasterHelp.gov—a Web site that provided local, state, and federal emergency managers with disaster management information. The E-government Act also created the Office of Electronic Government (led by an administrator appointed by the president) and the Chief Information Officers Council, which was to be made up of all the Chief Information Officers from the major government agencies. (Chief information officers generally oversee Web development in a government agency.) The council and the e-government administrator were to ensure that the various agencies complied with the goals and provisions of the act.

Many of these goals and provisions established standards for government Web sites that were already in operation. Existing government Web sites were required to provide links to organization policy and hierarchy on the front page and to present their information in a way that was easily searchable. Many agencies with multiple Web sites, such as NASA or the Environmental Protection Agency, were asked to consolidate their sites so that all the information for the public could be reached within a few clicks of the agency's main page. The E-government Act also supported new Web sites designed to provide basic services for American citizens. The FirstGov.gov (www.first-gov.gov) site was deemed the official portal for all federal government Web sites. Firstgov.gov provided links to more than 22,000 federal Web sites and state Web sites as well as a hierarchical index of all government organizations, according to an April 2003 White House report entitled *E-government Strategy*. In 2003 the site averaged over sixteen million page views per month from 5.5 million Internet users. Another Web site that the E-government Act officially authorized was Regulations.gov (www.regulations.gov), which was launched in January 2003. Regulations.gov lists pending regulations proposed by government agencies and allows citizens and non-governmental agencies to comment on the regulations. According to the E-government Act, the government agencies review the comments on Regulations.gov before putting a regulation into effect, effectively providing the American people with the ability to influence government regulation—a privilege previously reserved largely for lobbyists.

As a result of these White House initiatives and Congressional acts supporting e-government, federal agencies have come to offer many valuable online services to Americans. In 2002, for instance, the Department of Education made it possible for parents and students to apply online for a majority of the college grants and loans offered by the Department of Education. The Department of Housing and Urban Development (HUD) erected a number of Internet kiosks throughout cities across the United States where those in need of affordable housing could access the HUD database to find federally owned homes to buy. In 2003 nearly 300,000 people used such kiosks, according to the *FY 2003 Report to Congress on Implementation of the E-government Act*. Information technology has also been used to save citizens money and to protect Americans against possible terrorist threats. The Department of Homeland Security implemented the Student and Exchange Visitor Information System (SEVIS) in 2002. The system keeps track of the visa status of foreign students and their dependents and immediately flags those who overstay their visas. According to the report to Congress on E-government, the system reduced conventional visa monitoring costs for international students from $4.5 million annually to $0.8 million.

SATISFACTION WITH GOVERNMENT WEB SITES. Although some dissatisfaction exists with federal government Web sites, the American people seemed to be happy with the improvements in e-government. Since 2003 the

U.S. government has tracked Web sites in its annual American Customer Service Index (ACSI). The index measures how satisfied the American people are with various aspects of the federal government. Table 7.8 reveals that out of the Web sites on the survey, the American people were happiest with the National Institutes of Health's MedlinePlus Web site (www.medlineplus.gov) in 2004. Medline Plus scored eighty-six out of a possible one hundred on the index. The lowest score among the government Web sites was for the main site of the General Services Administration (www.gsa.gov) with a score of fifty-five in 2004.

Government Regulation

The federal government has passed very few laws designed to control Internet commerce or content compared with other broadcasting media. The Federal Communications Commission, which regulates all television and radio content, treats the Internet more like print media than like broadcast media. Unless a major law is being violated, people can publish all manner of pornography, illicit writing, and misleading information on the Internet without fear of repercussion. Activities that are illegal in many states or the United States as a whole, such as gambling or purchasing Cuban cigars, can be done online with little fear of prosecution. In addition, most purchases made on the Internet were not subject to local sales tax as of 2004, and states and municipalities were forbidden by federal law to tax Internet use.

For the most part, Congress has been wary of placing restrictions or taxes on the Internet. In fact, in November 2004 the Congress extended the tax ban on both interstate Internet commerce and Internet service to 2007. As for content, Congress is wary of potential public backlash that it would encounter if it regulated such activities as Internet pornography or gambling. Enforcing strict regulations would be difficult as well. Unlike radio or television, publishing content on the Web is exceedingly easy. Anyone, provided he or she has willing participants, can set up a Web server for a couple of thousand dollars, take pornographic pictures, and post them on the Internet. If the U.S. government did make gambling or pornography on the Internet illegal altogether, such sites could easily be moved offshore where U.S. laws would not apply. Another option would be to place restrictions and controls on all computers and Web browsers in the United States. Such a plan may have been feasible back in the early 1990s, when Internet backbones and browsers were still in the development phase. Placing such controls on the tens of millions of current computers and Web browsers now in use would neither be well received nor easily implemented.

CONTROLLING THE ASSAULT OF NON-SOLICITED PORNOGRAPHY AND MARKETING ACT OF 2003 (CAN-SPAM). The little Internet regulation that the government has

TABLE 7.8

American Consumer Satisfaction Index (ACSI) scores for e-government Web sites, 2004

ID	Agency/department	Customer segment	2004
	E-Government U.S. agency/department/office	Website	
	E-commerce/transactions		
Treasury	United States Mint, Treasury	Online Catalog—http://catalog.usmint.gov	81
FSA	Federal Student Aid, Education	Free Application for Federal Student Aid, FAFSA website—www.fafsa.ed.gov	81
SSA	SSA Retirement Planner	SSA Retirement Planner—http://www.socialsecurity.gov/r&m1.htm	78
PBGC	Pension Benefit Guaranty Corporation	PBGC main website—www.pbgc.gov	68
GSA	GSA Global Supply website	GSA Global Supply website—https://www.globalsupply.gsa.gov	67
GSA Advantage	General Services Administration	GSA Advantage website—https://www.gsaadvantage.gov	65
	Information/news		
NLM	National Library of Medicine, National Institutes of Health, HHS	MedlinePlus—http://medlineplus.gov	86
NLM	National Library of Medicine, National Institutes of Health, HHS	Medline Plus en español—http://medlineplus.gov/esp/	83
OWH	Office on Women's Health, HHS	National Women's Health Information Center (NWHIC) main website—www.4woman.gov	83
GSA	General Services Administration	Federal Citizen Information Center—www.pueblo.gsa.gov/	80
DOJ	National Criminal Justice Reference Service, Justice	NCJRS website—www.ncjrs.org	77
DOJ	National Institute of Justice, Justice	NIJ main website—http://www.ojp.gov/nij	77
NLM	National Library of Medicine, National Institutes of Health, HHS	TOXNET—http://toxnet.nlm.nih.gov	76
DOJ	Office of Juvenile Justice and Delinquency Prevention, Justice	OJJDP website—http://ojjdp.ncjrs.org	76
HHS	National Library of Medicine, National Institutes of Health, HHS	AIDSinfo—http://aidsinfo.nih.gov/	76
DOL	Bureau of Labor Statistics	BLS Occupational Outlook Handbook—www.bls.gov/oco/	75
HHS	National Institute of Allergies and Infectious Diseases, HHS	NIAID main website—www.niaid.nih.gov	75
CDC	Center for Disease Control, HHS	CDC main website—www.cdc.gov	74
SSA	Social Security Administration	SFA FAQ—http://ssa-custhelp.ssa.gov	73
Forest	Forest Service, Agriculture	Forest Service main website—http://www.fs.fed.us	72
State	Department of State	U.S. Department of State Education USA—http://educationusa.state.gov	72
EIA	Energy Information Administration, Energy	Energy Information Administration—www.eia.doe.gov	70
ERS	Economic Research Service, Agriculture	ERS main website—www.ers.usda.gov	70
NARA	National Archives & Records Administration	NARA main public website—www.archives.gov	70
DOJ	Bureau of Justice Assistance, Justice	BJA main website—http://www.ojp.usdoj.gov/BJA	69
FAS	Foreign Agricultural Service, Agriculture	FAS main website—www.fas.usda.gov	68
NAL	National Agricultural Library, Agriculture	NAL main website—www.nal.usda.gov	68
FSIS	Food Safety and Inspection Service, Agriculture	FSIS main website—www.fsis.usda.gov	67
State	Department of State	U.S. Embassy, Belgium website (Dutch)—www.usembassy.be/nl/nl.main.html	67
State	International Information Programs, State	IIP main website—http://usinfo.state.gov	66
State	Department of State	U.S. Embassy, Belgium main website—www.usembassy.be/main.html	64
State	Department of State	Student website—http://future.state.gov	64
State	Department of State	U.S. Embassy, Belgium website (French)—www.usembassy.be/fr/fr.main.html	63
CSREES	Cooperative State Research, Education, and Extension Service, Agriculture	CSREES main website—www.csrees.usda.gov	62
DOL	Employment Standards Administration, Labor	ESA main website—www.union-reports.dol.gov	61
NARA	National Archives & Records Administration	NARA AAD—Access to Archival Databases—http://www.archives gov/aad/index.html	59
	Portals/department main sites		
NCI	National Cancer Institute, National Institutes of Health, HHS	National Cancer Institute main website—www.cancer.gov	80
NARA	National Archives & Records Administration	NARA Presidential Library websites—http://.archives.gov/presidential_libraries/index.html	79
Commerce	National Institute of Standards and Technology, Commerce	NIST main website—www.nist.gov	77
NASA	National Aeronautics and Space Administration	NASA main website—www.nasa.gov	77
NLM	National Library of Medicine, HHS	NLM main website—www.nlm.nih.gov	76
FDIC	Federal Deposit Insurance Corporation	FDIC main website—www.fdic.gov	74
SSA	Social Security Administration	SSA main website—www.socialsecurity.gov	73
State	Department of State	Department of State main website—www.state.gov	73
GSA	General Services Administration	FirstGov.gov website (Spanish)—http://firstgov.gov/Espanol/index.shtml	72
GSA	General Services Administration	FirstGov.gov website—www.firstgov.gov	72
GAO	Government Accountability Office	GAO main public website—www.gao.gov	71
Treasury	Department of the Treasury	Treasury main website—www.treasury.gov	69
FAA	Federal Aviation Administration	FAA main website—www.faa.gov	68
USPTO	United States Patent & Trademark Office	USPTO main website—www.uspto.gov	66
GSA	General Services Administration	GSA main website—www.gsa.gov	55
	Recruitment/careers		
CIA	Central Intelligence Agency	Recruitment website—www.cia.gov/employment	79
OPM	Office of Personnel Management	Recruitment website—www.usajobs.opm.gov	76
State	Department of State	Recruitment website—www.careers.state.gov	76

SOURCE: Adapted from "ACSI Scores for U.S. Federal Government," Federal Consulting Group, a franchise of the U.S. Department of Treasury, December 14, 2004, http://www.theacsi.org/government/govt-04.html (accessed January 19, 2005)

enacted has met with mixed results. In January 2004 the CAN-SPAM Act went into effect. The act, passed by Congress in 2003, required that all spam contain a legitimate return address as well as instructions on how to opt out of receiving additional spam from the sender. Spam must also state in the subject line if the e-mail is pornographic in

TABLE 7.9

Public opinion on the amount of spam received after passage of CAN-SPAM legislation, February 2004

	Those with personal email accounts (N=1,099)	Those with work-related email accounts (N=576)
Getting more spam	24%	19%
Getting less spam	20%	11%
Haven't noticed a change	53%	53%
Never got spam or don't know	3%	18%

SOURCE: Lee Rainie and Deborah Fallows, "Since January 1, have you noticed any change in the amount of spam you receive?" in *Pew Internet and American Life Project Data Memo: the impact of the CAN-SPAM legislation*," Pew Internet and American Life Project, March 2004, http://www.pewinternet.org/pdfs/PIP_Data_Memo_on_Spam.pdf (accessed December 11, 2004). Used by permission of the Pew Internet and American Life Project, which bears no responsibility for the interpretations presented or conclusions reached based on analysis of the data.

TABLE 7.10

The types of Web sites people used to get political news and information, 2004

	Broadband users	Dial-up users
Web site of major news organizations, such as CNN.com	72%	51%
Web site of an international news site such as al Jazeera	24	14
Web site of alternative news site like AlterNet.org or NewsMax.com	16	7
Web site of politically liberal group such as People for the American Way or MoveOn.org	15	7
JohnKerry.com, the Democratic nominee's official site	14	8
GeorgeWBush.com, the president's official re-election site	13	7
RNC.com, the official site of the Republican National Committee	11	5
Web site of a politically conservative group such as the American Enterprise Institute or the Christian Coalition	10	11
DNC.com, the official site of the Democratic National Committee	6	6

SOURCE: John Horrigan, Kelly Garrett, and Paul Resnick, "The Kind of Web Sites People Use to Get Political News and Information," in *The Internet and Democratic Debate*, Pew Internet and American Life Project, October 27, 2004, http://www.pewinternet.org/pdfs/PIP_Political_Info_Report.pdf (accessed December 11, 2004). Used by permission of the Pew Internet and American Life Project, which bears no responsibility for the interpretations presented or conclusions reached based on analysis of the data.

nature. Violators of these rules were to be subject to heavy fines. According to Lee Rainie and Deborah Fallows in *The CAN-SPAM Act Has Not Helped Most Email Users So Far* (Washington, DC: Pew Internet & American Life Project, March 17, 2004), three months after the act took effect, no change had occurred in the level of spam received by Americans. Table 7.9 reveals that a vast majority of users with personal e-mail accounts surveyed (77%) reported receiving either the same amount of spam or more spam in the three months the act had been in effect.

CHILDREN'S INTERNET PROTECTION ACT (CIPA). A more successful regulation is the Children's Internet Protection Act (CIPA) of 2000. Under the act, public schools and libraries were required to keep minors from viewing explicitly sexual content on public school and library computers. If these organizations did not comply, they would no longer receive government assistance in buying IT equipment. According to a 2002 National Center for Education Statistics (NCES) survey, 99% of elementary and secondary public schools had complied with CIPA by 2002. Regulations involving children's welfare, however, have always been warmly received by the public, and this fact may account for CIPA's success.

ELECTIONS AND POLITICS

The Internet has not only influenced how people interact with the government, but how people approach politics as well. The number of people who read political news online increased dramatically between 2000 and 2004. According to an October 2004 Pew/Internet Report entitled *The Internet and Democratic Debate*, sixty-three million Americans got at least some of their political news from the Internet by the middle of 2004. Less than half that number of Americans (thirty million) had gone online to review political news in 2000. ComScore Media Metrix reported in a November 15, 2004, press release that some

twenty-five million Americans, one-sixth of all Internet users, visited a political Web site in October 2004. The JohnKerry.com Web site drew in 3.7 million visitors in the month before the presidential election, while GeorgeW-Bush.com logged 3.2 million visitors.

As Table 7.10 reveals, most Internet users did not look for their information and political news on official political candidate sites. A large majority of dial-up (51%) and broadband (72%) Internet users got their online political information from major news organizations such as CNN or MSNBC, according to the October 2004 Pew/Internet report *The Internet and Democratic Debate*. The second most popular Web sites were international sites, including those maintained by al Jazeera and the British Broadcasting Corporation (BBC). Alternative news sources, such as AlterNet.org and NewsMax.com, were the third most popular and tended to appeal to liberals. Individual candidate sites came in fifth and sixth in the survey. According to the Pew/Internet poll, Americans preferred not to get their news from a biased source. Nearly two-thirds (61%) of Americans replied that they wanted news sources that did not represent a political point of view. However, a quarter of the survey respondents (27%) did prefer news sources that shared their point of view, while 18% said they used sources that challenged their views.

Preferred News Sources

How does the Internet compare to other media with regard to where people get their news? Table 7.11 shows

TABLE 7.11

Basic news sources on an average day, June 2004

	All respondents	Broadband-at home	Dial-up at home	Non-internet users
Television	74%	72%	77%	73%
Radio	54	60	61	39
Newspapers	51	52	56	45
Email (including listservs) or the web	34	64	43	*
Magazines	21	26	22	15

Survey of 1,510 Americans adults (age 18 and older). "At home" internet users represent 93% of all internet users in the sample.

SOURCE: John Horrigan, Kelly Garrett, and Paul Resnick, "People's Basic News Sources on the Average Day," in *The Internet and Democratic Debate*, Pew Internet and American Life Project, October 27, 2004, http://www.pewinternet.org/pdfs/PIP_Political_Info_Report.pdf (accessed December 11, 2004). Used by permission of the Pew Internet and American Life Project, which bears no responsibility for the interpretations presented or conclusions reached based on analysis of the data.

TABLE 7.12

People's main sources of presidential campaign news over time, January 2000, January 2004, and June 2004

	June 2004	January 2004	January 2000
Television	78%	78%	86%
Newspaper	38	38	36
Radio	16	15	14
Internet and email (including listservs)	15	13	7
Magazines	4	2	4

Survey of 1,510 American adults (age 18 and older). Numbers add to more than 100 due to multiple responses.

SOURCE: John Horrigan, Kelly Garrett, and Paul Resnick, "People's Main Sources of Campaign News over Time," in *The Internet and Democratic Debate*, Pew Internet and American Life Project, October 27, 2004, http://www.pewinternet.org/pdfs/PIP_Political_Info_Report.pdf (accessed December 11, 2004). Used by permission of the Pew Internet and American Life Project, which bears no responsibility for the interpretations presented or conclusions reached based on analysis of the data.

that when it comes to the basic news sources people use on an average day, television was still number one in June 2004. Some 74% of respondents in *The Internet and Democratic Debate* reported that the television was their source for daily news. In terms of all people surveyed, the Internet came in fourth with only 34% of people citing the Internet as a daily news source. Having broadband Internet service, however, appeared to change things. Sixty-four percent of broadband users got their news from the Internet, beating out both newspapers and radio. On the whole, the Internet appeared to be slowly eroding television's political news audience. Table 7.12 reveals that from January 2000 to June 2004, the number of Americans who considered the television their primary source for campaign information dropped 8%. At the same time, those who turned mainly to the Internet for such information rose from 7% to 15%. As broadband continues to find its way into more and more American homes, these numbers will likely continue to shift in favor of the Internet.

Nearly half of those people who went looking for political information on the Internet, however, did not find what they were looking for. *Untuned Keyboards* (Washington, DC: Pew Internet & American Life Project, March 2003), a study by Michael Cornfield of the Institute for Politics, Democracy, and the Internet at George Washington University and Pew/Internet Project director Lee Rainie, revealed that only 55% of Internet users found what they were looking for the last time they searched for political information on the Internet. This rate of success was significantly lower than other Web searches involving complex subjects. For instance, some 78% of people found the health information they were looking for the last time they searched for it on the Web. The report cites the confusing nature of political rhetoric, the perceived lack of credibility associated with politicians, and the myriad opposing viewpoints as reasons why people felt

dissatisfied when searching for political information. On the whole, the study concludes that when it comes to politics, Americans are a suspicious, impatient, and beleaguered lot.

Political Web Sites and the Howard Dean Campaign

Extensive use of the Internet by political campaigns did not really begin until the 2004 presidential elections. *Untuned Keyboards* included the results of a survey taken of campaign staff from thirty-three Senate and Congressional campaigns in the 2002 elections. On the whole, the campaign staffers in these races found the Internet most useful for simply conducting campaign research and e-mailing the press. On a scale of one to five, with one indicating "not effective" and five being "very effective," the staffers rated research at a 3.9 in terms of effectiveness and press relations at a 3.8. Most campaign Web sites simply contained series of news releases and lists of endorsements for the candidate. A large percentage of campaign managers believed that Internet fundraising was neither effective nor easy to implement. Mobilizing volunteers using the Internet also received a mediocre rating of 3.2. Advertising on the Internet barely made a passing grade with an effectiveness score of two. The fact that most campaign offices did not maintain or know how to maintain a secure Web site compounded the problem. Without such security in place, constituents were reluctant to give out any personal information or make contributions online.

While some national and state politicians in the past had employed the Web piecemeal to raise money or to organize rallies, most pundits agree that the 2004 Howard Dean Democratic presidential primary campaign was the first to utilize the Internet to its potential. Using outside contractors from the public sector, the Dean campaign set up a Web site that provided a number of services for supporters. The site contained a link to Meetup.com (www.meetup.com), where supporters could log in, find like-minded Dean supporters in close proximity, and arrange a meeting. The matchmaking service brought together people all over the country and led to hundreds of ad-hoc campaign centers for Dean. The Web site also supported an official blog where supporters could read opinions from campaign staffers and comment on the campaign and political issues. By reading the blogs and responses, strategizers in the campaign could gain insight into what supporters wanted from Dean. Perhaps the most important feature on the Dean site was the "Contribute" button. According to Grant Gross in "Dean Profits from Web Campaign" (*CIO Magazine*, January 15, 2004), Dean collected $7.4 million in online donations between April 1 and September 30, 2003, from 110,786 separate online donations. The online donations represented 67% of the total $11 million in donations the campaign received. All told, by the end of September 2003, Dean had raised $25.4 million total, which was $5 million more than John Kerry, who ended up winning the Democratic nomination.

The campaign and the Internet donations also worked within the confines established by the McCain-Feingold law passed by Congress in March 2002 to reform campaign finance. This legislation was designed to prevent a relatively small number of organizations and individuals from having disproportionate influence in politics. The laws banned "soft money" campaign contributions (large donations by corporations, labor unions, wealthy individuals, and special interest groups that skirted federal campaign regulations by supporting political parties rather than individual candidates). The bill also set maximum campaign contribution that can be given by an individual to $25,000. As the Dean campaign revealed, the Internet provided a way for many Americans to contribute smaller sums of money to their favorite candidate, thus making campaign finance more democratic. Many of the other 2004 presidential candidates began implementing similar Internet strategies when they saw Dean's success.

Political Advertising on the Internet

According to Thomas B. Edsall and Derek Willis in "Fundraising Records Broken by Both Major Political Parties" (*Washington Post*, December 3, 2004), total spending on the presidential campaign topped $1.7 billion by all sources who had an interest in directing the outcome of the election. Of this, $925 million was spent on campaigning for John Kerry and $822 million was spent in support of President Bush. In "Election Ad Battle Smashes Record in 2004" (*USA Today*, November 25, 2004) Mark Memmott and Jim Drinkard reported that nearly all of the money raised ($1.6 billion) was spent on television ads. *Presidential Campaign Advertising on the Internet*, an October 2004 Pew/Internet data memo by senior research consultant Michael Cornfield revealed that roughly $1 was spent on Web ads for every $100 spent on television ads in the 2004 campaign. Using this

as a conversion ratio, total Web spending on the presidential campaign likely amounted to $16 million. The Pew/Internet data memo stated that between January and August 2004, the main candidates in the presidential election dropped an estimated $2.66 million on website banner ads. The Kerry campaign spent nearly three times as much money on online advertising in this time period ($1.3 million) than the Bush campaign ($419,000). At the same time, the Republican National Committee spent $487,000 on online advertising, as opposed to the $257,000 spent by the Democratic National Committee.

In general, the most common type of Internet ads centered on fundraising, typically asking voters for campaign contributions of $25 and $50. *Presidential Campaign Advertising on the Internet* indicated that most of the ads were fairly mild in content, carrying no endorsements or invitations to political events. Only rarely did the content presented in the ad attempt to rally voters or target voters in a specific groups or localities. The ads exhibited few of the negative attacks customary in television commercials.

Nearly 78% of Kerry ads centered on fundraising. Table 7.13 displays the top twenty Web sites where Kerry ads were posted. Most of these were top local and national news sites mixed with a few liberal-leaning Web sites such as www.villagevoice.com and www.salon.com. Many of the local Web sites serviced regions with a majority of Kerry supporters, such as San Francisco (www.sfgate.com) and Seattle (www.seattlepi.com and www.seattletimes.com). All of this fits with an attempt by the Kerry camp to utilize the Web to obtain contributions from people who already supported Kerry.

Cornfield suggested in *Presidential Campaign Advertising on the Internet* that the Bush campaign employed the Web to focus on recruiting and persuading Americans to vote for Bush. Table 7.14 lists those sites where Bush ad placement was highest. Many of the local news sites listed in the table were in hotly contested swing states in the 2004 campaign, such as Oregon (www.oregons12.com and www.kgw.com) and Missouri (www.stltoday.com). The Bush campaign also targeted women by advertising on such sites as www.parents.com, www.ladieshomejournal.com, and www.epicurious.com (which includes the Web sites of *Bon Appetit* and *Gourmet* magazines). The average visitor to Gourmet.com, for instance, was forty-four years old, college educated, and female, with an average income of over $74,000, according to the October 2004 Pew/Internet memo.

Cornfield concluded in *Presidential Campaign Advertising on the Internet* that while the presidential campaigns did a good job of using the Internet to raise money and gain supporters via their own sites, online advertising could have been much more aggressive. The memo points out that the $2.66 million spent on online advertising between January and August 2004 was only

TABLE 7.13

Top twenty campaign ad placements for John Kerry, January–September 2004

January–mid–September, 2004

1.	SFGate.com	1,144
2.	Newsweek.com	938
3.	Village Voice.com	766
4.	Reuters.com	462
5.	L.A.Weekly Media.com	437
6.	US News & World Report.com	435
7.	Seattle P-I.com	416
8.	Seattletimes.com	288
9.	Hollywood Reporter.com	195
10.	Salon.com	194
11.	MSN Slate.com	166
12.	TheBookMarc.com (textbook vendor)	151
13.	MSNBC.com	130
14.	Sun Times.com (Myrtle Beach SC)	97
15.	El Nuevo Herald.com (Miami FL)	87
16.	Washington Post.com	86
17.	CNN.com	77
18.	Ohio.com	69
19.	Monterey County Herald.com (CA)	46
20.	Sun Herald.com (Biloxi MS)	45

This information was compiled by a TNSMI/CMAG affiliate company, Evaliant Media Resources. Using its "spidering" technology, Evaliant searches thousands of Web sites seeking brand-related banner advertising. Once found, these advertisements are tagged and collated according to Web site location, daily frequency, and estimated media-buying expenditure. Thus, the numbers in the above table correspond to the number of times an ad with the brand name was encountered in daily sweeps for the first seven months of 2004.

SOURCE: Michael Cornfield, "Table 6. Kerry Top Twenty Placements: January–mid-September, 2004," in *Pew Internet Project Data Memo*, Pew Internet and American Life Project, October 2004, http://www.pewinternet .org/pdfs/PIP_Pres_Online_Ads_Report.pdf (accessed December 11, 2004). Used by permission of the Pew Internet and American Life Project, which bears no responsibility for the interpretations presented or conclusions reached based on analysis of the data.

TABLE 7.14

Top twenty campaign ad placements for George W. Bush, January–September 2004

January–mid-September, 2004

1.	KPTV Oregons12.tv.com (FOX, Portland OR)	970
2.	Parents.com	938
3.	KNVA-TV.com (WB, Austin TX)	551
4.	El Nuevo Herald.com (Miami FL)	471
5.	KPHO CBS 5 News.com (CBS, Phoenix AZ)	335
6.	AZFamily.com	303
7.	KGW.com (NBC, Portland OR)	272
8.	WOOD TV8.com (NBC, Grand Rapids MI)	233
9.	Bon Appetit.com	222
10.	KXAN-TV.com (NBC, Austin TX)	217
11.	CondeNet/Epicurious.com	215
12.	Ohio.com	214
13.	ParentCenter.com	201
14.	Gourmet.com	186
15.	ColumbusDispatch.com	176
16.	KHOU-TV.com (CBS, Houston TX)	165
17.	LadiesHomeJournalOnline	153
18.	Miami Herald Internet Edition.com	141
19.	STLToday.com (St. Louis MO)	118
20.	FoxNews.com	113

This information was compiled by a TNSMI/CMAG affiliate company, Evaliant Media Resources. Using its "spidering" technology, Evaliant searches thousands of Web sites seeking brand-related banner advertising. Once found, these advertisements are tagged and collated according to Web site location, daily frequency, and estimated media-buying expenditure. Thus, the numbers in the above table correspond to the number of times an ad with the brand name was encountered in daily sweeps for the first seven months of 2004.

SOURCE: Michael Cornfield, "Table 5. Bush Top Twenty Placements: January–mid-September, 2004," in *Pew Internet Project Data Memo*, Pew Internet and American Life Project, October 2004, http://www.pewinternet .org/pdfs/PIP_Pres_Online_Ads_Report.pdf (accessed December 11, 2004). Used by permission of the Pew Internet and American Life Project, which bears no responsibility for the interpretations presented or conclusions reached based on analysis of the data.

half of the $5.7 million brought in online via the Kerry Web site on the day Kerry gave his nomination speech.

IT and the Voting Booth

In 2002 Congress passed and the president signed the Help America Vote Act (HAVA) to bring IT into voting booths. The act was a direct response to the hotly contested 2000 presidential campaign in which disputes over punch-card ballots in Florida contributed to a month-long delay of nationwide presidential election results. The punch-card ballots were prone to human error in that people would sometimes punch out the wrong perforated circle or not punch the card all the way through. HAVA required states to upgrade to electronic voting systems. The bill allotted $3.9 billion to help states replace old punch-card and lever systems with new voting machines. Though HAVA did not specify precisely which voting machines states were required to use, the act did provide a list of features the machines should have. Among other things, the machines should keep an electronic and paper record of the votes, be accessible to those with disabilities, allow voters to review their ballots before they are cast, and notify voters if they misvote (for example, vote twice for the same office).

As of 2004 only two types of machines met HAVA's laundry list of requirements, and both were used heavily in the 2004 presidential election. The first type is the optical scanning (Marksense) voting system. This system operates much like the paper-based standardized tests given in high schools and colleges. Using a dark lead pencil or black ink pen, voters darken ovals next to candidates' names for whom they wish to vote. With the sheet in front of them, voters can review their ballots before casting them. The sheet is then fed into a scanner. If an error or misvote occurs on the ballot, the scanner spits the ballot out. It is then discarded and the voter votes again. If the ballot is acceptable, the machine scans the ballot using lasers and the votes are registered in the machine. Optical scanning systems, however, are not accessible to disabled people who have trouble seeing or do not have complete control of their fine motor skills.

The second type of machine, known as a direct recording electronic (DRE) voting system, covers all the requirements laid down by HAVA. DRE systems are akin to touch-screen ATM machines. The voter stands in front of the touch screen and a list of candidates for a given political contest is displayed on the screen. The voter simply touches the candidate's name to vote for that person, and the machine displays the next list of candidates. DRE systems can be equipped with Braille keyboards and headsets for the blind, and voting choices can be made larger on the screen for those who lack fine motor skills. The machine notifies the voter if he or she has misvoted, and the machines allow the voter to review the votes on a final checkout screen before they are cast. A paper record is printed out by the machine at the end of the voting day. Proponents claim that DRE is better than an optical system because the DRE system eliminates the potential human error involved in coloring in circles, and it is easier for the disabled.

Controversy has surrounded DRE systems nonetheless. Many people are concerned that hackers could somehow tap into these systems and change the votes. A second and perhaps more realistic concern is that the complicated computer hardware and software in these systems could malfunction. In "Is E-voting Safe?" (*PC World*, June 2004), Paul Boutin discusses a study on DRE systems conducted by computer scientists at California Institute of Technology and Massachusetts Institute of Technology in 2001. The study concluded that touchscreen machines were slightly more accurate than punchcard machines. The residual error of margin for the DRE machines, which equates to the percentage of votes thrown out due to error, was 2.3%. This is only marginally better than the 2.5% error generated by old punch-card systems. Optical-scan paper ballots, on the other hand, had an error rate of only 1.5%.

During the presidential election of 2004 most DREs functioned properly, but some developed unusual problems. In "E-voting Results: Mixed" (*Information Week*, November 8, 2004), George V. Hulme reported that some forty million Americans cast votes on 175,000 touchscreen voting machines. However, in Carteret County, North Carolina, 4,500 votes were lost when a DRE machine's memory became full and the machine stopped recording votes. In Florida's Miami-Dade county, voters reported that the checkout screens on various DREs displayed incorrect votes. A similar problem occurred in western Washington State when a few badly calibrated touchscreens recorded the wrong vote when touched. One possible solution for the DRE systems that some states have implemented is the use of redundant paper ballots. In this instance, receipt printers are attached to the DRE's. When the person is done voting, the printer prints a version of the person's vote. This paper can then be reviewed and placed into a ballot box for later review if necessary.

THE 511 TRAVEL INFORMATION SYSTEM

Using advanced technologies, the federal government and state governments have begun putting into place a nationwide travel information system known as 511. The 511 system is an attempt to unify the numerous automated information systems already operated by state and local governments. Dozens of cities and states set up these systems in the 1990s when cell phones and advanced communications became affordable. Callers and Internet users could retrieve information on traffic jams and road conditions over the phone or on the Web. ARTIMIS (Advanced Regional Traffic Interactive Management and Information Systems), for instance, was set up in 1995 to monitor traffic and alert people to traffic problems on eighty-eight miles of freeway in the Cincinnati metropolitan area. ARTIMIS uses cameras and hundreds of detectors to monitor the flow of traffic along these freeways. People can dial into the system at any time to retrieve the information.

Most of these systems, however, had one big flaw. To access them, drivers typically had to remember an unfamiliar, seven-digit number. Consequently these services were rarely used. Noticing this problem, the U.S. Department of Transportation (DOT) approached the Federal Communications Commission (FCC) and asked them to designate a three-digit number that would connect users to the local travel information anywhere in the country. The FCC chose 511. The number was short and would automatically be associated with the more widely used 411 and 911. Ultimately, the DOT wanted all driver information systems to adopt the 511 number, so that any driver in the country could receive information by simply dialing 511.

With the support of the DOT, a 511 Deployment Coalition was formed in 2001 by a number of federal and state agencies to establish guidelines and procedures for implementing local 511 travel information systems. According to the *Implementation and Operational Guidelines for 511 Service* published in September 2003 by the 511 Deployment Commission, 511 services should allow a driver to access automated recordings on travel conditions through a series of voice commands or touchtone commands on the phone. At bare minimum, the system should provide conditions for major arteries in the designated region.

Many widely developed systems such as ARTIMIS and TravInfo service in San Francisco adopted the number for their travel services right away. The DOT also began awarding $100,000 grants to states or cities without traffic advisory systems to fund implementation plans. Figure 7.1 displays the states, counties, and municipalities that used the 511 number and those that received funding to implement a system as of September 2004. The map shows that twenty-four separate locations had employed the 511 system. Usage statistics from www.deploy511.org revealed that in September, 1,239,607 calls had been placed in the 511 network, which was a 62% increase over the volume of calls placed in September 2003. The peak usage during the month corresponded to the hurricanes in the Southeast, Labor Day holiday travel, and inclement weather conditions. Usually, call volume is much greater in the winter and late fall than in the summer and spring.

FIGURE 7.1

Nationwide use of 511, September 2004

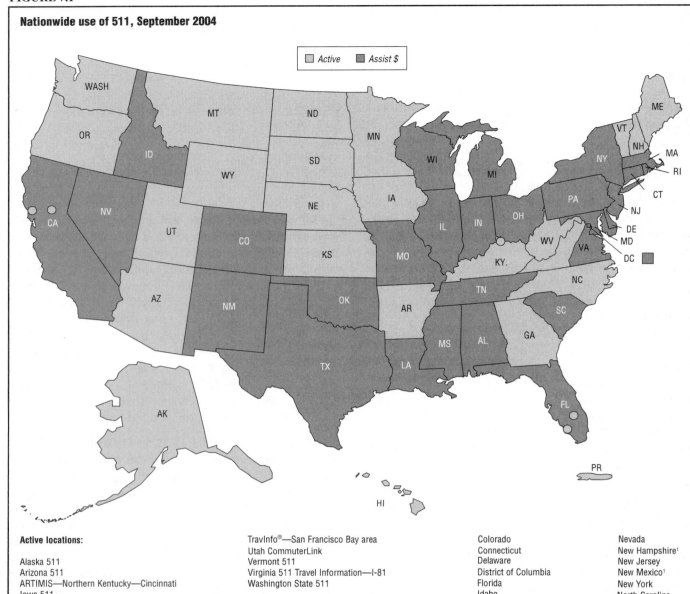

Active locations:

Alaska 511
Arizona 511
ARTIMIS—Northern Kentucky—Cincinnati
Iowa 511
Kansas 511
Kentucky 511
Maine 511
Minnesota 511
Montana 511
Nebraska 511
New Hampshire 511
North Carolina 511
North Dakota 511
Oregon 511
Orlando/I-4, Florida
Sacramento Region 511
South Dakota 511
South Florida—Miami—Dade area
Tampa Bay area 511

TravInfo®—San Francisco Bay area
Utah CommuterLink
Vermont 511
Virginia 511 Travel Information—I-81
Washington State 511

Adopter[1] overview reports:

Arizona
Greater Detroit
Kentucky
Minnesota
San Francisco Bay Area
Shenandoah Valley, Virginia (Full report)
Utah

States that received assistance funding:

Alabama
Alaska[2]
Arizona
California

Colorado
Connecticut
Delaware
District of Columbia
Florida
Idaho
Illinois
Indiana
Iowa[2]
Kansas
Kentucky
Louisiana
Maine[2]
Maryland
Massachusetts
Michigan
Minnesota[2]
Mississippi
Missouri
Montana
Nebraska

Nevada
New Hampshire[1]
New Jersey
New Mexico[1]
New York
North Carolina
North Dakota
Ohio
Oklahoma
Oregon
Pennsylvania
Rhode Island
South Carolina
South Dakota
Tennessee
Texas
Utah
Vermont[2]
Virginia
Washington State
Wisconsin

[1]Adopters are locations that were among the first to investigate implementing 511 traveler information services.
[2]CARS-511 Pooled Fund States

SOURCE: "511 Deployment," Federal Highway Administration, United States Department of Transportation, September 2004, http://www.fhwa.dot.gov/trafficinfo/511.htm (accessed December 11, 2004)

CHAPTER 8

ONLINE HEALTH RESOURCES

Prior to the Internet, finding the latest information on a health issue typically required access to a university or medical library and specialized knowledge of the subject. Most medical studies and information existed in expensive books and journals, which were generally written for those with formal training. The Internet gave rise to a plethora of accessible, informative Web sites that average consumers could comprehend. The rise of online pharmacies also allowed people the convenience of ordering and receiving prescription drugs from home. However, these conveniences have come with their share of problems. Online pharmacies that sell counterfeit medications run rampant on the Internet as of 2005, and some Americans rely on self-diagnosis when they should be consulting a medical professional. Overall, however, Americans' experiences with online health care information have been positive. According to Susannah Fox and Deborah Fallows in *Internet Health Resources* (Washington, DC: Pew Internet & American Life Project, July 2003), roughly eight out of ten online Americans who searched for health information found what they were looking for at least most of the time in 2002. Eighty to ninety percent of people who sought health resources on the Web appreciated the convenience, the breadth of information, and the anonymity of online medical sources.

The Internet has benefited those who work in health-care fields as well. The Internet allows medical researchers to share information as never before. Enormous databases accessible on the Internet contain references to nearly all published medical papers, sparing researchers the misery of hunting through print indexes. The Internet also provides the perfect medium for posting health-care research data, such as statistics on disease prevalence, and research organizations have posted data from thousands of disease studies. The availability of the research data has fostered a new era of scientific cooperation wherein medical results from labs halfway around the world can be brought together with a click of a mouse.

HEALTH CARE ON THE INTERNET

According to the Pew/Internet study *Internet Health Resources*, 80% of adult American Internet users (ninety-three million people) had gone online at least once to reference medical and health information as of late 2002. This represented close to half of the adult American population in 2002 and made searching for health care the second most popular online activity (next to e-mailing). In addition, the number of people engaged in this activity was growing at a rapid rate. In a previous Pew/Internet study, *The Online Health Care Revolution* (Washington, DC: Pew Internet & American Life Project, November 2000), Susannah Fox and Lee Rainie estimated that only 55% of adult Internet users (fifty million people) had researched a medical or health-related topic at that time.

Most of the people who go online for health information, however, do it infrequently. Some 80% of people who conducted health searches in or before 2002 said that they performed such a search every few months or less. Only 6% of health seekers reported going online in a typical day. Over half (57%) of all people turning to the Internet for medical advice said they went looking on behalf of someone else, such as a relative, a spouse, or a friend. Roughly half of all online Americans (54%) visited a Web site that provided information or support for people interested in a specific disease.

The July 2003 Pew/Internet report found that fewer online men (75%) surfed the Web for health and medical information than online woman (85%). (See Figure 8.1.) Elderly Americans sought out health advice less than those under sixty-five years of age. In fact, 80% of Web users eighteen to sixty-four had searched for medical knowledge online, as opposed to 70% of seniors sixty-five and older. This age discrepancy did not have as much to do with disease prevalence in the two groups as it did with the fact that many seniors were not online in 2002. As the general population ages, the percentage of online health seeking seniors should grow. Not surprisingly, online

FIGURE 8.1

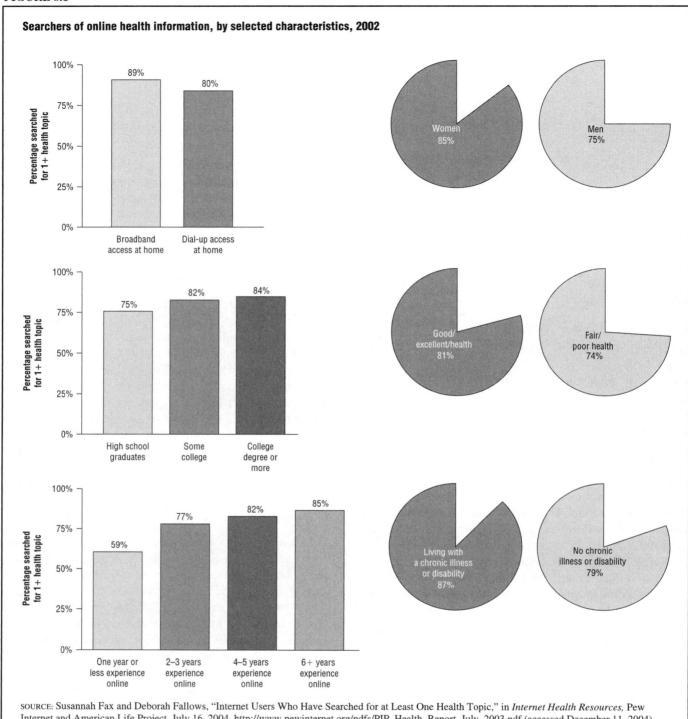

Searchers of online health information, by selected characteristics, 2002

SOURCE: Susannah Fax and Deborah Fallows, "Internet Users Who Have Searched for at Least One Health Topic," in *Internet Health Resources,* Pew Internet and American Life Project, July 16, 2004, http://www.pewinternet.org/pdfs/PIP_Health_Report_July_2003.pdf (accessed December 11, 2004). Used by permission of the Pew Internet and American Life Project, which bears no responsibility for the interpretations presented or conclusions reached based on analysis of the data.

Americans with higher incomes and education levels also searched for health information more than those with less education and income. The only discrepancies within racial groups could be attributed to the differences in income and education levels among those groups. Finally, Internet users with high-speed connections searched for medical information more than those without. A full 89% of Americans with broadband connections reported looking for health information on the Internet.

The Types of Health-Related Searches Made by Americans

Table 8.1, which appears in *Internet Health Resources,* lists the types of health-care searches Americans engaged

TABLE 8.1

Health topics researched online, 2002

Health topic	Internet users who have searched for info on it (%)
Specific disease or medical problem	63%
Certain medical treatment or procedure	47
Diet, nutrition, vitamins, or nutritional supplements	44
Exercise or fitness	36
Prescription or over-the-counter drugs	34
Alternative treatments or medicines	28
Health insurance	25
Depression, anxiety, stress, or mental health issues	21
A particular doctor or hospital	21
Experimental treatments or medicines	18
Environmental health hazards	17
Immunizations or vaccinations	13
Sexual health information	10
Medicare or Medicaid	9
Problems with drugs or alcohol	8
How to quit smoking	6

SOURCE: Susannah Fax and Deborah Fallows, "Health Topics Searched Online," in *Internet Health Resources*, Pew Internet and American Life Project, July 16, 2004, http://www.pewinternet.org/pdfs/PIP_Health_Report_July_2003.pdf (accessed December 11, 2004). Used by permission of the Pew Internet and American Life Project, which bears no responsibility for the interpretations presented or conclusions reached based on analysis of the data.

TABLE 8.2

Health topics researched online, by disability or chronic illness status of seeker, 2002

Health topics	Non-disabled Internet users (%)	Those with disabilities (%)
Specific disease or medical problem	61	85
Certain medical treatment or procedure	45	66
Diet, nutrition, vitamins or nutritional supplements	42	59
Prescription or over-the-counter drugs	31	55
Alternative treatments or medicines	26	48
Depression, anxiety, stress, or mental health issues	19	37
Experimental treatments or medicines	16	37

N = 1,220.

SOURCE: Susannah Fax and Deborah Fallows, "Online Americans living with a chronic illness or disability are fervid health seekers," in *Internet Health Resources,* Pew Internet and American Life Project, July 16, 2004, http://www.pewinternet.org/pdfs/PIP_Health_Report_July_2003.pdf (accessed December 11, 2004). Used by permission of the Pew Internet and American Life Project, which bears no responsibility for the interpretations presented or conclusions reached based on analysis of the data.

in by topic in 2002. Sixty-three percent of Internet users searched for facts on a specific disease or medical problem. A much higher percentage of women (72%) than men (54%) reported searching for information on specific diseases and problems. Far fewer people searched for information on preventive health measures, such as diet, nutrition, and fitness. Forty-four percent of Internet users reported looking for information on diet and nutrition, and 36% said they surfed the Internet looking for fitness information. In January the number of people looking for diet and nutrition advice spiked as people aimed to fulfill their New Year's resolutions. A majority (51%) of Internet users aged eighteen to twenty-nine went online to view fitness information, compared with roughly one-third (35%) of those aged thirty to forty-nine. Health insurance, which has always been a big concern for American adults, ranks seventh, according to Table 8.1. A larger percentage of online parents (29%) researched health insurance topics than those without children (23%). Drugs, alcohol, and tobacco were the least popular topics mentioned.

The health of Internet users and the health of the people around them also influenced the type of health information they looked for on the Web. Disabled and chronically ill people as a group had the least Internet access. Pew/Internet research found that only 38% of disabled Americans typically went online in 2002. According to *Internet Health Resources*, of those disabled people who did go online, nearly 87% had surfed the Web for health information. Table 8.2 reveals the health topics that online disabled people searched for most. On the whole they researched the same topics as the general population, but at higher rates. Researching a specific disease or med-

ical problem topped the disabled Internet users' list, with 85% claiming to have performed this activity. Looking for fitness information and for a particular doctor or hospital did not rank high among disabled Internet users. The online habits of the roughly one-tenth of Americans who lived with someone chronically ill or disabled also differed from the general Internet population. Those living with the chronically ill generally searched for practical information to help their loved ones. Sixty-two percent of caregivers on the Internet searched for a specific medical treatment or procedure, as opposed to 47% of the general online population. Over half (55%) of online caregivers used the Internet to find information on drugs, versus only a third of the Internet population (34%) as a whole. A higher percentage of caregivers also searched for material on mental health (37% vs. 21%) and looked into experimental treatments (35% vs. 18%).

The Impact of the Internet on Health Care Information

For the most part, Americans are positive about the health information available to them on the Web. According to *Internet Health Resources*, roughly 70% of online health-information seekers reported that the Internet has influenced medical decisions related to their own health or to that of someone close to them. Seventy-three percent said that the Internet has improved the health care they received. This number was up from 2001, according to Susannah Fox and Lee Rainie in *Vital Decisions* (Washington, DC: Pew Internet & American Life Project, May 2002), when only 61% of those seeking online medical advice believed the Internet improved their health care. Table 8.3 displays the percentage of people affected favorably by health Web sites. Forty-four percent thought that information gleaned from the Internet affected a decision on how to treat an illness, and 25% said the information

TABLE 8.3

Impact of online health information, 2001

SUCCESSFUL SEARCHERS WHO SAY ONLINE HEALTH INFORMATION. . .

	%
Affected a decision about how to treat an illness or condition	44
Led them to ask a doctor new questions or get a second opinion	38
Changed approach to maintaining own health or health of someone they care for	34
Changed the way they think about diet, exercise, and stress	30
Changed the way they cope with a chronic condition or manage pain	25
Affected a decision about whether to see a doctor or not	17

SOURCE: Susannah Fox and Lee Rainie, "Information's Impact," in *Vital Decisions,* Pew Internet and American Life Project, May 22, 2002, http://www.pewinternet.org/pdfs/PIP_Vital_Decisions_May2002.pdf (accessed December 11, 2004). Used by permission of the Pew Internet and American Life Project, which bears no responsibility for the interpretations presented or conclusions reached based on analysis of the data.

TABLE 8.4

Factors deterring users from some health information Web sites, 2001

Health seekers	%
Site was too commercial	47
User couldn't determine the source of the information	42
User couldn't determine when information was last updated	37
Site lacked endorsement of a trusted independent organization	30
Site appeared sloppy or unprofessional	29
Site contained information you knew to be wrong	26
Information disagreed with own doctor's advice	20

SOURCE: Susannah Fox and Lee Rainie, "Evaluating Information," in *Vital Decisions,* Pew Internet and American Life Project, May 22, 2002, http://www.pewinternet.org/pdfs/PIP_Vital_Decisions_May2002.pdf (accessed December 11, 2004). Used by permission of the Pew Internet and American Life Project, which bears no responsibility for the interpretations presented or conclusions reached based on analysis of the data.

changed the way they coped with pain. Fox and Rainie concluded that those typically in the most need obtained the greatest benefits from e-medicine. In fact, 51% of those surveyed who were treated for a serious illness said they or someone they knew benefited significantly from online Internet advice in the year prior to the 2001 Pew/Internet survey. Two percent of those who searched for health advice online said that they knew someone who was seriously harmed by following medical information gleaned from the Internet.

Many health-care officials worry that Americans use the Internet to diagnose their own ailments in the hope of avoiding time-consuming but necessary visits to the doctor's office. The biggest problem with self-diagnosis is that it is rarely objective. Using advice from online Web sites is especially problematic in that it is often incomplete. Gretchen K. Berland, Marc N. Elliott, and others affiliated with the California HealthCare Foundation and RAND Health undertook a study of medical Web sites on breast cancer, depression, obesity, and childhood asthma between January and December 2000. The team published their results in "Health Information on the Internet: Accessibility, Quality, and Readability in English and Spanish" (*JAMA*, May 23, 2001). According to the researchers, key medical information was missing from most Web sites: "On average, 45% of the clinical elements on English- and 22% on Spanish-language Web sites were more than minimally covered and completely accurate and 24% of the clinical elements on English- and 53% on Spanish-language Web sites were not covered at all. All English and 86% of Spanish Web sites required high school level or greater reading ability."

The Medical Library Association (MLA) has a list of recommendations that those seeking health information on the Internet should follow. These include identifying each site's sponsor, checking the date of information posted, and verifying that the material is factual, as opposed to

opinion. The California HealthCare Foundation warns that online Americans looking for health information should take their time searching for advice, visit at least four to six sites, and discuss what they find with a doctor before taking action. Most people surveyed for the May 2002 Pew/Internet study entitled *Vital Decisions* did not adhere to these guidelines. A majority of people only visited a few sites in their medical searches. Seventy-two percent of people looking for health information online uncritically accepted most of the health information they found. For the most part, online health-care seekers used the Web to confirm what they already thought they knew. Roughly 90% of health-conscious online Americans said that the information they found on their last online search generally supported their beliefs. Only 4% reported that the information differed from what they had read or heard before.

There were, however, a number of factors that did turn people away from medical information, which are displayed in Table 8.4. The biggest deterrent for people was commercialism. Generally, too many banners or pop-up ads caused people to lose confidence in a medical Web site. Some 42% of online health seekers did not trust information if they could not determine the source, and 37% were wary of information when they could not determine whether it had been recently updated. All in all, the report revealed that only one quarter of people surveyed follow the recommendations given by the MLA and the California HealthCare Foundation.

Despite Americans' abuse of e-medicine, the Pew/Internet study *Internet Health Resources* revealed that people who surfed the Web for health topics were also more likely to visit the doctor. Nearly 80% of Internet users interviewed for the report had been to the doctor in the year prior to the survey. Eighty-four percent of those who went to the doctor also said they searched for online health information. Only two-thirds (66%) of online survey respondents who did not see a doctor said they had gone online for health information. According to *Vital Decisions*, nearly

FIGURE 8.2

Use of MedlinePlus, by quarter, 1999–2004

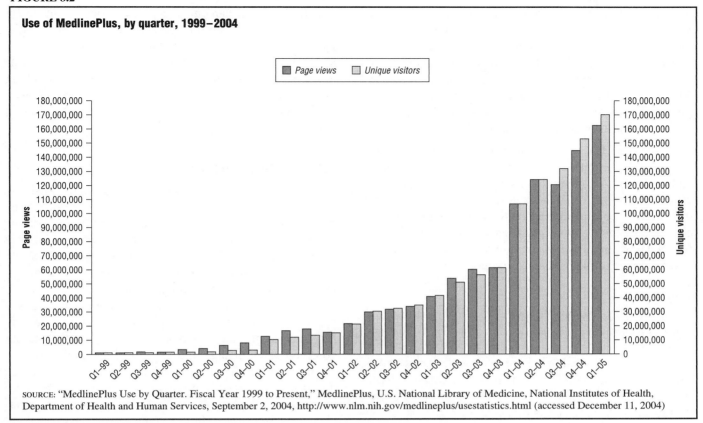

SOURCE: "MedlinePlus Use by Quarter. Fiscal Year 1999 to Present," MedlinePlus, U.S. National Library of Medicine, National Institutes of Health, Department of Health and Human Services, September 2, 2004, http://www.nlm.nih.gov/medlineplus/usestatistics.html (accessed December 11, 2004)

one-third of all successful Internet medical searches led to someone visiting their doctor. For the most part, people said that their health-care professionals were open to them bringing online material to a visit. A third (31%) of people in *Vital Decisions* who went to their doctor with Internet-based information said their doctor thought the material was "very interesting." Forty-eight percent said the doctor was "somewhat interested," and only 13% reported that the doctor simply dismissed the information.

Top Web Sites for Health Information

According to the MLA, the ten most useful medical Web sites as of November 2002 were (listed alphabetically):

- Cancer.gov, National Cancer Institute (www.cancer.gov)
- Centers for Disease Control and Prevention (www.cdc.gov)
- Familydoctor.org, American Academy of Family Physicians (familydoctor.org)
- Healthfinder, National Health Information Center (www. healthfinder.gov)
- HIV InSite, University of California, San Francisco Center for HIV Information (www.hivinsight.com)
- KidsHealth, Nemours Foundation (www.kidshealth.com)
- Mayo Clinic (www.mayoclinic.org)
- MEDEM, Inc.: Connecting Physicians and Patients Online (www.medem.com)

- MedlinePlus, National Library of Medicine (www. medlineplus.gov)
- NOAH: New York Online Access to Health (www. noah-health.org)

These Web sites were evaluated in part on their credibility, content, sponsorship/authorship, purpose, and design. MedlinePlus made its debut on the Web in October 1998 with twenty-two health topics in its library. The site received 116,000 page hits in its first month. By late 2004 the site was getting over 120 million page hits every three months (see Figure 8.2), and contained information from the National Institutes of Health (the largest medical research institution in the world) as well as other top medical institutions. All in all, the site held information on more than 650 diseases and conditions. Content from the *ADAM* medical encyclopedia (www.adam.com) and *Merriam-Webster's Medical Dictionary* are integrated onto the site. Users of the site can also obtain current facts on most prescription and nonprescription drugs. The site displays no advertising, and all the information on MedlinePlus is reviewed by experts in the medical profession. A search on MedlinePlus for a disease typically yields definitions, fact sheets, drug information, the latest news on the disease, and links to places where further information could be found. Of all e-government Web sites included in the American Customer Satisfaction Index (ACSI), MedlinePlus received the highest rating (86 out of 100) in 2004.

Other general medicine Web sites noted by the MLA included healthfinder.gov, familydoctor.org, medem.com, noah-health.org, and mayoclinic.com. Like MedlinePlus, these sites contain information on numerous medical diseases and conditions. Not-for-profit kidshealth.org focuses on health care for children from prenatal care through adolescence. This Web site maintains separate areas for kids, teenagers, and parents, and as of late 2004, the site received more than 200,000 visitors a day.

Facts on HIV are available at hivinsight.com, and cancer.gov presents information on cancer types, causes, and treatments. Cancer.gov also maintains a database of clinical trials all over the country for those who seek information on alternative treatments. Finally, cdc.gov, operated by the Centers for Disease Control and Prevention (CDC), contains information on communicable diseases, immunization, and disease prevention.

E-mail and Health Care

E-mail has also proven useful for those seeking medical information and advice. E-mail provides a great way for Americans with health problems to commiserate with friends and family and to stay in touch with their doctors. The July 2003 Pew/Internet report *Internet Health Resources* revealed that 30% of adult American e-mail users (thirty-two million people) have at some time sent or received an e-mail regarding health care. Roughly 25% of e-mailers swap health related e-mails with friends and family members. Typically those who are caring for a sick loved one do not have the time or energy to call friends and family members to update them on the patient's condition. E-mail provides the perfect medium for many to transmit such news. E-mail also has proven beneficial when used in conjunction with support groups and counseling. According to Deborah Tate and her colleagues at Brown University, people who participated in Internet weight-loss programs were much more successful if they received e-mail counseling ("Effects of Internet Behavioral Counseling on Weight Loss in Adults at Risk for Type 2 Diabetes," *JAMA*, April 9, 2003). Of ninety-two adults enrolled in online weight-loss programs, those who communicated with their weight-loss counselors via e-mail lost 4.8% of their original body weight, which was double that lost by those without e-mail counseling.

E-mail is also useful for communicating with health-care professionals. Roughly 6% of people who use e-mail employed it to communicate with a doctor, according to *Internet Health Resources*. E-mail provides an easy way to make appointments or to renew prescriptions. E-mail also is ideal for those who have minor health problems to discuss such as an upper respiratory infection or a rash. Quite a few people surveyed for *Internet Health Resources* lived in rural areas far from their doctors' offices and found that e-mail helped to bridge the distance. E-mail allows a patient to relate symptoms to the doctor without having to play phone tag, and based on the e-mail, the doctor can either ask the patient to come in for a diagnosis or can simply give advice via e-mail reply. Disabled and chronically ill e-mail users relied on e-mail more than most to communicate with their doctors as many of them typically have trouble moving about. In fact, a full 19% of chronically ill and disabled people who use e-mail communicated with their doctor via e-mail at some time.

MEDICATION ONLINE

Since the late 1990s, the online pharmacy business has been growing at a steady rate. Most major online pharmacies, such as drugstore.com and Wal-Mart's online pharmacy, are legitimate. They carry the Verified Internet Pharmacy Practice Sites (VIPPS) seal of approval (issued by the National Association of Boards of Pharmacy), meaning they comply with all state and federal laws. Much like traditional pharmacies, these online drug stores require that a prescription be faxed or called in by a doctor. Such pharmacies also send the drug to the patient complete with dosage and warning information on the bottle. However, illegitimate virtual pharmacies, which do not follow U.S. state and federal regulations, have begun operating on the Internet as well. Some of these pharmacies are based in the United States and some operate on foreign soil.

The lure of illegal pharmacies is low cost and convenience. Many illegitimate pharmacies will send patients prescription drugs without a prescription. Pharmacy Web sites located in other countries typically sell their drugs for much less than U.S. pharmacies as well. Many foreign pharmacies that cater to the U.S. market are located in Canada. Clifford Krauss reported in "Internet Drug Exporters Feel Pressure in Canada" (*New York Times*, December 11, 2004) that the 270 online Canadian pharmacies made more than $800 million from U.S. customers in 2003. While many of the Canadian pharmacies follow the same strict standards as American pharmacies, it is illegal for individuals in the United States to buy pharmaceuticals from foreign countries.

Illegitimate online pharmacies have generated a great deal of concern among health-care professionals and government lawmakers in the United States. One problem is that state medical boards, who typically oversee brick-and-mortar operations, have difficulty monitoring pharmaceutical Web sites. While some of these pharmacies follow many of the same standards as legitimate operations, others disregard them altogether. In addition to providing drugs without a prescription, many send patients drugs without warnings or dosage information. Such a practice is exceedingly dangerous. Accutane, an acne treatment medication, has been known to cause severe birth defects and mental problems in select patients. If a

TABLE 8.5

Prescription drugs ordered and received from Internet pharmacies, 2004

Drug ordered	Orders placed[1]	Drug samples received[2]	Drug samples obtained without a prescription provided by the patient
Accutane	10	6[3]	3
Celebrex	10	9	7
Clozaril	9	0	0
Combivir	6	5	1
Crixivan	6	6	2
Epogen	1	1	0
Humulin N	7	4	3
Lipitor	10	9	6
OxyContin	1	1	1
Percocet	0	0	0
Viagra	10	9	7
Vicodin/hydrocodone	10	9[3,4]	9
Zoloft	10	9	6
Total	**90**	**68**	**45**

Note: The samples were shipped by FedEx (24), UPS (3), the U.S. Postal Service (39), and other couriers (2).

[1]Does not include attempted orders that were not accepted. We did not reach our goal of placing 10 orders for each drug because we could not always locate 10 sources from which we could purchase the drugs in a manner consistent with our methodology's protocols.
[2]We did not receive a drug sample for every order placed. Reasons included the drug being out of stock, a requirement that physicians prescribing certain drugs be part of a registry, and pharmacy requests for follow-up information we could not provide. In several instances, we could not determine why an order placed was not received.
[3]Includes one sample we could not link to an order we placed.
[4]Although we placed orders for Vicodin, we did not receive any samples of the brand name version of the drug; all nine samples received were of the generic equivalent hydrocodone.

SOURCE: "Table 2. Prescription Drugs Ordered and Received from Internet Pharmacies," in *Internet Pharmacies: Some Pose Safety Risk to Consumer,* United States General Accounting Office, June 2002, http://www.gao.gov/new.items/d04820.pdf (accessed December 11, 2004)

TABLE 8.6

Prescription requirements of domestic and non-U.S. Internet pharmacies, 2004

Prescription requirement	U.S. Internet pharmacies	Canadian Internet pharmacies	Other foreign Internet pharmacies
Prescription from patient's physician must be provided	5	18	0
Web site provides prescription based on questionnaire	24	0	3
No prescription required	0	0	18

SOURCE: "Table 3. Prescription Requirements of Pharmacies from which We Obtained Samples," in *Internet Pharmacies: Some Pose Safety Risk to Consumer,* United States General Accounting Office, June 2002, http://www.gao.gov/new.items/d04820.pdf (accessed December 11, 2004)

pregnant woman were to receive an unlabeled bottle of Accutane and did not know of the warnings, the results could be disastrous. Another concern is that many of these sites have been known to deal in counterfeit drugs with diluted ingredients or no ingredients at all. Counterfeit heart medication or even cholesterol medication could result in a patient's death. When federal and state agencies become aware of one of these illegitimate pharmacies in the United States, they attempt to shut it down. However, government regulators can do very little about controlling pharmacies outside of U.S. borders.

In the first six months of 2004 the United States General Accounting Office (GAO) conducted a study of Internet pharmacies. The investigators placed up to ten orders for each of thirteen different drugs from online pharmacies located in the United States, Canada, and other foreign countries, including Argentina, Costa Rica, Fiji, India, Mexico, Pakistan, and Turkey. (See Table 8.5.) When the GAO received the drugs they forwarded them to drug manufacturers for chemical verification. The results were reported in *Internet Pharmacies: Some Pose Safety Risks for Consumers*, which was published in June 2004 by the GAO. As Table 8.6 shows, all the Canadian Internet pharmacies required prescriptions from a patient's physi-

cian. Only five U.S. Internet pharmacies followed this convention. The other twenty-four sent out prescriptions based on questionnaires that inquired about a patient's history—a practice condemned by the Food and Drug Administration (FDA), the American Medical Association (AMA), and many state medical boards. Most of the foreign Internet pharmacies outside of Canada did not even require a questionnaire.

Some of the sites, particularly in Canada and the United States, followed every rule that brick-and-mortar pharmacies did in the United States. In one case, a U.S. pharmacy refused to send the investigators a prescription for Accutane since the doctor who wrote the prescription was not on an official list of doctors qualified to do so. Table 8.7 lists some of the problems encountered with the sixty-eight online pharmacies that did send drug samples to the GAO investigators. For the most part, the samples that were sent from U.S. online pharmacies had only a few problems, including improper labeling. Many Canadian pharmacies sent versions of popular U.S. drugs that were not licensed for sale in the United States. Much like generic medications, these drugs have the same medicinal ingredients as their U.S. equivalents and pose no additional threat to those taking them.

Drugs sent from foreign countries other than Canada were riddled with problems. Five foreign pharmacies took the investigators' money and sent them no drugs. Of the drugs received from these other foreign countries, none of them had an instruction label and only six out of twenty-one had warning labels. Some of these drugs, particularly narcotics, were packaged in strange ways to disguise the contents of the package. The supposed shipment of Oxy-Contin arrived in a used CD case wrapped in brown packing tape. Several of the foreign drugs were counterfeit as well, including the OxyContin, which did not contain any of the actual drug. When the GAO investigators attempted to track down the origin of the foreign packages, they came up with some bizarre locations. A sample of Lipitor from Argentina was apparently shipped from a shopping

TABLE 8.7

Problems observed among prescription drug samples obtained from online sources, 2004

Pharmacy location	No pharmacy label with instructions for use (23 samples)	No warning information (21 samples)	Improperly shipped or dispensed (4 samples)	Unconventional packaging (6 samples)	Damaged packaging (5 samples)	Not approved for U.S. market (35 samples)	Counterfeit or otherwise not comparable to product ordered (4 samples)
Canadian		Celebrex (2) Zoloft (2)				Accutane (3) Combivir (3) Crixivan (3) Humulin N (1) Lipitor (2) Viagra (1) Zoloft (3)	
Other foreign	Accutane (3) Celebrex (3) Combivir (1) Crixivan (2) Humulin N (3) Lipitor (3) OxyContin (1) Viagra (2) Zoloft (3)	Accutane (2) Celebrex (3) Crixivan (2) Lipitor (3) OxyContin (1) Viagra (2) Zoloft (2)	Humulin N (3)	Accutane (1) Celebrex (1) Crixivan (2) OxyContin (1) Viagra (1)	Accutane (2) Celebrex (1) Crixivan (1) Lipitor (1)	Accutane (2) Celebrex (3) Combivir (1) Crixivan (1) Humulin N (3) Lipitor (3) OxyContin (1) Viagra (2) Zoloft (3)	Accutane (1) OxyContin (1) Viagra (2)
U.S.	Celebrex (1) Zoloft (1)	Lipitor (1) Zoloft (1)	Crixivan (1)				

Notes: Drug names indicated are those that General Accounting Office (GAO) ordered. The samples we received were not the brand name drugs we ordered in all instances. Drug samples do not add to 68 because some samples exhibited more than one problem.

SOURCE: "Table 4. Problems Observed Among Prescription Drug Samples Received," in *Internet Pharmacies: Some Pose Safety Risk to Consumer,* United States General Accounting Office, June 2002, http://www.gao.gov/new.items/d04820.pdf (accessed December 11, 2004)

mall in Buenos Aires. An order of Humulin N and Zoloft were traced to private residences in Lahore, Pakistan.

Who Is Ordering Online Medications?

Though the number of people purchasing drugs online has grown since the turn of the century, the overall percentage of Americans buying pharmaceuticals on the Internet was still fairly low as of mid-2004. According to Susannah Fox in *Prescription Drugs Online* (Washington, DC: Pew Internet & American Life Project, October 2004), only 5% of American adults (ten million people) had bought prescription drugs online for themselves or others by spring 2004, compared with the 64% (129 million people) of American adults who took prescription drugs on a regular basis or lived with someone who did. Predictably, most people who bought online drugs said that convenience and savings were the two biggest reasons they bought drugs online. Roughly 75% of people who made an online drug purchase bought a drug for a chronic medical condition such as high blood pressure. The rest said they went online to purchase a drug for other purposes such as weight loss or sexual performance.

The vast majority of people surveyed in the Pew/Internet report who bought online drugs said they had a prescription from a doctor. Almost all of these people received their prescription drug from an online pharmacy based in the United States. Only a few people replied that they found their online pharmacy by responding to a spam e-mail advertisement. In the end, most people who went online for their drugs were happy with their experience. Roughly 90% of those who purchased online pharmaceuticals said they planned to do it again. The biggest complaint people had was that their packages were lost in the mail. Given these positive experiences, one would expect that more people would fill their prescriptions online. Even with all the reputable online pharmacy Web sites, a full 62% of Americans surveyed still believed that purchasing prescription drugs online was more dangerous than buying them at a local pharmacy. Only 20% felt online purchases were as safe.

THE MEDICAL DATA REVOLUTION

Since the 1980s, information technologies and the Internet have transformed the field of medical research. Before launching a medical research project, a scientist first must know what has been done in the area he or she plans to study. The initial step, for instance, for a researcher who wants to find a cure for Alzheimer's would be to analyze previous data on the subject. Only then could the researcher formulate new theories and design experiments that advance the field. Before the Internet and the widespread use of computer databases, researchers seeking such information were required to spend days at medical libraries, sifting through thick journal indexes that cataloged thousands upon thousands of past journal articles by subject. The advent of computer databases changed all that. Huge medical indexes were put in digital form, which allowed researchers to compile a full list of research articles in minutes instead of days. As of late 2004 a number of databases existed online. Medline/PubMed, which is maintained by the National Library of Medicine, is one of the most comprehensive and widely used of these databases. In 2004 PubMed contained citations and abstracts summarizing papers published in nearly 4,800 biomedical journals in the United States and seventy other countries. By simply going online to PubMed and typing a query, a researcher can track down every published paper on most medical topics.

The ability of computers and the Internet to store and transmit scientific data also has transformed the way medical research is conducted. The Internet allows scientists from all over the world to share data on diseases and patient attributes. Computers can then perform statistical analysis on disease data in relation to various aspects of patient histories, such as age, geographic location, and even the presence of other diseases.

The Centers for Disease Control's National Center for Health Statistics (NCHS) database contains statistics on a variety of diseases including arthritis, heart disease, HIV, and even tooth decay. All this information is freely available for scientists to use in their research. In 1999, for example, West Virginia University and scientists with the CDC combined data from the NCHS and the U.S. Census to build a U.S. atlas showing heart disease in women by location, age, race, and income. Among other things, the atlas confirmed earlier studies that revealed that women in poorer communities had higher levels of heart disease than their counterparts in affluent communities. The atlas also provided a reference resource for government officials and health-care workers, letting them know exactly where their time and money should be spent on heart disease awareness programs. The State Center for Health Statistics in North Carolina employed CDC data to determine the mortality and life expectancies of its residents. The resulting January 2002 study—entitled "Healthy Life Expectancy in North Carolina, 1996–2000," by Paul Buescher and Ziya Gizlice—determined that the life span of the average North Carolinian was 75.6 years. They also calculated that the average person would likely spend some 12.6 years toward the end of life in poor to fair health. Using such a study, the state could forecast how

TABLE 8.8

Number of candidates waiting for organ transplants, January 2005

*All	87,189
Kidney	60,418
Pancreas	1,661
Kidney/pancreas	2,432
Liver	17,244
Intestine	195
Heart	3,270
Lung	3,895
Heart/lung	171

*All candidates will be less than the sum due to candidates waiting for multiple organs

SOURCE: "Waiting List Candidates as of Today," The Organ Procurement and Transplantation Network, January 2005, http://www.optn.org/data/ (accessed January 17, 2005)

much money would be required to support the state's elderly population far into the future.

Computer databases and the Internet have also become invaluable resources for organ and tissue donor programs. Treatments for cancers such as leukemia sometimes destroy the bone marrow that produces red blood cells, white blood cells, and platelets in the blood stream. To replace the bone marrow, a transplant from another person is needed. Finding compatible bone marrow, however, is very difficult. Typically, a match will not even exist within the same family. The National Bone Marrow Donor Registry is a computer database of people who have agreed to donate their bone marrow to those in need. A doctor with a patient in need of a transplant can simply log onto the registry via the Internet and pull up all possible matches in the country. The Organ Procurement and Transplantation Network (OPTN) maintains a similar database for internal organ transplants, including kidney, pancreas, heart, lung, and intestine. OPTN's secure transplant information database keeps track of exactly which patients are in need of a transplant. Table 8.8 displays the list of candidates who were waiting on the OPTN on January 17, 2005. All necessary forms and patient histories are also included in the database. Should a donor's heart become available in a medical facility anywhere in the United States, the attending physician can access the database to find patients who are waiting for a new heart.

CHAPTER 9

HIGH TECH AND DAILY LIFE

Since the early 1980s, high tech has been creeping into every aspect of life, becoming as invisible in many Americans' everyday lives as running water or refrigeration. Many Americans think nothing of going online to check the weather, buy tickets, plan holidays, look for religious inspiration, or find information on hobbies from coin collecting to rock climbing. The Internet also contains an endless list of resources that most people would never have room for on the bookshelf but take for granted nonetheless, including maps, dictionaries, phone books, and even manuals on most products. The Internet has become a great way to communicate with others, and millions have used it to make a date, schedule appointments, or find old friends. In August 2004 Deborah Fallows reported in *The Internet and Daily Life* (Washington, DC: Pew Internet & American Life Project) that 88% of online Americans surveyed said that the Internet had become part of their daily routines.

The Internet is not the only new technology to have become ubiquitous in everyday American life. Microchips, sensors, and display screens can be found on or in just about every appliance in the home. They allow people to do everything from control the home thermostat from a remote computer to heat water with microwave radiation. Complex sensors and systems also control most American automobiles, monitoring engine performance, regulating gas flow, sensing obstacles, and in some instances pinpointing the car's location. As of 2004 robots were also beginning to make their way into American homes to complete time-consuming tasks such as mowing the lawn or vacuuming the living room.

EVERYDAY ACTIVITIES AND THE INTERNET

The more Americans are exposed to the Internet, the more the Internet comes into play a role in seemingly every facet of day-to-day American life. According to Fallows in *The Internet and Daily Life*, nine out of ten (92%)

TABLE 9.1

Everyday online activities, 2003

Activity and percentage (in parentheses) of those who do this activity at all in their lives, either online or offline	Internet users who do this activity online
Get map or directions (88%)	87%
Communicate with friends/family (95)	79
Check weather (86)	69
Get news (88)	63
Get sports scores (47)	55
Buy tickets (74)	55
Send cards, etc. (81)	52
Get addresses, zip codes, phone numbers (74)	50
Play games (74)	46
Plan gatherings (66)	46
Pay bills, banking (82)	44
Pursue hobbies (80)	34
Buy daily items (78)	33
Find new people (25)	26
Listen to music (87)	23
Schedule appointments (69)	22
Read for fun (83)	18
Watch videos (70)	16

N = 1,358.

SOURCE: Deborah Fallows, "Everyday Online Activities," *The Internet and Daily Life,* Pew Internet and American Life Project, August 11, 2004, http://www.pewinternet.org/pdfs/PIP_Internet_and_Daily_Life.pdf (accessed December 19, 2004). Used by permission of the Pew Internet and American Life Project, which bears no responsibility for the interpretations presented or conclusions reached based on analysis of the data.

online Americans surveyed during November and December 2003 believed the Internet was good for obtaining everyday information. Three-quarters (75%) considered the Internet a great way to conduct everyday transactions. Table 9.1 lists some of the specific everyday activities online Americans engaged in on the Internet. (Each percentage on the right side of the table represents the percentage of Internet users who take part in the activity who have at some point gone on the Internet to do so.) Many of the activities involved referencing practical information. Over two-thirds (69%) of Internet users who checked the weather regularly checked it on the Internet. Half (50%) of

TABLE 9.2

Everyday online activities of broadband and dial-up users, 2003

Activity	Broadband at home and work	Broadband at home or work	Dial-up only
Get maps or directions	94%	91%	83%
Communicate with friends/family	92	83	77
Check weather	91	77	62
Get sports scores	89	66	43
Get news	83	73	52
Get addresses, zip codes, phone numbers	77	60	39
Buy tickets	74	62	48
Do bills, banking	70	53	36
Send cards, invites	67	56	50
Plan gatherings	64	51	42
Buy daily items	51	40	25
Play games	48	47	45
Pursue hobbies	45	38	30
Schedule appointments	45	30	13
Find new people	43	30	21
Listen to music	38	29	15
Watch videos	32	22	9
Read for fun	30	20	16

N = 1,358.

SOURCE: Deborah Fallows, "Broadband Users Do More Everyday Activities Online Than Dial-up Users," *The Internet and Daily Life,* Pew Internet and American Life Project, August 11, 2004, http://www.pewinternet.org/pdfs/ PIP_Internet_and_Daily_Life.pdf (accessed December 19, 2004). Used by permission of the Pew Internet and American Life Project, which bears no responsibility for the interpretations presented or conclusions reached based on analysis of the data.

TABLE 9.3

Everyday activities done exclusively offline or online, 2003

Activity	Percent of Internet users who do this activity only *offline*	Percent of Internet users who do this activity only *online*
Get maps or directions	14%	56%
Communicate with friends/family	20	21
Check weather	31	31
Get news	38	17
Get sports scores	45	26
Buy tickets	45	28
Send cards, invites	47	17
Get addresses, zip codes, phone numbers	50	19
Play games	54	20
Plan gatherings	53	20
Do bills, banking	56	20
Pursue hobbies	66	10
Buy daily items	68	9
Find new people	76	12
Listen to music	77	6
Schedule appointments	78	9
Read for fun	82	5
Watch videos	84	4

N = 1,358.

SOURCE: Deborah Fallows, "Everyday Activities Done Exclusively Offline or Online," *The Internet and Daily Life,* Pew Internet and American Life Project, August 11, 2004, http://www.pewinternet.org/pdfs/PIP_Internet _and_Daily_Life.pdf (accessed December 19, 2004). Used by permission of the Pew Internet and American Life Project, which bears no responsibility for the interpretations presented or conclusions reached based on analysis of the data.

online adults who typically found themselves looking up addresses, zip codes, and numbers did so on the Internet.

Communications were a big part of people's everyday Web experience as well. In the 2003 survey conducted by Pew/Internet, eight out of ten (79%) Web users who usually communicated with friends and family used the Web to communicate with them. Over one-quarter (26%) of online Americans who were dating or interested in meeting someone new did so on the Internet. The type of Internet service Americans had also greatly affected the likelihood of their engaging in online activities. As Table 9.2 displays, the percentage of people who took part in activities online jumped significantly when people had access to broadband.

According to Fallows in the August 2004 Pew/Internet report, quite a few online Americans used the Internet exclusively to take part in everyday activities during 2003. (See Table 9.3.) In fact, far more Internet users found maps or directions exclusively online than offline. A full 20% of Internet users (thirty-five million people) did all their banking and paid all their bills online, and 9% of Internet users (fifteen million Americans) bought such everyday items as groceries, kitchen utensils, and appliances on the Internet. Only 4% to 5% of those who participated in the Pew/Internet survey said they read for fun or watched videos exclusively on the Web.

A third of the people surveyed for *The Internet and Daily Life* reported that the Internet plays a major role in

their lives. (As opposed to the two-thirds who felt it played a minor role.) Fallows labeled these people "major players." Major players tended to be wealthier, more educated, and online longer than other American Internet-users. Forty-nine percent of major players graduated from college, versus 30% of the other people on the Internet. Only 21% of nonmajor players had a household income exceeding $75,000. Some 38% of major players, on the other hand, brought in that much money. Roughly three-quarters (76%) of major players had broadband, compared with under half (42%) of other Internet users. As Table 9.4 predictably displays, major players were much more likely to do everyday activities online.

Parenting and the Internet

The Internet has aided parents in their efforts to plan the daily activities of their children. According to *Parents Online*, a November 2002 Pew/Internet report by Katherine Allen and Lee Rainie, 26% of parents said that the Internet has improved the manner in which they spent time with their children. Parents went online to look for everything from parental ratings on television shows to advice on how to pacify children afraid of the dark. Thirty-four percent of parents said the Internet was helpful in planning weekend outings for the family. Twenty-seven percent of parents said the Internet made finding birthday and holiday gifts for the family easier. Parents also employed the Internet to get in touch with their children's teachers and the

TABLE 9.4

TABLE 9.5

Use of Internet for everyday activities, by level of Internet use, 2003

Activity	MP	Others
Get maps or directions	95%	83%
Communicate with friends/family	91	75
Check weather	83	62
Get news	83	53
Get sports scores	75	46
Get addresses, zip codes, phone numbers	73	38
Send cards, invites	69	45
Buy tickets	68	49
Plan gatherings	65	36
Do bills, banking	64	35
Play games	58	42
Buy daily items	51	23
Pursue hobbies	46	28
Find new people	42	20
Schedule appointments	39	14
Listen to music	36	16
Watch videos	33	8
Read for fun	30	13

N=1,358.

SOURCE: Deborah Fallows, "The online Americans who say the Internet plays a major role in their daily life are more likely to do everyday activities online than others," *The Internet and Daily Life,* Pew Internet and American Life Project, August 11, 2004, http://www.pewinternet.org/pdfs/PIP _Internet_and_Daily_Life.pdf (accessed December 19, 2004). Used by permission of the Pew Internet and American Life Project, which bears no responsibility for the interpretations presented or conclusions reached based on analysis of the data.

E-mails sent for the holidays, 2002

	2001	2002
To/from family members about holiday plans and events	42%	48%
To/from friends about holiday plans and events	39%	45%
Holiday letters/cards via email	24%	27%
To/from someone I had not spoken with in several years to exchange holiday greetings	11%	16%
To/from members of my church/synagogue to plan religious activities	N/A	10%

Sample = 1,220 Internet users.

SOURCE: Lee Rainie and John Horrigan, "The Kinds of Emails Holiday Celebrants Sent," in *Holidays Online—2002,* Pew Internet and American Life Project, January 7, 2003, http://www.pewinternet.org/pdfs/PIP _Holidays_Online_2002.pdf (accessed December 19, 2004). Used by permission of the Pew Internet and American Life Project, which bears no responsibility for the interpretations presented or conclusions reached based on analysis of the data.

parents of their children's friends. In a December 2000 Pew/Internet survey discussed in *Parents Online*, nearly one-third of parents (28%) replied that they keep in touch with their children's teachers through e-mail.

Parents also relied on the Internet to care for their children's health. *Parents Online* revealed that nearly 67% of online parents said they surfed the Internet for online health information, compared with 60% of adults without children. Parents were also generally more likely than adults without children to say the Internet improved the level of health care in their homes. More mothers than fathers logged onto the Internet to look for heath advice. Some 72% of wired mothers said they went online to find health and medical information, versus 57% of fathers. In a 2001 survey cited in *Parents Online*, mothers who went online to look for health information were asked about their most recent health search. Thirty-four percent of the health-seeking mothers said they went online on behalf of their children. Some 27% said they went online for their husbands, and 16% of these mothers went online for their parents.

Holidays and the Internet

The holiday season is a hectic time for any household, and the Internet provides an easy and convenient way to send holiday greetings, buy gifts, and stay in touch with family members. In fact, 78% of wired adults in America used the Web or e-mail to engage in some sort of holiday activity, according to *Holidays Online—2002*, a January

2003 Pew/Internet study by Lee Rainie and John Horrigan. E-mail was among the most popular applications, and Table 9.5 lists the ways e-mailing Americans employed their e-mail over the holiday season. Over one-quarter (27%) of e-mail users decided to save the expense and hassle of paper cards and instead opted to send them out electronically in 2002. Roughly half (48%) of e-mail users sent or received e-mail to and from family to arrange holiday plans, and slightly fewer (45%) employed e-mail to discuss plans with friends. Sixteen percent in 2002 said they had gotten in touch with someone via e-mail who they had not spoken to in years.

The World Wide Web also proved useful in planning holiday activities and trips. According to Rainie and Horrigan in *Holidays Online—2002*, 25% of wired adults, primarily women, went on the Internet to find ideas about crafts, food, or other ways to celebrate the holidays. Roughly 33% of online Americans used the Internet to plan seasonal activities, such as looking up the hours for Santa's workshop or a holiday light show. Another 11% of online Americans, typically heavy users of the Internet, made travel plans and reservations for the holidays online.

As most major retailers now have a Web site, shopping online has become easier than ever. *Holidays Online— 2002* revealed that some 46% of wired adults (forty-seven million people) used the Internet to look for gifts, and 28% (twenty-nine million people) actually bought something. (See Table 9.6 for a breakdown of who shopped online for the holidays.) A majority of adults (75%) who took part in e-commerce pointed to convenience and saving time as among their main reasons for shopping online. Roughly half (51%) said that the reason they shopped online was because they could find hard-to-locate gifts, and another one-third (31%) reported cost savings as their main reason for purchasing items on the Internet. All together, Americans spent close to $11 billion online during the 2002 holiday season, according to the January 2003 Pew/Internet

TABLE 9.6

Online holiday gift shoppers, by selected characteristics, 2002

Men	41%
Women	59%
By race and ethnicity	
Whites	79%
Hispanics	10%
Blacks	4%
Others	7%
By age	
18–29	24%
30–49	52%
50–64	20%
65+	4%
By household income	
<$30,000	13%
$30,000–$49,999	23%
$50,000–$74,999	25%
>$75,000	39%
By Internet experience	
1 year or less	3%
2–3 years	14%
4–5 years	37%
6 or more years	45%

Sample = 1,220 Internet users.

SOURCE: Lee Rainie and John Horrigan, "Who the Holiday Shoppers Were," in *Holidays Online—2002*, Pew Internet and American Life Project, January 7, 2003, http://www.pewinternet.org/pdfs/PIP_Holidays_Online_2002.pdf (accessed December 19, 2004). Used by permission of the Pew Internet and American Life Project, which bears no responsibility for the interpretations presented or conclusions reached based on analysis of the data.

TABLE 9.7

Growth of online holiday season shopping, 2001–02

	2002 holiday season sales in millions	% change vs. the same period a year ago
Home & garden	$555	78%
Furniture & appliances	$171	75%
Toys	$396	61%
Sports & fitness	$233	54%
Jewelry & watches	$216	45%
Movies & video	$205	36%
Apparel & accessories	$1,455	31%
Video games	$130	24%
Consumer electronics	$1,027	21%
Event tickets	$250	16%

Data for period between Nov. 1–Dec. 20, 2002.

SOURCE: Lee Rainie and John Horrigan, "Largest Growth Categories in Online Sales," in *Holidays Online—2002*, Pew Internet and American Life Project, January 7, 2003, http://www.pewinternet.org/pdfs/PIP_Holidays_Online_2002.pdf (accessed December 19, 2004). Used by permission of the Pew Internet and American Life Project, which bears no responsibility for the interpretations presented or conclusions reached based on analysis of the data.

report. Online holiday shoppers spent an average of $407 in 2002. More than one-third (34%) of these shoppers spent more than $300 on Web retail. As can be seen in Table 9.7, more apparel and accessories sold online throughout the 2002 holiday season than any other product, according to data from comScore Networks cited by Rainie and Horrigan. Consumer electronics came in second, and sales in home and garden grew by the largest percentage from the year before.

Religion, Spirituality, and the Internet

Nearly 64% (eighty-two million people) of Internet users as of late 2003 had taken part in religious or spiritual activities online. An April 2004 Pew/Internet report entitled *Faith Online* by Stewart Hoover, Lynn Clark, and Lee Rainie revealed that 38% of wired American adults sent, received, or forwarded e-mail with spiritual content. (See Table 9.8.) Thirty-two percent of Internet users went online to read religious news, and 17% searched for places to attend religious services. More online people seemed interested in activities that enhanced their spiritual and religious lives (e.g., sending a spiritual or religious e-mail) rather than those related solely to the organizational side of religion such as scheduling church workshops. At the same time, those who attended church once a week were much more likely to engage in online activities for spiritual or religious reasons. (See Table 9.9.)

According to *Faith Online*, those who used the Internet for religion or spirituality were more likely than general Internet users to be white, female, college-educated, and married. They were also more likely to live in the South or Midwest and to reside in households earning an income of $75,000 or more. Not all of the online faithful used the Internet to focus on their own religion. A little more than one-quarter (26%) said they had utilized the Internet to explore faiths other than their own. Of those, a little over half (51%) said they were curious about other religions, and 13% said that they did it to enhance spiritual growth. The study also found that most online believers (54%) described themselves as religious and spiritual, as opposed to spiritual but not religious (33%), religious but not spiritual (6%), or not religious and not spiritual (4%). Overall, online religious and spiritual people considered the Internet to be a supplement to rather than a substitute for their everyday religious life.

THE HOME ELECTRONICS REVOLUTION

In the 1970s and early 1980s, advances in circuit manufacturing lowered the price of integrated electronic components from hundreds of dollars to less than $10 in some instances. Since then electronics chips, displays, and sensors have worked their way into everything from washing machines to hair dryers to coffeemakers. Overall, such electronics have given people more control over the settings on their appliances, lighting, and heating and cooling systems.

High Tech Home Features

By late 2004, many home appliances and systems had become fully programmable and even Internet accessible.

TABLE 9.8

Religious and spiritual uses of the Internet, 2003

Sent, received, or forwarded email with spiritual content	38%
Sent an online greeting card for a religious holiday such as Christmas, Hanukah, or Ramadan	35%
Read online news accounts about religious events/affairs	32%
Sought information on the Web about how to celebrate holidays or other significant religious events	21%
Searched for places in their communities where they could attend religious services	17%
Used email to plan a meeting for a religious group	14%
Downloaded or listened online to music with religious or spiritual themes	11%
Made or responded to a prayer request online	7%
Made a donation to a religious organization or charity	7%

N = 1,358 Internet users.

SOURCE: Stewart Hoover, Lynn Clark, and Lee Rainie, "Religious and Spiritual Uses of the Internet," in *Faith Online,* Pew Internet and American Life Project, April 7, 2004, http://www.pewinternet.org/pdfs/PIP_Faith _Online_2004.pdf (accessed January 11, 2005). Used by permission of the Pew Internet and American Life Project, which bears no responsibility for the interpretations presented or conclusions reached based on analysis of the data.

TABLE 9.9

Church attendance and Internet activities, 2003

	Those who get religion news online	Those who use the Internet for personal religious and spiritual purposes	Those who use the Internet for institutional religious and spiritual reasons
Attend church at least once a week	39%	67%	51%
Once a month	36	56	45
Several times per year	27	50	26
Don't attend services	23	38	16

N = 1,358 Internet users.

SOURCE: Stewart Hoover, Lynn Clark, and Lee Rainie, "Church Attendance and Internet Activities," in *Faith Online,* Pew Internet and American Life Project, April 7, 2004, http://www.pewinternet.org/pdfs/PIP_Faith_Online _2004.pdf (accessed January 9, 2005). Used by permission of the Pew Internet and American Life Project, which bears no responsibility for the interpretations presented or conclusions reached based on analysis of the data.

Interactive, online thermostats, for instance, were installed in many new homes. These thermostats, which can be connected to the Web, give the homeowner the option of setting and monitoring the temperature of the house remotely from a computer or a laptop. The thermostat also alerts the user of a malfunction or a gas leak in the system. Zone lighting systems contain electronics that enable homeowners to program lighting configurations for multiple areas of the same room. With the touch of a button, one side of a room can be illuminated for reading while the other side remains dark for watching television.

Another programmable fixture that was available in many newer homes was the electronic keypad locking system. The advantage of the keypad over the normal lock is that it can be reprogrammed easily. If a homeowner wants to keep someone out, it can be done by changing the lock code. The lock can also be set to let in certain people, such as a painter, only during certain times of the day. Some keypad locks contain circuit boards that can be plugged into a broadband connection, which gives the homeowner the option of changing the lock codes remotely or keeping a record of who came and went. By 2004 some companies offered automated home systems that tied the lights, the door locks, the thermostat, and home security system into one control center that could be accessed by the Internet. According to "Building an Electronic Fortress" by Charlie Wardell in the November 2004 issue of *Popular Science*, these systems can be placed in different modes for when the homeowner is awake, asleep, or away. When the homeowner goes out of town all that he or she has to do is press a button and the lights are turned off, the alarm is set, and the thermostat is turned down. These systems could be installed for $1 to $2 per square foot in 2004.

Smart Appliances

As technologies progress and electronics become even more affordable, makers of appliances will likely continue to add additional electronic features. Whirlpool, for instance, has been working with engineers at Michigan State University to create a talking washing machine to aid blind people when they do their laundry, according to "Students Make Washing Machine Talk" by Geoff Adams-Spink (*BBC News World Edition*, September 12, 2004). In addition to containing Braille instructions, the washing machine tells the user what command he or she has selected as each button is pushed or knob is turned. A status button has also been incorporated, which reads back the current settings when pressed. The additional circuitry costs only about $30 to install, and the prototype unit was being tested in the home of a blind couple as of September 2004.

A number of technologies were emerging in 2004 that may someday allow people to operate every major and minor appliance via a remote control or telephone. One such device, known as the ZigBee, was being developed by the ZigBee Alliance, a consortium of seventy companies that included Motorola, Honeywell, Samsung, and Mitsubishi Electric. According to "Radio Chip Heralds the Smarter Home" by Duncan Graham-Rowe (*New Scientist*, August 7, 2004), the ZigBee is a networkable, low-power, two-way radio microchip with a range of about 250 feet that can receive and send data. Such chips could be implanted into everyday appliances and tied into their controls. A PDA (personal digital assistant) or some type of universal remote control would then be employed by the homeowner to transmit and receive signal to and from the chips. In this way, every appliance or entertainment system in the house could be monitored and activated via remote control. A base station capable of communicating with the ZigBee chips could easily be attached to a phone line as well. By calling into the base station via phone, the homeowner could check the status of an oven or a coffeemaker using the touch-tone commands.

ROBOTS

Around the turn of the twenty-first century, the first practical, automated robots went on sale for the consumer market. Far from the convenient marvels depicted on futuristic television shows, these robots could perform only simple tasks such as vacuuming. As of October 2004, five models of robotic vacuum cleaners were on the market. Most of these vacuum cleaners use various sensors to feel their way around the room, picking up dirt as they go. The Electrolux Trilobite, for instance, shoots out ultrasonic signals like a bat to detect and avoid obstacles in its way as it goes back and forth across the room for forty-five minutes, sucking up dirt and recording where it has been. In "Run for Your Lives, Dust Bunnies!" (*Popular Science*, October 2004), Jonathon Keats found the performance of most of the robot vacuum cleaners lacking, with the exception of the Trilobite.

Another robotic device available in 2004 was the Robomower by Friendly Robotics. True to its name, the Robomower automatically zigzags back and forth over a lawn, cutting the grass as it goes. Sensors are imbedded in bumpers that surround the entire mower, and if it bangs into something bigger than a large piece of bark, it backs off. A low voltage guide wire set up by the user around the perimeter of the yard lets the mower know if it is crossing the boundaries of the lawn, in which case it turns around.

Programmable Robots

Yet another type of robot that made its debut in 2005 was the PC-Bot by White Box Robotics. In "Plug-and-Play Robots" (*Scientific American*, April 2004), W. Wayt Gibbs remarked that the knee-high robots "look like R2-D2 droids that have been redesigned by Cadillac." These PC-Bots are built from everyday computer components and accessories. Each one has a digital camera, speakers, slots for peripheral components such as a disc drive, and sensors mounted on the outside. A standard hard drive, microprocessor, a drive motor, and a stabilizer are contained within the chassis. The whole thing is mounted on wheels. The innovation behind the PC-Bots, however, does not lie in its components, but rather in the fact that the machine is fully programmable. Face and object recognition software, for instance, can be placed on a PC-Bot, which allow it to recognize various people and objects in its environment and then act on that information, according to Gibbs. One variation of the PC-Bot that White Box Electronics sold was the 912 HMV. This robot was designed to roam around the owner's house when the owner is out of town. If the robot spots a strange figure or detects a loud noise, it can e-mail or send a page to the owner.

Humanoid Robots

Several large companies and academic labs around the world have been experimenting with complex humanoid robots as well. The most famous of these is probably Honda's ASIMO (Advanced Step in Innovation Mobility) robot. Researchers at Honda have been working on the ASIMO design since 1986. As of late 2004 the robot could recognize up to ten faces, run at a clip of three kilometers an hour, respond to a handshake, and even climb stairs, according to the Honda Web site (http://asimo.honda.com). Honda's goal was to create a robot that could be controlled remotely by a handicapped person to complete basic chores around the house such as retrieving the mail, doing the dishes, or moving items from one place to another.

Another group of robot scientists at Purdue University and Japan's Advanced Institute of Science and Technology were working on ways to design robots that had the agility and precision of humans. According to Natalie Goel in "Will New Robots Kick Honda's ASIMO?" (*PC Magazine*, December 8, 2004), Purdue scientists were placing sensors on human bodies (the same used to create human animation in video games and movies) and then recording precisely how people performed simple tasks in three dimensions. They planned to use these computer analyses of human movement to design robots that moved more like humans. However, given the current cost to produce and maintain humanoid robots, the immediate future of robots will likely resemble the PC-Bot more than the ASIMO.

HIGH TECH AUTOMOBILES

Technological innovations for everyday life are not just occurring in the home. Many advanced IT technologies have made it into the car as well. As of 2004, car buyers had the option to choose certain models of sedans and minivans with proximity sensors in their bumpers. These sensors help to prevent accidents by alerting the driver if something such as a parked car or a small child is too close to the bumper. Global positioning systems (GPS) have also become an option on just about any new car. GPS systems continuously pick up signals broadcast from a network of stationary (nonorbiting) satellites positioned above the Earth. By analyzing its proximity in relation to three of the satellites in the network, the GPS system can pinpoint its location on the surface of the Earth. Most systems then combine this information with an up-to-date map of the local roads to display the car's position on a street map.

In-Vehicle Communications Systems

Combining GPS, cell phone, and sensor technology, several companies have developed what are known as in-vehicle communications systems. In the United States, OnStar was the most widely used of these in-vehicle systems, with over two million subscribers as of 2004.

OnStar, which is a subsidiary of General Motors, was first offered on GM vehicles in 1996. The system is activated when the user either presses either a red or a blue button in the car or when the car's airbags are deployed. Pressing the blue button instructs the OnStar cellular unit to dial the main OnStar switchboard. A GPS then relays the vehicle's coordinates through the built-in mobile phone to the operator, telling him or her exactly where the car is. Sensors planted on the car's major systems let the operator know how the car is functioning. The car owner can then request roadside assistance, directions, or information on the status of the car. In the event of a life-threatening emergency, the red button contacts an OnStar emergency service operator who then calls the nearest emergency service provider. The system is also triggered if the air bags go off. In this event, the emergency OnStar operator is called. The operator then notifies the nearest emergency service provider, telling them where the accident took place, as well as the make and model of the car. Finally, the user can call the operator from a phone outside the car to open the car door locks or to report a stolen car. The OnStar operator can assist the police in tracking down a stolen car.

Advances in Safety and Vehicle Communications

According to "The Future of the Car: Intelligence" by Paul Horrell (*Popular Science*, September 2004), cars will not only likely continue to become more fuel efficient and faster, but more intelligent as well. Companies were experimenting with numerous ways of using external sensors to inform the driver and systems within the car of impending danger. French carmaker Peugeot Citroën, for instance, was experimenting with a system of infrared sensors that scan painted road markings on each side of the car and alert the driver if he or she is straying out of the lane. If the blinker is not on and the driver strays left, the sensors perceive the car crossing the line in the road and the left side of the driver's seat vibrates. If the driver strays right, the right side of the seat vibrates.

Other car companies are tinkering with systems that allow cars to communicate with one another in order to warn drivers of delays or dangerous road conditions ahead. DaimlerChrysler was experimenting with such a system in their European Smart cars. The system employs a bevy of sensors and wireless local area networks (WLAN) much like those used in wireless home computing set-ups. When this intelligent car encounters a traffic jam or black ice, for instance, sensors on the car would detect the problem. The car then would send the information via the WLAN to another car equipped with the system some 500 feet away, which would relay the information on to another car and so on until every car and driver in the area would be made aware of the traffic jam or the black ice.

CHAPTER 10
PUBLIC OPINION ABOUT THE INTERNET AND INFORMATION TECHNOLOGIES

Since the advent of the Internet, the Gallup Organization, headquartered in Washington, D.C., has polled Americans about everything from their general use of computers and the Internet to the trust people place in online health-care advice. Data from a Gallup poll conducted in April 2003 revealed that 79% of Americans used a personal computer at their office, place of work, or school. A December 2004 Gallup poll found that 75% of respondents also logged on to the Internet at some point during the past year. Sixteen percent of Americans said they went online up to one hour a day, and a full 32% spent more than an hour a day on the Web. For the most part, Internet usage appeared as if it was beginning to plateau in 2004. A December 2002 poll reported that 72% of Americans used the Internet, with 26% of respondents saying they went online more than an hour a day. As a comparison, only 47% of people said they used the Internet in a poll conducted during November 1998.

In December 2003 Gallup also collected data on how online Americans used the Internet. As with surveys by the Pew Internet & American Life Project, e-mail came in number one. Nine out of ten people (93%) responded that they had used e-mail. Roughly two-thirds (65%) of respondents claimed they used e-mail frequently. Checking the news or weather came in second with eight out of ten (83%) people responding that they engaged in this activity online. The poll found that seven out of ten Internet users (69%) shopped online. This number matches up with a "Pew Internet Project Data Memo" by Lee Rainie (April 13, 2004), which reported that two-thirds (65%) of American Internet users over age eighteen had bought something online. The Gallup poll also found that six out of ten (63%) online adults made travel plans and looked up medical advice online. Half (51%) of those polled contacted someone else with instant messaging (IM), five out of ten (49%) played a game online, and four out of ten (39%) paid bills online. A higher percentage of online Americans engaged in some of these activities than in pre-

vious years. According to a February 2000 Gallup poll, at that time only 89% of people sent e-mails and 45% shopped online.

In "Internet Use: What's Age Got to Do with It?" Linda Lyons calls attention to the discrepancy in Internet use between adults aged eighteen to forty-nine and those over fifty (Gallup Organization, March 16, 2004). The report, which employed aggregated data from 2002 and 2003, reveals that 52% of adults under the age of fifty said they log on to the Internet everyday, compared with 17% of those aged sixty-five and older. Different age groups engaged in different activities on the Internet. Roughly every age group sent and received e-mail in the same proportion. However, 36% of young adults aged eighteen to twenty-nine used instant messaging, compared with 18% of the thirty to forty-nine-year-old group and 12% of fifty- to sixty-four-year-olds. Twenty-six percent of those thirty to forty-nine paid their bills online, compared with the 9% of those over fifty. Surprisingly, roughly equal percentages in each age group logged on to play games.

Other demographic differences exist among those who use the Internet extensively. According to the March 2004 Gallup report by Linda Lyons, a higher percentage of men (49%) went online every day than women (40%). In addition, nearly half of urban (47%) and suburban (49%) people went online every day, as opposed to only one-third (34%) of those living in rural areas. Forty-four percent of whites used the Internet every day, versus 46% of non-whites, suggesting that the digital divide between races has evaporated. According to "Minority Teens Less Likely to Socialize via Web" by Steve Hanway (Gallup Organization, June 10, 2003), however, the U.S. Department of Commerce reported in February 2002 that whites were still ahead of African-Americans and Hispanics in their Internet use. Gallup poll data on teen Internet usage from January and February 2003 appeared to corroborate these findings to a certain extent. The data revealed that 79% of online black and Hispanic teenagers sent and received e-mails, compared with 89% of online white teens. Seventy percent of wired white youth also used instant messaging to chat with friends, as opposed to 56% of wired Hispanics and African-Americans. Hispanics and African-Americans, however, sought out information on the Internet just as much as whites (92% vs. 93%) and chatted more with people they did not know in online chat rooms. Hanway suggested that these findings indicate that black and Hispanic Internet users do not have as extensive a network of friends and family with Internet connections as white teens did. The June 2003 report, however, ended on an optimistic note. Hanway pointed out that Internet and computer companies would in the future likely lower the prices of basic Internet access to reach all audiences and that at that point people in various racial and socioeconomic demographics should be online in equal proportions.

E-MAIL

As noted earlier, e-mail is the most popular application on the Internet. More than nine out of ten (97%) e-mail users felt that e-mail had made their lives better, according to a Gallup poll survey taken in June 2001. The data, which appeared in "Almost All E-mail Users Say Internet, E-mail Have Made Lives Better" by Jeffrey Jones (Gallup Organization, July 23, 2001), also revealed that 52% of e-mailers agreed that e-mail was the online activity that they engaged in most. Over 50% said that they had come to use e-mail more often than the telephone or the U.S. mail. Most e-mailers, however, would give up e-mail before they would give up more traditional means of communication. When asked which form of communication they would be least likely to sacrifice, 63% said the telephone, 15% said U.S. mail, 12% said e-mail, and 10% said cellular phones.

Slightly more e-mail users reported using e-mail at home as opposed to work (90% vs. 83%), and roughly half (53%) used e-mail in both places. Most people had more than one e-mail address, which is likely not only due to work and home accounts but to the proliferation of spam as well. In fact, only 23% of e-mailers had one address. Thirty-three percent had two addresses, 14% had three addresses, 7% had four addresses, and a full 22% claimed to have five or more e-mail addresses. People who used e-mail at work sent and received e-mails much more than those who just used e-mail at home. Fifty-one percent of people who said they had e-mail at work also said they check it once an hour, whereas only 6% of those with home accounts checked in on their e-mail every hour. This may have to do with the volume of e-mails received at home and at work. The average e-mail user with a work account reported receiving twelve e-mails per day. The median home user only received eight. As to who people sent and received messages from, the June 2001 Gallup survey revealed that 39% of people traded e-mails with

coworkers and business associates most. Family came in second with 33%, and 28% replied that they e-mailed friends most often. For the most part, men were more likely to e-mail a business associate than women were (44% vs. 32%), and women were more likely to e-mail family than men were (38% vs. 29%).

Overall in 2001, women tended to use e-mail more than men did, according to Jones in "Almost All E-mail Users Say Internet, E-mail Have Made Lives Better." Nearly two-thirds (61%) of females who used e-mail said e-mailing was the activity they engaged in the most online. Fewer than half (44%) of male e-mailers cited e-mailing as their number one activity. Oddly, women were more likely than men to be willing to give up e-mail. Fifteen percent of men responded that they were less willing to give up their e-mail rather than other forms of communication, as opposed to 8% of women. Other than these slight gender differences in e-mail use, very few demographic differences existed among the general population of e-mailers. As to instant messaging, most adults (58%) said they never used it online. Only one-third of adults reported using IM occasionally.

Spam

As anyone who uses e-mail knows, spam continues to be a growing problem. According to "American E-mailers Increasingly Fed up with Computer Spam" by Frank Newport and Joseph Carroll (Gallup Organization, May 20, 2003), Earthlink estimated that nearly 40% of the e-mail coursing through its system each day consisted of spam in 2003. America Online (AOL) claimed that up to 80% of the e-mail in its network was spam. *USA Today* calculated that two trillion spam messages were likely to have been sent over all of 2003.

Most Americans were not happy with the amount of spam they were receiving. An April 2003 CNN/USA Today/Gallup poll revealed that 67% of e-mail users reported that spam was a problem. This was a sharp increase from March 2000 when a Pew/Internet poll reported that only 37% of people said they received too much spam. In fact, the problem was so bad that 13% had quit their e-mail service in the year prior to the April 2003 CNN/USA Today/Gallup poll. Nearly one-quarter (24%) of e-mail users had considered leaving their service because of spam.

CELLULAR PHONES

As of late 2003 cell-phone ownership among Americans was still rising at a fairly brisk rate. A mid-November 2003 Gallup poll found that some 67% of Americans owned a cell phone, according to "Cell Phone Users Have Little Interest in Number Portability" by Joseph Carroll (Gallup Organization, December 8, 2003). A similar Gallup poll in March 2000 found that only 50% of Americans had a cell phone. The rise in users occurred at a fairly steady rate over those three years. In the summer of 2001, 55% of Americans owned cell phones, and in early 2002 cell-phone ownership was at 60%. (See Figure 10.1.) When it came to choosing a cell-phone carrier, the November 2003 Gallup poll revealed that the calling plan was the most important feature to Americans. In fact, 44% of cell-phone users selected their carrier because of the calling plan. The next most important factor was network coverage, with 31% of people choosing this factor. Only 12% of cell-phone users thought customer service was important, and 5% felt strongly about the features on the cell phone.

Not all demographic groups had equal access to cell phones. Eight out of ten (83%) Americans who earned $50,000 annually or more owned a mobile phone, as opposed to 35% of people who earned less than $20,000. The age group in which cell-phone ownership was most prevalent was the thirty- to forty-nine-year-old group. Seventy-four percent in this age range owned a cell phone. Roughly the same percentage of those aged eighteen to twenty-nine (69%) and those aged fifty to sixty-four (69%) owned cell phones. Only four out of ten (43%) of those sixty-five or older had their own mobile phone.

As the number of cell phones has grown, so too has the practice of talking on a cell phone while driving. Generally, people consider this behavior to be unsafe. Nearly two-thirds (84%) of people responding to a Gallup poll conducted in early November 2003 disagreed with the statement, "using a cellular phone while driving is safe." Only 78% of cell-phone users believed that driving while speaking on a cell phone was unsafe, whereas a full 95% on nonusers felt this way. Despite this sentiment, 38% cell-phone users openly admitted to using their cell phones frequently while driving. Many of these people did not use a hands-free device as only 35% of all cell-phone users reported using a hands-free cell phone.

In mid-2001 New York became the first state to pass a law banning the use of hand-held cell phones while driving. Since then many other states have followed suit. According to "Public Favors Ban on Use of Cellular Phones While Driving" by Darren Carlson (Gallup Organization, July 12, 2001), 70% of Americans supported the idea that their state should ban the use of hand-held cell phones while driving. Sixty-two percent of respondents believed that a full ban should be put into place. Once again, many of those who admitted driving while on the phone seemed to think it was unsafe. Roughly half (49%) of these cell-phone drivers reported that they were in favor of such a ban. Two-thirds (67%) of the general public and half (52%) of all cell-phone users did not feel that the ban would be an inconvenience to them.

E-COMMERCE

The number of Americans who have shopped online increased from 45% to 69% between 2000 and 2004. The

FIGURE 10.1

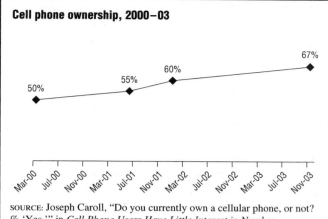

SOURCE: Joseph Caroll, "Do you currently own a cellular phone, or not? % 'Yes,'" in *Cell Phone Users Have Little Interest in Number Portability,* Gallup News Service, The Gallup Organization, December 8, 2003, http://www.gallup.com/poll/content/default.aspx?ci=9856 (accessed January 9, 2005). Copyright © 2003 by The Gallup Organization. Reproduced by permission of The Gallup Organization.

growth in e-commerce did not appear to be slowing as of 2004. In her commentary "Good News for E-tailers from Tomorrow's Retired Investors" (Gallup Organization, December 14, 2004), Raksha Arora pointed to the fact that e-commerce brought in $17.6 billion in the third fiscal quarter of 2004, according to the U.S. Department of Commerce. This number represented a 21.5% increase over e-commerce sales in the third quarter of 2003. Arora reasons that as the large American generation born in the post–World War II era become retirees this trend will only likely continue.

The growth in overall e-commerce has been reflected in the growth in online holiday shopping. An early December 2004 Gallup poll revealed that three in ten planned to use the Internet to shop for holiday gifts in 2004. Mark Gillespie reported in "Average American Will Spend $797 on Gifts This Holiday Season" (Gallup Organization, November 27, 2000) that 21% of people surveyed said they were at least somewhat likely to do their holiday shopping online. This figure represented a dramatic increase from 1998 when only 10% said they would go online to buy gifts.

Some differences existed between those who shopped online and those who did not. According to "Online Shopping Grows, but Department, Discount Stores Still Most Popular with Holiday Shoppers" by Mark Gillespie (Gallup Organization, December 3, 2002), men were more likely than women to do holiday shopping online. Age also seemed to make a difference. Roughly one out of ten (13%) of those eighteen to twenty-nine interviewed said they were very likely to shop online, compared to two-tenths (22%) of those between the ages of thirty and forty-nine. Only 9% of Americans over fifty said they were likely to shop online.

Banking

By the early 2000s more and more banks were offering electronic banking options that allowed customers to conduct banking business without ever walking up to a teller. (See Chapter 3.) According to "Banking Customers Still Love Bricks and Mortar" by Dennis Jacobe (Gallup Organization, June 10, 2003), Americans were taking advantage of these electronic services. In a March 2000 Gallup poll, only 7% of Americans reported any experience with online banking. By 2003 29% of Americans said that they banked online from home at least once a month, and 17% responded they banked online more than four times a month. (See Figure 10.2.) ATM usage also increased between 2000 and 2003, but at a lower rate. Forty-eight percent of Americans used an ATM at least once a month in 2000, compared with 57% in 2003.

Due to the high costs of hiring tellers and leasing branch space, banks have encouraged the use of electronic banking among customers as a whole. While Americans have taken advantage of online banking, debit cards, and ATM services, most still make regular trips to a bank branch location. Jacobe's Gallup report revealed that in 2003 83% of Americans still visited their bank once a month on average, and three out of ten visited the bank four or five times a month. In the March 2000 Gallup poll, 87% of respondents said they were bank customers, and 78% said they used the bank once a week. Between 2000 and 2003, the frequency of visits appeared to have gone down, but the number of banking customers did not change. Overall, Jacobe concluded that seeing a teller face to face was still very important to Americans. In particular, when faced with a complicated transaction, people would rather deal with someone in person. Consumers were also willing to pay the additional fees for the added convenience of ATM and online banking where applicable.

E-CRIME

A Gallup poll conducted in October 2004 found that 8% of American households had been victims of a computer- or Internet-based crime. This figure represented twenty-four million people who had experienced such crimes as fraud or computer hacking. This was a 33% increase from October 2003 when only 6% of Americans (seventeen million people) said they had been victims of e-crime. Internet crime drove the overall incidence of household crime up from 25% to 30%, according to David W. Moore in "Crime Rate Steady: 3 in 10 Households Victimized Past Year" (Gallup Organization, December 3, 2004).

Privacy and Security Issues

At the heart of Internet crime lies identity theft and fraud. Most Americans seem to be aware of the problems surrounding identity theft, according to "Majority of E-

FIGURE 10.2

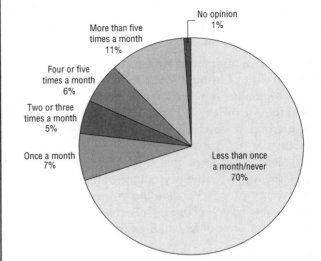

Consumer use of online banking, April 2003

DURING THE PAST TWELVE MONTHS, WHAT IS THE AVERAGE NUMBER OF TIMES YOU USED YOUR BANK'S ONLINE BANKING SERVICE — ONCE A MONTH, TWO OR THREE TIMES A MONTH, FOUR OR FIVE TIMES A MONTH, OR MORE OFTEN?

April 2003

No opinion 1%

More than five times a month 11%

Four or five times a month 6%

Two or three times a month 5%

Once a month 7%

Less than once a month/never 70%

SOURCE: Dennis Jacobe, "Consumer Use of Online Banking," in *Banking Customers Still Love Bricks and Mortar,* Gallup Poll News Service Commentary, The Gallup Organization, June 10, 2003, http://www.gallup.com/poll/content/?ci=8593 (accessed January 9, 2005). Copyright © 2003 by The Gallup Organization. Reproduced by permission of The Gallup Organization.

mail Users Express Concern about Internet Privacy" by Jeffrey Jones and Darren Carlson (Gallup Organization, June 28, 2001). Eighty-two percent of e-mailing Americans polled in June 2001 by the Gallup Organization were at least somewhat concerned about giving out personal information on the Internet. The same percentage of e-mailers was wary of the misuse of credit card information provided over the Internet as well.

Figure 10.3 displays the information that those with e-mail were very/somewhat comfortable giving out over the Internet. Only 11% of those who responded were at ease with giving out their social security number, and only 33% felt comfortable with providing their credit card number. Close to 50%, however, were comfortable with releasing their work phone number, street address, and home phone. (Though 78% said they were fine with relinquishing their e-mail address, all those who took the poll were required to do so.) A February 2000 Gallup poll revealed that roughly 88% of people who purchased information or products online used their credit card to do so.

In late January 2003 the Slammer/Sapphire worm spread worldwide around the Internet in thirty minutes, affecting thousands of host computers and shutting down servers of many major companies, including American

FIGURE 10.3

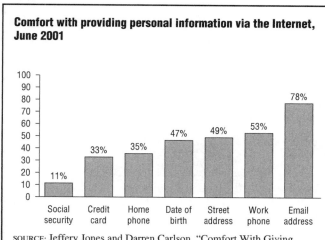

Comfort with providing personal information via the Internet, June 2001

SOURCE: Jeffery Jones and Darren Carlson, "Comfort With Giving Information Out Over the Internet," in *Majority of E-mail Users Express Concern about Internet Privacy,* Gallup News Service, The Gallup Organization, June 28, 2001, http://www.gallup.com/poll/content/default.aspx?ci=4558 (accessed January 9, 2005). Copyright © 2001 by The Gallup Organization. Reproduced by permission of The Gallup Organization.

Express and Countrywide Financial Corporation. Shortly after this worm hit the Internet, the Gallup Organization asked Internet users about how the incident affected their perception of the Internet. Nearly 9% of those polled in February responded that the problems on the Internet affected them personally. A resounding 81% said that the viruses either delayed or prevented their getting to a Web site. Many peoples' overall confidence in the Internet was shaken. Twenty percent of Internet users said that the stories of the worms made them less likely to use the Internet, and 47% said they were less likely to use credit cards online.

According to Jones and Carlson in "Majority of E-mail Users Express Concern about Internet Privacy," two-thirds of e-mail users in 2001 believed the government should pass more laws to ensure online privacy. In September 2000 Gallup had found that exactly half of all Internet users maintained that opinion. At the same time, however, Internet users in 2000 were wary of the type of government surveillance that could be used to effectively capture hackers or creators of viruses. Roughly two-thirds (63%) of online Americans said they were "very concerned" about government software that allowed law enforcement to tap into Internet e-mail to search for incriminating evidence. Sixty percent of Web users also said they were worried about powerful government databases, such as those proposed by the Department of Homeland Security, that contain extensive information on ordinary Americans.

The idea of corporations gathering personal information online and constructing databases troubled American Internet users as well. Jones and Carlson found in June 2001 that nearly three-quarters (73%) of e-mailing Americans were concerned about companies keeping track of

their Internet usage, and roughly the same number (71%) were wary of Internet "cookies" that monitor their comings and goings on the Web. In addition, many (61%) were anxious about their Internet service provider monitoring their use of the Internet and e-mail.

ENTERTAINMENT MEDIA

Since the early 1960s Americans have preferred to spend their evenings in front of a television more than anywhere else. According to "There's No Place Like Home to Spend an Evening, Say Most Americans" by Lydia Saad (Gallup Organization, January 10, 2002), 27% of Americans in a 1960 poll replied that their favorite way of spending their evening was in front of a television. Reading, resting, and entertaining and visiting friends were ranked second, third, and fourth. Television watching appeared to hit its peak between the mid-1960s and early 1970s. A full 46% of people polled by Gallup in February 1974 rated television as their favorite evening activity, followed by the somewhat ambiguous response of "staying at home with the family" (14%), and reading (8%). Listening to music was also very popular in 1974. Five percent of Americans said that they listened to music in their free time, which was the highest percentage compared with all other years.

By December 2001, watching television (including videos and DVDs) had dropped back down to 1960 levels, with only 26% of people saying that watching television was their favorite leisure activity. Twenty-five percent of respondents replied that they enjoyed spending time with family the most. (The poll, however, did not delve into what activities American families enjoyed during time spent together.) Reading came in at 9%, listening to music was at 2%, and only 1% of people replied that they preferred to work on the home computer in 2001.

Hobbies

For years Gallup has also been asking Americans about their favorite hobbies. The 2001 press release by Lydia Saad listed the results for this survey from February 1948 and December 2001. In 1948, 42% of Americans replied that they were not interested in any hobbies. The hobbies that generated the highest response were handiwork, which included everything from knitting to model aviation (15%), athletics and sports (10%), and amateur craftsmanship, including carpentry and photography (6%). By comparison, only 19% of survey respondents in 2001 said they did not have a hobby. A full 33% listed sports. The number of people who engaged in handiwork grew to 17%. Spending time on the computer, which included programming, surfing the Internet, and playing games, was the favorite hobby of 4% of survey respondents.

A September 2002 Gallup poll took a different approach in trying to determine how Americans entertain themselves in their free time. The poll, which appeared in "Does Reading Still Stack Up?" by Jennifer Robison (Gallup Organization, September 3, 2002), asked computer users how much time they spent on a number of activities. (See Figure 10.4.) Once again, television won out. Computer users reported that they watched 2.5 hours of television a day. Using the Internet, however, came in second in this poll, with computer users saying they spent 1.5 hours a day on the Internet. The poll reported that both computer users and noncomputer users spent 1.1 hours reading books on average.

Music and Movie File Sharing

Since the creation of Napster in the late 1990s, file sharing of music, and to a lesser extent movies, has become commonplace in America. (See Chapters 4 and 5.) According to "Downloads Are Music to Teen Ears" by Linda Lyons (Gallup Organization, June 24, 2003), 47% of U.S. teenagers (aged thirteen to seventeen) said they used the Internet for file-sharing purposes. Many of these music files were undoubtedly downloaded from sites and file-sharing networks, such as Kazaa, that were not approved or licensed by the recording industry. When asked if they had downloaded music from an Internet site not authorized by a record company, 18% of adult Internet users responded that they had, according to a spring 2002 Gallup poll. This same survey also revealed that 3% of Internet users had downloaded a movie illegally. If downloading movies could be done quickly and easily, 21% said they would do so.

According to "A New Spin on Music Distribution" by Steve Crabtree (Gallup Organization, July 16, 2002), the International Federation of Phonographic Industries (IFPI) claimed that music sales around the world dropped 5% in 2001 due to music piracy (i.e., illegal file sharing) and economic downturn. As a response to this loss in profit and infringement of music artists' copyrights, the Recording Industry Association of America began to go after organizations and individuals who were downloading music without the record industry's approval. In 2002 the infringement of copyrighted material could be punished with $250,000 in fines or three years in prison.

Public sentiment on the issue was mixed. A March 2002 Gallup poll showed that 43% of people thought copying songs from a CD onto a computer and then trading songs over the Internet should be legal, and 46% thought the practice should be illegal. Eight out of ten adults polled in May 2002 said that the ability to share music files over the Internet had no affect on their likelihood of buying a CD. A clear majority of adults were against laws that would require electronics manufacturers to make CD players in such a way that music could not be copied. Sixty-three percent opposed such laws in March 2002, and only 32% were in favor. Feelings were again

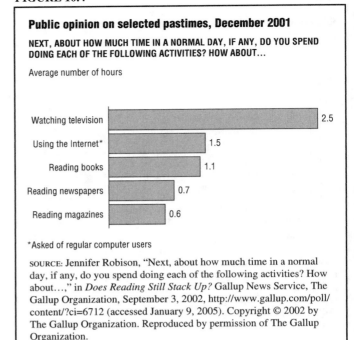

FIGURE 10.4

Public opinion on selected pastimes, December 2001

NEXT, ABOUT HOW MUCH TIME IN A NORMAL DAY, IF ANY, DO YOU SPEND DOING EACH OF THE FOLLOWING ACTIVITIES? HOW ABOUT…

Average number of hours

Activity	Hours
Watching television	2.5
Using the Internet*	1.5
Reading books	1.1
Reading newspapers	0.7
Reading magazines	0.6

*Asked of regular computer users

SOURCE: Jennifer Robison, "Next, about how much time in a normal day, if any, do you spend doing each of the following activities? How about…," in *Does Reading Still Stack Up?* Gallup News Service, The Gallup Organization, September 3, 2002, http://www.gallup.com/poll/content/?ci=6712 (accessed January 9, 2005). Copyright © 2002 by The Gallup Organization. Reproduced by permission of The Gallup Organization.

mixed when people were asked if record companies should make CDs where songs could only be copied a few times. Forty-eight percent of adults favored this solution, versus the 42% who opposed it.

Teens and Entertainment

Despite the unprecedented variety of entertainment choices available to teenagers in 2003, Figure 10.5 shows that most teens (aged thirteen to seventeen) had adopted the favorite pastime of their parents. When asked in 2004 what they did yesterday for entertainment, 90% of teens said they watched television, according to "Teens' Leisure Habits: TV on Top" by Heather Mason (Gallup Organization, October 26, 2004). Television superseded every other activity by far. Listening to music on the radio and listening to music on CD/MP3 players came in second and third in the poll, with 77% and 76% of teens claiming to have participated in these activities during the previous day. Reading was not at the top of the list. Only 33% of teens had read a book for pleasure. Roughly the same percentage (29%) had read a magazine or newspaper (28%).

As Figure 10.5 reveals, two-thirds of teens used the Internet the day before they were polled in October 2004. In "What Are Teen Webheads Doing Online?" (Gallup Organization, May 6, 2003), Steve Hanway reported that teens' use of the Internet varied markedly. A full quarter (26%) of teenagers with Internet access responding to a January/February 2003 Gallup poll said they went online an hour or less a week. Roughly a third (38%) replied that they went on for one to five hours a week. Most of the remaining teens were on the Internet five hours or more,

FIGURE 10.5

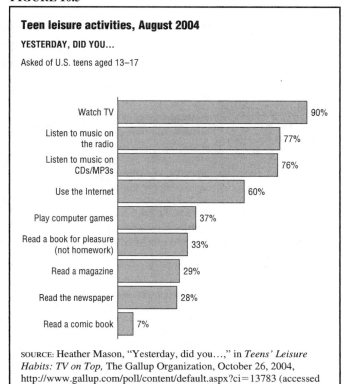

Teen leisure activities, August 2004

YESTERDAY, DID YOU...

Asked of U.S. teens aged 13–17

- Watch TV — 90%
- Listen to music on the radio — 77%
- Listen to music on CDs/MP3s — 76%
- Use the Internet — 60%
- Play computer games — 37%
- Read a book for pleasure (not homework) — 33%
- Read a magazine — 29%
- Read the newspaper — 28%
- Read a comic book — 7%

SOURCE: Heather Mason, "Yesterday, did you…," in *Teens' Leisure Habits: TV on Top,* The Gallup Organization, October 26, 2004, http://www.gallup.com/poll/content/default.aspx?ci=13783 (accessed January 9, 2005). Copyright © 2004 by The Gallup Organization. Reproduced by permission of The Gallup Organization.

FIGURE 10.6

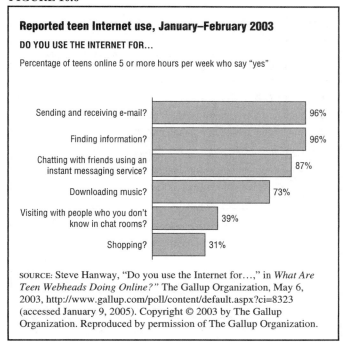

Reported teen Internet use, January–February 2003

DO YOU USE THE INTERNET FOR...

Percentage of teens online 5 or more hours per week who say "yes"

- Sending and receiving e-mail? — 96%
- Finding information? — 96%
- Chatting with friends using an instant messaging service? — 87%
- Downloading music? — 73%
- Visiting with people who you don't know in chat rooms? — 39%
- Shopping? — 31%

SOURCE: Steve Hanway, "Do you use the Internet for…," in *What Are Teen Webheads Doing Online?"* The Gallup Organization, May 6, 2003, http://www.gallup.com/poll/content/default.aspx?ci=8323 (accessed January 9, 2005). Copyright © 2003 by The Gallup Organization. Reproduced by permission of The Gallup Organization.

with 7% spending over twenty hours on the Internet. Figure 10.6 displays what teens did online. As with adults, teens' favorite activities were finding information (96%) and sending and receiving e-mail (96%). Chatting with friends over IM came in third, and downloading music was the fourth-most popular activity. A full 73% of those teens who spent more than five hours a week on the Internet reported using the Internet to download music.

Another popular activity listed in Figure 10.5 was playing video games. An August 2003 Gallup poll found that nearly three-quarters of teens (74%) played video games at least one hour a week. Forty percent of the respondents said that they played between one and five hours a week, 12% replied that they played eleven to twenty hours per week, and a whopping 13% reported gaming for twenty-one hours or more. The August 2003 poll appeared in "Grand Theft of Innocence? Teens and Video Games" by Steve Crabtree (Gallup Organization, September 16, 2003). The article points out that many parents and educators were concerned about the violence in video games such as Grand Theft Auto. Grand Theft Auto allows players to roam around a fictitious city committing countless crimes. Not only do such games give teens a false impression of adult life, but studies have shown that the games may hinder social development in some teens. According to Crabtree, a study at Tokyo University in 2001 found that violent games stunt the devel-

opment of the brain's frontal lobe, which is the part of the brain that controls antisocial behavior. Regardless, 60% of teens reported playing games in the Grand Theft Auto series. Only sports games were more popular. Sixty-nine percent of respondents to the August 2003 poll said they had played sports game. Generally, when it came to video games, girls played less than boys. The exception was The Sims series of games. Forty-five percent of girls played games in this series, compared to 43% of boys.

NEWS MEDIA

Where people get their news is often a good measure of which media they favor. Figure 10.7, which appeared in "How Americans Get Their News" by Darren K. Carlson (Gallup Organization, December 31, 2002), reveals the ways in which people received their daily news from August 1995 and December 2002. In general, cable news networks, talk radio, and Internet news sources increased in popularity over these years, while the nightly network news programs and the local paper fell out of favor. Evening news programs on ABC, CBS, and NBC took the biggest hit, with viewership dropping 19 percentage points from 1995 to 2002. Newspaper popularity increased slightly between March 1998 and July 1999 to a peak of 54% before declining again to 47%. The biggest increase occurred among Americans who got their news from cable, which rose from 23% to 41%. The number of people who said they received their news from the Internet increased from 3% to 15%.

A Gallup poll conducted in December 2004 revealed that some of these trends continued for two more years. In

FIGURE 10.7

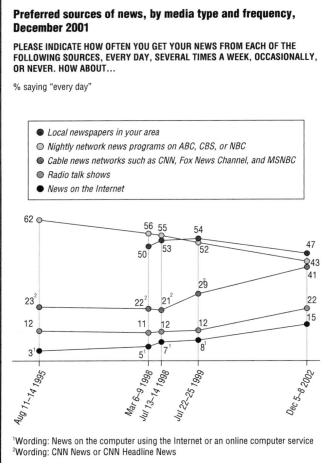

Preferred sources of news, by media type and frequency, December 2001

PLEASE INDICATE HOW OFTEN YOU GET YOUR NEWS FROM EACH OF THE FOLLOWING SOURCES, EVERY DAY, SEVERAL TIMES A WEEK, OCCASIONALLY, OR NEVER. HOW ABOUT...

% saying "every day"

- ● Local newspapers in your area
- ○ Nightly network news programs on ABC, CBS, or NBC
- ◐ Cable news networks such as CNN, Fox News Channel, and MSNBC
- ◑ Radio talk shows
- ● News on the Internet

[1]Wording: News on the computer using the Internet or an online computer service
[2]Wording: CNN News or CNN Headline News

SOURCE: Darren Carlson, "Please indicate how often you get your news from each of the following sources, every day, several times a week, occasionally, or never. How about...," in *How Americans Get Their News,* Gallup News Service, The Gallup Organization, December 31, 2002, http://www.gallup.com/poll/content/default.aspx?ci=7495 (accessed January 9, 2005).

FIGURE 10.8

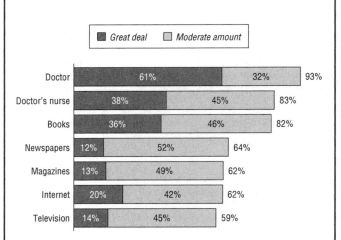

Public opinion on trustworthy sources of health information, September 2002

SOURCE: Frank Newport, "Amount of Trust in Health and Medical Information," in *Americans Get Plenty of Health News on TV, but Tend Not to Trust It,* September 27, 2003, http://www.gallup.com/poll/content/default.aspx?ci=6883 (accessed January 9, 2005). Copyright © 2003 by The Gallup Organization. Reproduced by permission of The Gallup Organization.

particular, the number of people getting their daily news from the Internet increased to 20%. Daily local newspaper readership declined to 44% and daily viewership of the nightly network news dropped precipitously to 26%. Cable network news did not continue its rise, with daily viewership dropping slightly from 41% to 39%. A likely explanation could be that more people are turning away from television in general and to the Internet to get their daily news. In the 2002 report, Carlson pointed out that the Internet was not necessarily driving the established news organizations out of business. Many newspapers put their content online. Networks such as NBC have invested a lot of money and talent into developing Web sites, which received much of the Internet traffic from those looking for news.

HEALTH INFORMATION

Despite the increased reliance on the Internet for health information, it still came in last as a source of medical information. Only 37% of those interviewed for a Sep-

tember 2002 Gallup poll said that they found at least some of their health advice on the Web, according to "Americans Get Plenty of Health News on TV, but Tend Not to Trust It" by Frank Newport (Gallup Organization, September 2002). The Internet fell in behind every other popular source, including the doctor (70%), television (64%), books (56%), and the doctor's nurse (49%). Generally the Internet was more popular among those forty-nine and younger. Nearly 43% of those under fifty received health-care information on the Internet, as opposed to 28% of those fifty and over. However, the Internet was still the least-used source among younger people.

Although television came in second as a source of health information, Figure 10.8 shows that Americans trusted it the least. Where trust is concerned, the Internet came in next to last with 62% of people saying they trust information on the Internet. When looking at the percentage of people who trust the sources they used greatly, the Web moves to fourth place behind books. This could be a reflection of the fact that the Internet yields higher quality information for those who spend a long time looking for it. The September 2002 poll revealed that media sources of health and medical news tended to confuse as many people as they helped. Forty-five percent of respondents said that they felt more confused about a health issue after reviewing a medical or health news report, versus 50% who said they were better able to make a health decision. In fact, Newport suggested that health reports in the media or on the Internet actually caused more people to go to the doctor and ask him or her questions about health care. Nearly one-third (32%) of Americans said that they question a doctor about medical information they found on the Internet or in the media somewhat often, and 16% claim they ask questions very often. Only 20% of Americans said they never asked the doctor about information they see.

INTERNET AND POLITICS

In 2004 many politicians began using the Internet as a primary tool for communicating with the electorate. (See Chapter 7.) In addition, more and more voters used the Internet to look up information on politicians. According to "2004 Campaign Trail Winds through Cyberspace" by Darren Carlson (Gallup Organization, January 20, 2004), only 31% of Americans said they used the Internet to get news or information about the political candidates in 2000. By January 2004 this number increased to 49% of Americans. As Figure 10.9 reveals, the number of people who never looked for political information on the Internet decreased significantly, while the number of those who frequently looked for political information increased sharply.

Demographic differences existed, however, between those who sought political information online and those who did not. Thirty-four percent of men logged onto the Internet frequently to enhance their political knowledge, as opposed to only 22% of women in 2004. Generally, one-third of adults between the ages of eighteen and sixty-five looked for political information frequently on the Web, but at age sixty-five this behavior dropped dramatically. In fact, only 11% of Americans over sixty-five went to the Web frequently to delve into politics. Income and education also made a big difference. Nearly half of those with a graduate degree surfed the Internet frequently for political information, compared with 16% of those with a high school education or less. As to income, 45% of Americans making over $75,000 a year went online for political news and views, versus 23% of those making less than $30,000.

TEENS AND CLASSROOM TECHNOLOGY

According to "System Failure? Teens Rate School Technology" by Julie Ray (Gallup Organization, July 29, 2003), the student-to-computer ratio in 2003 was 3.8 to 1, which was down considerably from 1983 when the student to computer ratio in public schools was as high as 125 to 1. A January/February 2003 Gallup poll asked

FIGURE 10.9

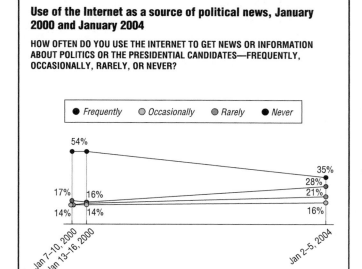

Use of the Internet as a source of political news, January 2000 and January 2004

HOW OFTEN DO YOU USE THE INTERNET TO GET NEWS OR INFORMATION ABOUT POLITICS OR THE PRESIDENTIAL CANDIDATES—FREQUENTLY, OCCASIONALLY, RARELY, OR NEVER?

● Frequently   ○ Occasionally   ● Rarely   ● Never

SOURCE: Darren Carlson, "Internet for Political News," in *2004 Campaign Trail Winds Through Cyberspace,* The Gallup Organization, January 20, 2004, http://www.gallup.com/poll/content/default.aspx?ci= 10321 (accessed January 9, 2005). Copyright © 2004 by The Gallup Organization. Reproduced by permission of The Gallup Organization.

teens how they rated the technology in their schools. Most teens seemed appreciative, with 28% giving their school's technology an *A* and 33% giving it a *B*. Roughly one-third (38%) gave their school a grade of either a *C* or *D* and only 5% issued their school's technology a failing grade. Some trends emerged among students, which suggested that the students were as much a factor in the grades given as the technology. Thirty-one percent of boys, for instance, gave an *A*, while only 24% of girls did so. Ray suggested that this may be due to the gender gap in technology. As a whole, male students still embrace high technology more than female students do, and manufacturers of software, especially in the entertainment industry, tend to gear software to male tastes (i.e., plenty of violence and scantily clad women). Another trend that emerged from the January/February data was that students at the top of their classes tended to award more *A*s than average or below average students did. One-third of students in the top of their classes gave *A*s, as opposed to 23% of average/below average students. Overall, Ray concluded that students expect a lot when it comes to technology, and that budget cuts to school technology would likely lead to a lot of complaints.

IMPORTANT NAMES AND ADDRESSES

American Customer Satisfaction Index (ACSI)
E-mail: tfelker@cfigroup.com
URL: http://www.theacsi.org

The Center for Academic Integrity
P.O. Box 90434
Duke University
Durham, NC 27708
(919) 660-3045
FAX: (919) 660-3049
E-mail: integrity@duke.edu
URL: http://www.academicintegrity.org

Centers for Disease Control and Prevention
1600 Clifton Rd.
Atlanta, GA 30333
(404) 639-3311
Toll-free: 1-800-311-3435
URL: http://www.cdc.gov

CERT Coordination Center (E-Crime and Viruses)
Software Engineering Institute
Carnegie Mellon University
Pittsburgh, PA 15213-3890
(412) 268-7090
FAX: (412) 268-6989
E-mail: cert@cert.org
URL: http://www.cert.org

Computer Security Institute
600 Harrison St.
San Francisco, CA 94107
Toll-free: 1-866-271-8529
FAX: (818) 487-4550
E-mail: rrichardson@cmp.com
URL: http://www.gocsi.com

comScore Networks
11465 Sunset Hills Rd., Suite 200
Reston, VA 20190
(703) 438-2000
FAX: (703) 438-2051

E-mail: info@comscore.com
URL: http://www.comscore.com

Economics and Statistics Administration, U.S. Department of Commerce
1401 Constitution Ave. NW, Rm. 4855
Washington, DC 20230
(202) 482-2235
FAX: (202) 482-2889
E-mail: ER.Anderson@esa.doc.gov
URL: https://www.esa.doc.gov/

Federal Communications Commission
445 12th St. SW
Washington, DC 20554
Toll-free: 1-888-225-5322
FAX: (866) 418-0232
E-mail: fccinfo@fcc.gov
URL: http://www.fcc.gov

Federal Deposit Insurance Corporation (FDIC)
550 17th St. NW
Washington, DC 20429-9990
(202) 736-0000
Toll-free: 1-877-275-3342
E-mail: publicinfo@fdic.gov
URL: http://www.fdic.gov

Federal Election Commission
999 East St. NW
Washington, DC 20463
(202) 694-1100
Toll-free: 1-800-424-9530
E-mail: info@fec.gov
URL: www.fec.gov

Federal Trade Commission
600 Pennsylvania Ave. NW
Washington, DC 20580
(202) 326-2222
URL: http://www.ftc.gov

The Gallup Organization
901 F St. NW

Washington, DC 20004
Toll-free: 1-888-274-5447
URL: http://www.gallup.com

Government Accountability Office
441 G St. NW
Washington, DC 20548
(202) 512-3000
E-mail: webmaster@gao.gov
URL: http://www.gao.gov

Governors Highway Safety Association
750 First St. NE, Suite 720
Washington, DC 20002
(202) 789-0942
URL: http://www.statehighwaysafety.org/

ICSA Labs
1000 Bent Creek Blvd., Suite 200
Mechanicsburg, PA 17050
(717) 790-8100
E-mail: gjapak@icsalabs.com
URL: http://www.icsalabs.com

Intelligent Transportation Society of America
1100 17th St. NW, Suite 1200
Washington, DC 20036
(202) 484-4847
FAX: (202) 484-3483
E-mail: editor@itsa.org
URL: www.itsa.org

Intelligent Transportation Systems Joint Program Office (HOIT), U.S. Department of Transportation
400 Seventh St. SW
Washington, DC 20590
(202) 366-9536
Toll free: 1-866-367-7487
E-mail: itsweb.master@fhwa.dot.gov
URL: www.its.dot.gov

Internet Society
1775 Wiehle Ave., Suite 102

Reston, VA 20190-5108
(703) 326-9880
FAX: (703) 326-9881
E-mail: info@isoc.org
URL: http://www.isoc.org

Internet2
1000 Oakbrook Dr., Suite 300
Ann Arbor, MI 48104
(734) 913-4250
E-mail: info@internet2.edu
URL: http://www.internet2.edu

Medical Library Association
65 East Wacker Pl., Suite 1900
Chicago, IL 60601-7298
(312) 419-9094
FAX: (312) 419-8950
E-mail: info@mlahq.org
URL: http://www.mlanet.org

Motion Picture Association of America
15503 Ventura Blvd.
Encino, CA 91436
(818) 995-6600
E-mail: webhost@mpaa.org
URL: http://www.mpaa.org

National Center for Education Statistics
1990 K St. NW
Washington, DC 20006
(202) 502-7300
FAX: (202) 502-7466
E-mail: NCESwebmaster@ed.gov
URL: http://nces.ed.gov

National Science Foundation
4201 Wilson Blvd.
Arlington, VA 22230
(703) 292-5111
Toll-free: 1-800-877-8339
E-mail: info@nsf.gov
URL: http://www.nsf.gov/

Office of Electronic Government and Technology
725 17th St. NW

Washington, DC 20503
(202) 395-3080
FAX: (202) 395-3888
URL: www.estrategy.gov

Office of Management and Budget
725 17th St. NW
Washington, DC 20503
(202) 395-3080
FAX: (202) 395-3888
E-mail: president@whitehouse.gov
URL: http://www.whitehouse.gov/omb/

On-Line Gamers Anonymous
P.O. Box 724
Hudson, WI 54016
(612) 245-1115
E-mail: olga@olganon.org
URL: http://www.olganon.org

Organ Procurement and Transplantation Network
P.O. Box 2484
Richmond, VA 23218
(804) 782-4876
FAX: (804) 782-4994
E-mail: webmaster@unos.org
URL: http://www.optn.org

Pew Internet & American Life Project
1615 L St. NW, Suite 700
Washington, DC 20036
(202) 419-4500
FAX: (202) 419-4505
E-mail: data@pewinternet.org
URL: http://www.pewinternet.org

Recording Industry Association of America
1330 Connecticut Ave. NW, Suite 300
Washington, DC 20036
(202) 775-0101
FAX: (202) 775-7253
E-mail: webmaster@riaa.com
URL: http://www.riaa.com

Technical Support Working Group
E-mail: ADP@tswg.gov
URL: http://www.tswg.gov

TV Parental Guidelines Monitoring Board
P.O. Box 14097
Washington, DC 20004
(202) 879-9364
E-mail: tvomb@usa.net
URL: http://www.tvguidelines.org

U.S. Census Bureau
4700 Silver Hill Rd.
Washington, DC 20233-0001
(301) 763-3030
E-mail: pio@census.gov
URL: http://www.census.gov

US-CERT
1110 North Glebe Rd.
Arlington, VA 22201
(703) 235-5110
E-mail: info@us-cert.gov
URL: http://www.us-cert.gov

U.S. Department of Homeland Security
Washington, DC 20528
(202) 282-8000
URL: http://www.dhs.gov

U.S. Department of Justice—Computer Crime and Intellectual Property Section
950 Pennsylvania Ave. NW
Washington, DC 20530-0001
(202) 514-2000
E-mail: askDOJ@usdoj.gov
URL: http://www.usdoj.gov

U.S. Department of Labor
Frances Perkins Bldg.
200 Constitution Ave. NW
Washington, DC 20210
Toll-free: 1-866-4-USA-DOL
URL: http://www.dol.gov

RESOURCES

The Pew Charitable Trust established the Pew Internet & American Life Project in 1999. Since then, the Pew Internet Project has conducted dozens of surveys to determine just who in America uses the Internet and how they use it. All of their publications can be found online at www.pewinternet.org. *America's Online Pursuits* (2003), *The Internet and Daily Life* (2004), and *E-mail at Work* (2002) paint a general picture of what Americans do online. For information on how various demographic groups employ the Internet, see *Internet Use by Region in the United States* (2003), *Rural Areas and the Internet* (2004), and *Older Americans and the Internet* (2004). *The Internet Goes to College* (2002), *Teenage Life Online* (2001), and *Let the Games Begin* (2003) reveal what young people are doing online. *How Americans Get in Touch with Government* (2004), *Digital Town Hall* (2004), *The Internet and Democratic Debate* (2004), and *Untuned Keyboards* (2003) all illustrate how influential the Internet has become in politics. With regards to health care and the Internet, *Wired for Health* (2003), *Prescription Drugs Online* (2004), and *Vital Decisions* are all good resources. *Spam: How It Is Hurting E-mail and Degrading Life on the Internet* (2003) and *Fear of Online Crime* (2001) expose some of the problems facing the Web. Other useful publications issued by Pew/Internet include *Holidays Online* (2002), *Faith Online* (2004), *Consumption of Goods and Services in the United States* (2003), and *How Americans Use Instant Messaging* (2004).

The Gallup Organization, headquartered in Washington, D.C., provides valuable results from recent polls on such topics as Internet and cell-phone use, e-crime, e-commerce, and entertainment, among others. Reports consulted for this book include "Internet Use: What's Age Got to Do With It?" by Linda Lyons (March 16, 2004), "American E-mailers Increasingly Fed up with Computer Spam" by Frank Newport and Joseph Carroll (May 20, 2003), "Public Favors Ban on Use of Cellular Phones While Driving" by Darren Carlson (July 12, 2001), and "Banking Customers Still Love Bricks and Mortar" by Dennis Jacobe (June 10, 2003).

In addition to *Hobbes' Internet Timeline*, a number of excellent accounts of Internet history can be found online. Most of these histories are listed on the Internet Society's Web site (http://www.isoc.org/internet/history/). *A Brief History of the Internet*, also located on the Internet Society's site, was written by some of those people who gave rise to the Internet, including Vint Cerf, the creator of TCP/IP. Public Broadcasting Service's *Nerds 2.0.1* (http://www.pbs.org/opb/nerds2.0.1/) and Walt Howe's *A Brief History of the Internet* provide a less technical account of Net history. For a historian's point of view on how the Internet came to be, see *History of the Internet, Internet for Historians* by Richard T. Griffiths (http:// www.let.leidenuniv.nl/history/ivh/frame_theorie.html) and *Hardy: The History of the Net* by Henry Hardy (http://www.vrx.net/usenet/history/hardy/). *Cyber Geography* by Martin Dodge displays map after map of the Internet networks that have spanned the United States since the creation of ARPANET. The Internet2 Web site contains a great deal of information on the Internet2 consortium as well as the future of the Net. An in-depth history of cell phones can be found at privateline.com along with detailed explanations on how cell phones work.

A number of magazines and Web sites report on the latest developments in technology. In print, *Wired* magazine, *PC World*, *New Scientist*, *Popular Science*, and *Scientific American* typically contain a wealth of articles on the most recent trends in electronics and software. On the Web, ZDNet.com, CNet.com, Wired.com, TechWeb.com, and eWeek.com post the latest news in high-tech on a daily basis.

The Federal Communications Commission is the government agency responsible for regulating which devices can use the various portions of the electromagnetic spectrum. The agency also regulates television and radio programming. The FCC Web site (www.fcc.gov) provides information on radio spectrum allocation, closed captioning, high definition television, the Children's Internet Protection Act, and the V-Chip.

The United States Census Bureau's *Statistical Abstracts of the United States* (http://www2.census.gov/prod2/statcomp/index.htm) contains a number of statistics illustrating the impact of technology on American life. These include the percentage of households with computer and Internet access, the amount of time and money Americans spend on various media and media systems (e.g., television and radio), the percentage of public schools with Internet access, and the number of Americans with credit card and debit card accounts. *E-Stats* (www.census.gov/estats), also produced by the Census Bureau, provides financial statistics on e-commerce in the United States. The Economics and Statistics Administration (ESA), the agency that oversees the Census Bureau, independently compiles reports on Internet usage as well as the impact of high-tech on the economy. The ESA's *Digital Economy* delves into how high technology has transformed the American economy since the 1980s.

The Federal Trade Commission's (FTC's) identity theft Web site (http://www.consumer.gov/idtheft/stats.html) houses a number of reports and informational brochures on identity theft and Internet fraud. Publications consulted for this book include *Federal Trade Commission—Identity Theft Survey Report* (2003), *ID Theft—What's It All About* (2003), *National and State Trends in Fraud and Identity Theft* (2003), and the *Federal Trade Commission Overview of the Identity Theft Program* (2003). The U.S. Department of Justice maintains a Web site on cybercrime (www.cybercrime.gov) rife with reports on identity theft and Internet fraud. The site also includes several reports on intellectual property theft, including the *Report of the Department of Justice Task Force on Intellectual Property* (2004).

The Computer Emergency Response Team Coordination Center (CERT/CC) at Carnegie Mellon University monitors and responds to major threats to the Internet such as large-scale hacking incidents and virus attacks. The CERT/CC home page (www.cert.org) provides useful information on the incidents reported and vulnerabilities found within the Net. Each year CERT/CC, in conjunction with *CSO* magazine and the U.S. Secret Service, publishes the *E-Crime Watch Survey*, which outlines the e-crime incidents reported each year by hundreds of businesses, organizations, and government agencies. These crimes include anything from Internet fraud to hacking incidents to viruses. A similar report entitled *CSI/FBI Computer Crime and Security Survey* is issued by the Computer Security Institute (www.gocsi.com) and the Federal Bureau of Investigation. ICSA Labs (http://www.icsalabs.com/), a division of

TruSecure Corporation, releases the *Computer Virus Prevalence Survey* each year, detailing virus activity among large corporations. The Technical Support Working Group Web site (www.tswg.gov), the Department of Homeland Security Web site (www.dhs.gov), and the US-CERT Web site (www.us-cert.gov) all contain reports on how the government is using high-tech to combat threats to national security.

To learn more about how national elections are conducted and information on optical scan and digital recording electronic voting machines, visit the Federal Election Commission Web site (www.fec.gov). The Intelligent Transportation Systems Joint Program Office, located within the U.S. Department of Transportation, contains reports on 511 deployment and operations (http://www.its.dot.gov/511/511.htm). The American Customer Satisfaction Index (ACSI) scores for many of the federal government's most popular sites can be found at www.customerservice.gov. The Office of Management and Budget e-government Web site provides information on President George W. Bush's e-government initiatives as well as the E-Government Act of 2003. Reports available on this site include the *FY 2003 Report to Congress on Implementation of the E-Government Act* (2004) and *Implementing the President's Management Agenda for E-Government* (2003). The 1998 Government Paperwork Elimination Act (GPEA), the predecessor to the E-Government Act, required government agencies to render all their forms in electronic format. In 2000 the U.S. General Accounting Office (GAO) assessed the success of the GPEA in their report *Electronic Government: Government Paperwork Elimination Act Presents Challenges for Agencies*.

In 2004 the GAO released a report on Internet pharmacies entitled *Internet Pharmacies: Some Pose Safety Risks for Consumers*. The report outlines some of the problems GAO agents encountered when they ordered drugs from Internet pharmacies. The National Institutes of Health's MedlinePlus Web site (www.medlineplus.gov) contains accurate and valuable information on a myriad of diseases and drugs. The Medical Library Association's Web site (www.mlanet.org) lists the ten most useful medical Web sites on the Net. The Centers for Disease Control Web site (www.cdc.gov) reports on how researchers are employing the Internet, GPS systems, and other high-tech equipment to analyze the risks associated with major diseases.

The National Center for Education Statistics (http://www.nces.ed.gov/) has released a number of reports detailing the use of computers and the Internet in the classroom. The two reports discussed in this book are *Internet Access in U.S. Public Schools and Classrooms: 1994–2002* and *Distance Education at Degree-Granting Postsecondary Institutions: 2000–2001*. The Center for Academic Integrity (academicintegrity.org) documents and addresses the growing problem of cheating in the classroom.

INDEX

Ashcroft, John
    agreement with Microsoft, 41
    intellectual property theft and, 54
Asian and Pacific Islander Americans
    Internet access, percent of households
        with, 9f
    Internet usage by, 9
ASIMO (Advanced Step in Innovation
    Mobility) robot, 112
Association for Research Libraries, 78
ASTA (American Society of Travel Agents),
    36
Asteroids, 59
AT&T (American Telegraph and Telephone
    Company), 19, 20
Atari Historical Society, 59
Atari, Pong, 59
Atari VCS (Atari 2600), 59
ATM (automated teller machine)
    debit cards and, 38–39
    use of, 118
Auctions
    fraud, 46–47
    online auctions, 32–33
Automated clearing house (ACH) system,
    39–41
automated teller machine (ATM)
    debit cards and, 38–39
    use of, 118
Automatic bill payment, 40
Automobiles
    cell phone use in, 21, 117
    high tech, 112–113
    onboard computers on trucks, 31
"Average American Will Spend $797 on
    Gifts This Holiday Season" (Gillespie),
    117

B

B2B. *See* Business-to-business
Bankcard fraud, 43
Banking
    bill payment, 40, 115
    consumer use of online banking, 118f
    identity theft and, 43–45
    IT and currency, 38–41
    online banking, public opinion on, 118
"Banking Customers Still Love Bricks and
    Mortar" (Jacobe), 118
Baran, Paul, 3
Battery life, cell phone, 22–23
Bell Laboratories, 19
Bell System, 19–20
Berland, Gretchen K., 100
Berners-Lee, Tim, 6
Bertelsmann (German media conglomerate),
    53
Bill payment
    ACH system for, 40
    participation in online bill payment, 115
BITNET, 4, 14
Black/African-Americans. *See* African-
    Americans
BlackBerry devices, 21–22
Blaster worm, 48
Blocking, Internet material, 73
Blog (Web log), 69, 93

BLS (U.S. Bureau of Labor Statistics), 30
Bone marrow transplant, 105
Books, 68
Borland, John, 55
Boutin, Paul, 95
Broadband
    adult Internet users with broadband at
        home, 12f
    everyday activities on the Internet and,
        108
    everyday online activities of
        broadband/dial-up users, 108 (t9.2)
    growth of, 11
    news from the Internet with, 92
    public schools with broadband access,
        74t
    VoIP and, 18
"Broadband Web Link Goes Wireless"
    (Ananthaswamy), 12
Brokerage accounts, online, 36, 38
Brown, Sharon P., 30
BugBear virus, 48
"Building an Electronic Fortress" (Wardell),
    111
Bungie Studios, 57–58
Bush, George W.
    campaign ad placements for, 94 (t7.14)
    Check Truncation Act signed by, 41
    E-government Act of 2002 and, 88–89
    political advertising on Internet, 93
    visitors to Web site of, 91
Business-to-business (B2B)
    ACH system for, 40
    e-commerce, 31
    shipments, sales, revenues, by total and
        e-commerce, 31t
Businesses. *See* American businesses
Bytes, 5

C

Cabir virus, 2
Cable News Network (CNN), 65
Cable television
    digital cable, 67
    history of, 64–66
CAI (Center for Academic Integrity), 71,
    81–82
California HealthCare Foundation, 100
Calling plan, 117
Cambridge University, 58
Campaign finance, 93–94
CAN-SPAM. *See* Controlling the Assault of
    Non-Solicited Pornography and
    Marketing Act of 2003
*The CAN-SPAM Act Has Not Helped Most
    Email Users So Far* (Pew Internet &
    American Life Project), 91
Canada, online pharmacies in, 102, 103
Cancer, 105
Cancer.gov, 101, 102
Car-mounted telephone, 20
Caregivers, 99
Carlson, Darren
    cell phone ban, 117
    "How Americans Get Their News,"
        121–122

"Majority of E-mail Users Express
    Concern about Internet Privacy," 118,
    119
    "2004 Campaign Trail Winds through
        Cyberspace," 123
Carroll, Joseph, 116–117
Cars. *See* Automobiles
Casinos, online, 61
Catholic schools, 71
CD. *See* Compact discs
CD players (compact disc players), 61–62
CD-ROMs, 80
CDC. *See* Centers for Disease Control and
    Prevention
CDMA (code division multiple access), 20
Cell-phone carrier, 117
"Cell Phone Users Have Little Interest in
    Number Portability" (Carroll), 116
"Cell Phones and Kids: Do They Mix?"
    (Sullivan), 21
Cellular phones
    3G cell phone service, 12
    Cabir virus, 2
    cellular telecommunications industry, 14t
    future of, 22–23
    growth of phone system/subscribers, 13
    history/development, 19–20
    issues/concerns, 21
    networks, 20
    ownership, 117f
    proliferation of, 1
    public opinion on, 116–117
    radio frequencies for analog cell phone
        access, 21 (f2.4)
    radio frequencies for digital cell phone
        encoding/decoding, 21 (f2.5)
    state distracted driving laws, 22f
Cellular towers
    cellular phone development and, 19, 20
    modern cell-phone networks, 20
Center for Academic Integrity (CAI), 71,
    81–82
Centers for Disease Control and Prevention
    (CDC)
    National Center for Health Statistics
        database, 105
    Web site of, 101, 102
Cerf, Vint, 4
CERN (European Organization for Nuclear
    Research), 6
CERT. *See* Computer Emergency Response
    Team
CERT Coordination Center (CERT/CC), 2,
    49
Chat, 3
Cheating
    Internet and, 81–82
    plagiarism, 71
Check Truncation Act, 41
Checking account, 45
Checks, 40
Chicago (IL), 20
Chief Information Officers, 88
Child pornography, Internet, 43
Children
    cell phones and, 21

public school instructional rooms with Internet access, 75*t*

public school students to instructional computers with Internet access, 74*f*

public school students to instructional computers with Internet access, ratio of, 76*t*

public schools allowing student access to Internet outside of school hours, 79*t*

public schools using procedures to prevent student access to inappropriate material on the Internet, 77*t*

public schools with broadband access, 74*t*

public schools with Internet access, 72*t*

teen Internet use compared to adult Internet use, 81 (*t*6.12)

Web site or Web page, percent of public schools with, 80 (*t*6.9)

Web sites that received disproportionate number of hits from college campuses, 82*t*

what teens did online, 80 (*t*6.11)

where teens logged on, 80 (*t*6.10)

"Effects of Internet Behavioral Counseling on Weight Loss in Adults at Risk for Type 2 Diabetes" (Tate), 102

EFTPS (Electronic Federal Tax Payment System), 40

"Election Ad Battle Smashes Record in 2004" (Memmott and Drinkard), 93

Elections

campaign ad placements for George W. Bush, 94 (*t*7.14)

campaign ad placements for John Kerry, 94 (*t*7.13)

Internet and politics, 123

political advertising on Internet, 93–94

political Web sites, 92–93

presidential campaign news, people's main sources of, 92 (*t*7.12)

visitors to political Web sites, 91

voting booth and IT, 94–95

voting systems replacement, 85

Electrolux Trilobite, 112

Electronic Delay Storage Automatic Calculator (EDSAC), 58

Electronic Federal Tax Payment System (EFTPS), 40

Electronic keypad locking system, 111

Electronic payment methods

consumer payment systems by method of payment, 40*t*

credit card use, 39 (*t*3.10)

credit cards, use of general purpose credit cards by families, 39 (*t*3.11)

credit/debit cards, 38–39

electronic money transfer, 39–41

IT and currency, 38

payment instruments, households that use selected, 41*t*

Electronic shopping and mail-order house businesses

online sales, 32

total and e-commerce sales of electronic shopping and mail-order houses, 36*t*

Electronic signature systems, 88

Electronic transfer of money, 39–41

Electronic voting systems, 94–95

Electronics

appliances, smart, 111–112

electronic innovations, spread of, 1–2

high tech home features, 110–111

Elementary schools, 71–75

"Elk Cloner" virus, 48

Elliott, Marc N., 100

Emarketer.com, 17

Emergency Alert System (EAS), 55

Employee, e-crimes by, 50

Employment

by copyright industries, 51

in information technology producing industries, 28*t*–29*t*

loss of IT jobs, 27, 30

Enhanced definition TV (EDTV), 67

Entertainment

CD, cross-section of, 62*f*

college students' use of Internet for, 76, 78–79

digital television standards, 67*t*

gaming, 57–61

journalism, 68–69

KaZaa media desktop application usage, 65*f*

media usage and consumer spending, 58*t*

new technologies and, 57

news, estimated revenue, printing expenses, inventories for newspaper, periodical, database, directory publishers, 68*t*

online music services, visitors to, 65*t*

public opinion on, 119–121

public opinion on selected pastimes, 120*f*

recorded music, 61–64

recording media, manufacturers' shipments and value of, 62*t*

sound recordings, profile of consumer expenditures for, 64*t*

teen Internet use, 121 (*f*10.6)

teen leisure activities, 121 (*f*10.5)

television, 64–68

utilization of selected media, 66*t*

Entertainment Software Rating Board (ESRB), 60

Environmental Protection Agency, 89

Escrow company, 47

ESRB (Entertainment Software Rating Board), 60

Ethernet, 3

Ethnicity. *See* Race/ethnicity

European Organization for Nuclear Research (CERN), 6

EverQuest, 60

Everyday activities. *See* Daily life

"Evidence for Striatal Dopamine Release during a Video Game" (*Nature*), 60

F

Faith Online (Pew Internet & American Life Project), 110

Fallows, Deborah

CAN-SPAM Act, 91

The Internet and Daily Life, 107, 108

Internet Health Resources, 97–100

number of e-mails per day, 13

spam findings, 15–16

Family

e-mails to, 116

Internet and parenting, 108–109

spending time with, 119

Familydoctor.org, 101, 102

Fanning, Shawn, 52–53

FastWeb, 76

FBI (Federal Bureau of Investigation), 50–51

FCC. *See* Federal Communications Commission

FDMA (frequency division multiple access), 20

Fear of Online Crime (Pew Internet & American Life Project), 43, 43*t*

Federal Bureau of Investigation (FBI), 50–51

Federal Communications Commission (FCC)

closed captioning and, 66

digital television standards, 67, 67*t*

511 system and, 95

Internet regulation and, 89

regulation of radio spectrum frequencies, 19, 20

Federal Deposit Insurance Corporation, 38, 39, 40

Federal Emergency Management Agency (FEMA), 88

Federal government

511 information system, 95

Government Paper Elimination Act, compliance, 88*t*

information technology and, 85

Internet technologies and, 88–91

See also Government

Federal Reserve, 40–41

Federal Trade Commission (FTC), 43, 44–46

FedForms.gov, 88

FEMA (Federal Emergency Management Agency), 88

File sharing

college students' use of Internet for, 79

intellectual property theft and, 51–54

KaZaa media desktop application usage, 65*f*

peer-to-peer file sharing, 63–64

public opinion on music/movie file sharing, 120

visitors to selected online music services, 65*t*

Filtering, Internet material, 73

Financial industries, 25

FirstGov.gov, 89

Fitness information, 99

511 Deployment Coalition, 95

511 system

function of, 85

implementation of, 95

nationwide use of, 96*f*

Floppy disks, 48

Florida

DRE systems in, 95

punch-card ballots in, 94

Web boards, 76
Web browser
  development of, 6
  e-mail use and, 14
  Microsoft Internet Explorer antitrust
    litigation, 41
Web log (blog), 69, 93
Web server, 6
Web sites
  contacting government via, 85–86
  federal government, 88–91
  for health information, 101–102
  Government Paper Elimination Act,
    compliance, 88t
  government Web sites, ACSI scores for,
    90t
  government Web sites, problems
    encountered with, 87 (t7.5)
  government Web sites, reasons
    Americans contact, 86–87
  growth of, 6
  Internet health care information, impact
    of, 99–101
  MedlinePlus, use of, 101f
  municipal Web sites, features found on,
    87 (t7.6)
  online retail sales, 32
  percent of public schools with Web site
    or Web page, 80 (t6.9)
  political news and information, types of
    Web sites people used to get, 91 (t7.10)
  political Web sites, 91–94
  real estate brokerage, 38
  school, 73–74
  that received disproportionate number of
    hits from college campuses, 76, 82t
Weight loss, 102

West Virginia University, 105
"What Are Teen Webheads Doing Online?"
  (Hanway), 120–121
Whirlpool, 111
White Americans
  e-mail users, 15
  instant messaging users, 18
  Internet access, percent of households
    with, 9f
  Internet use by, 9, 115, 116
  Internet use by college students, 76
White Box Robotics, PC-Bot, 112
Whitman, Meg, 32–33
Wholesalers
  e-commerce sales, 32
  total and e-commerce wholesale trade
    sales, 34t
Who's Not Online (Pew/Internet survey), 8,
  9
Wi-MAX (Worldwide Interoperability for
  Microwave Access), 12
WildList Organization International, 48
"Will New Robots Kick Honda's ASIMO?"
  (Goel), 112
Willis, Derek, 93
Windows, Microsoft
  antitrust litigation and, 41
  MSBlaster worm and, 48, 49
Wireless technologies, 11–12
Women
  e-mail use by, 15, 116
  gaming of college students, 79
  health search online by, 97, 99
  holidays and Internet, 109, 117
  Internet use by, 9, 115
  Internet use by college students, 76
  politics and Internet, 123

Woolley, Elizabeth, 60
Work, 116
  See also Employment; Jobs
Workers
  productivity growth of, 30
  productivity trends, 30f
The World (Internet service provider), 6
World Wide Web
  development of, 6
  invention of/e-mail and, 14–15
Worldwide Interoperability for Microwave
  Access (Wi-MAX), 12
Worms
  damage to businesses, 48
  definition of, 48
  growth of, 2
  Internet worms, viruses, hacking
    attempts reported, 3t
  Slammer/Sapphire worm, 118–119

X

Xbox console, Microsoft, 57–58, 60
Xbox Live, Microsoft, 60

Y

Yaha virus, 48
Yahoo, 17
YS-CERT, 49

Z

Zakon, Robert H., 6
ZigBee, 111–112
ZigBee Alliance, 111–112
Zone lighting systems, 111